NORTHEAST MILAN
Pages 104–123
Street Finder maps 3, 4

HISTORIC CENTRE
Pages 42–59
Street Finder maps 3, 4, 7, 8

SOUTHEAST MILAN
Pages 92–103
Street Finder maps 7, 8

NORTHEAST
MILAN

HISTORIC
CENTRE

SOUTHEAST
MILAN

0 metres   600

0 yards   600

D1110005

EYEWITNESS TRAVEL GUIDES

MILAN
& THE LAKES

EYEWITNESS TRAVEL GUIDES

MILAN
& THE LAKES

DORLING KINDERSLEY
LONDON • NEW YORK • MUNICH • MELBOURNE • DELHI

www.dk.com

A DORLING KINDERSLEY BOOK

www.dk.com

Produced by Fabio Ratti
Editoria Libraria e Multimediale, Milan, Italy

PROJECT EDITORS Barbara Cacciani, Giovanni Francesio
EDITORS Emanuela Damiani, Mattia Goffetti,
Alessandra Lombardi, Marco Scapagnini
DESIGNERS Oriana Bianchetti, Silvia Tomasone

Dorling Kindersley Ltd
PROJECT EDITOR Fiona Wild
SENIOR ART EDITOR Marisa Renzullo
DTP DESIGNERS Maite Lantaron, Samantha Borland, Sarah Meakin
PRODUCTION Marie Ingledew

CONTRIBUTOR Monica Torri

ILLUSTRATORS
Giorgia Boli, Alberto Ipsilanti,
Daniela Veluti, Nadia Viganò

ENGLISH TRANSLATION
Richard Pierce

Film output by Quadrant Typesetters, London
Reproduced by Lineatre, Milan

Printed and bound by
L. Rex Printing Company Limited, China
First published in Great Britain in 2000 by
Dorling Kindersley Ltd,
80 Strand, London WC2R 0RL

Reprinted with revisions 2003

Copyright 2000, 2003 © Dorling Kindersley Ltd
A Penguin Company

ISBN 0 7513 4810 4

FLOORS ARE REFERRED TO THROUGHOUT IN ACCORDANCE WITH EUROPEAN
USAGE; IE THE "FIRST FLOOR" IS THE FLOOR ABOVE GROUND LEVEL.

CONTENTS

Statue, entrance to the Pinacoteca
di Brera *(see pp114–7)*

INTRODUCING MILAN AND THE LAKES

Naviglio Grande, in the southern
district of Milan *(see p89)*

Leonardo da Vinci's *Last Supper*, in Santa Maria delle Grazie *(see pp72–3)*

Sant'Ambrogio Basilica dating from the 4th century *(see pp84–7)*

HOW TO USE THIS GUIDE

THIS GUIDE helps you to get the most out of your visit to Milan and the lakes of Northern Italy by providing detailed descriptions of sights, practical information and expert advice. *Introducing Milan*, the first chapter, sets the city in its geographical and historical context, and *Milan at a Glance* provides a brief overview of the architecture and cultural background. *Milan Area by Area* describes the main sightseeing areas in detail, with maps, illustrations and photographs. A special section is dedicated to the lakes of Northern Italy, which are all within easy travelling distance of Milan's city centre. Information on hotels, restaurants, bars, cafés, shops, sports facilities and entertainment venues is covered in the chapter *Travellers' Needs*, and the *Survival Guide* section contains invaluable practical advice on everything from personal security to using the public transport system. The guide ends with a detailed Street Finder map and a map of the public transport network in Milan.

FINDING YOUR WAY AROUND THE SIGHTSEEING SECTION

The city of Milan is divided into five sightseeing areas, each with its own colour-coded thumb tab. Each area has its own chapter, which opens with a numbered list of the sights described. The lakes of Northern Italy are covered in a separate chapter, also colour coded. The chapter on the lakes opens with a road map of the region. The major sights are numbered for easy reference.

1 Introduction to the Area
On this page the major sights are numbered, listed by category and plotted on an area map, which also shows where public transport stops, taxi ranks and car parks are located.

A locator map shows where you are in relation to the other areas of the city.

Each area has a colour-coded thumb tab.

Locator map

The area shaded pink is shown in greater detail on the Street-by-Street map.

2 Street-by-Street Map
This gives a bird's-eye view of the most interesting parts of each sightseeing area. The numbering of the sights ties in with the area map on the preceding page as well as with the fuller descriptions provided on the pages that follow.

A suggested route for a walk covers the most interesting streets in the area.

MILAN AREA BY AREA

The five coloured areas shown on this map *(see pp12–13)* correspond to the main sightseeing areas of Milan – each of which is covered by a full chapter in the *Milan Area by Area* section *(see pp40–123)*. These areas are also highlighted on other maps, for example in the section *Milan at a Glance (see pp26–35)*. The colours on the margins of each area correspond to those on the colour-coded thumb tabs.

Numbers refer to each sight's position on the area map and its place in the chapter.

Practical information provides everything you need to know to visit the sights, including map references to the *Street Finder (see pp216–29)*.

3 Detailed Information on Each Sight

All the most important monuments and other sights are described individually. They are listed in order, following the numbering on the area map. The key to the symbols used is shown on the back flap for easy reference.

The story boxes discuss particular aspects of the places described.

Stars indicate the features you should not miss.

4 The Top Sights

All the most important sights are described individually in two or more pages. Historic buildings and churches are dissected to reveal their interiors. and museums and galleries have colour-coded floorplans to help you locate the major works on exhibit.

The Visitors' Checklist provides all the practical information needed to plan your visit.

INTRODUCING MILAN

ALLI LETTORI.

Quanto la nobilissima Città di Milano sia bella, grande, forte, e populata, e d'acque, per le quali anco uengono barche abondantissima, e d'ogni sorti d'arti piena, e d'il suo territorio fertilissimo. Ciascuno che l'habbia uiste, o praticata, o che leggerà chi di essa ne hà scritto facilmente lo può sapere e pero qui si lassa di narrarlo, ma solo si metterà nell'altro spatio quello che di essa più notabile ne appare.

Putting Milan on the Map

MILAN IS THE CAPITAL OF LOMBARDY (LOMBARDIA), the most densely populated and economically developed region in Italy. The population of Milan is over 1,300,000 (second only to Rome). This figure does not include the many people who live in the suburbs – which have spread outwards over the years – who depend on the city both for work (there are large numbers of commuters) and entertainment. The city lies in the middle of the Po river valley (Valle Padana) and has always been a key commercial centre. Today it forms part of an industrial triangle with the cities of Turin and Genoa. Milan's position makes it an ideal starting point for visits to the Alpine lakes. Lake Maggiore and Lake Como are close to Milan, whereas Lake Garda is further east, with the western shore part of Lombardy, the eastern part of the Veneto.

Europe

The new international airport, Malpensa 2000, in addition to Linate airport, has brought Milan even closer to the other European capitals. Train connections are also excellent.

MILAN AND ENVIRONS

Milan and its Environs

The city, which is described in detail on pages 40–123, is surrounded by a motorway network. A ringroad (beltway), East and West, connects all the incoming roads and is always crowded with traffic.

0 kilometres   5

0 miles

Tangenziale Ovest

Trento

L. d'Idro

L. d'Iseo

Brescia

L. di Garda

Verona

Mantova

Modena

Bologna

Ravenna

Lucca

Pisa

Adriatic Sea

Sea

0 kilometres   40

0 miles   40

Satellite image of lakes Maggiore and Como and the Milan area

KEY

—— Motorway

—— Major road

—— Minor road

—— Railway line

✈ Airport

🚉 Railway station

⛴ Ferry port

Central Milan

ALTHOUGH MILAN is a major city in all
respects, it is comparatively small. The
city has been divided into five areas in this
guide. The historic centre, which you can
visit on foot, takes in the Duomo and Teatro
alla Scala; in the northwestern district are the
Castello Sforzesco and Santa Maria delle
Grazie, whose refectory houses Leonardo da
Vinci's famous *Last Supper*. Sant'Ambrogio
and San Lorenzo lie in the southwest; the
southeast boasts the Ca' Granda, now the
university. The large northeastern district
includes the Brera quarter, with its famous
art gallery, Corso Venezia and the so-called
Quadrilateral, with its designer shops.

Via Montenapoleone
*This is the most famous street in
the area known as the "Quadrilateral", where the
leading fashion
designers are
located*
(see pp
106–7).

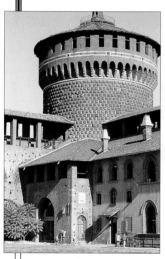

Castello Sforzesco
*The Visconti built this fortress
in 1368 and it was later
rebuilt by the Sforza dynasty,
creating one of Europe's
most elegant Renaissance
residences* (see pp64–7).

| 0 metres | 600 |
| 0 yards | 600 |

**San Lorenzo
alle Colonne**
*This church is one of
the Early Christian
basilicas built for
Sant'Ambrogio (St
Ambrose) in the 4th
century. It is the only
one that still preserves
some of its original
parts* (see pp80–81).

Duomo
*Milan's Lombard-Gothic
cathedral is the third largest
church in the world and took
four centuries to finish. On top
is the* Madonnina, *a statue of
the Madonna that has become
a symbol of the city
(see pp46–9).*

KEY

▢	Major sight
Ⓜ	Metro station
🚖	Taxi stand
🅿	Car park
ℹ	Tourist information
✝	Church
✚	Hospital
👮	Police station

Abbazia di Chiaravalle
*The abbey, founded in 1135 by Cistercian Benedictines,
lies 7 km (4 miles) southeast of Milan (see pp102–3).*

THE HISTORY OF MILAN

ACCORDING TO *the words of a 17th-century ambassador, "Milan never fails to be a great city, and when it declines it soon becomes great again". The sentiments encapsulate one of the characteristics of the city – its ability to rise from the ruins of wars, epidemics, sieges and bombings suffered over the centuries, and to regain dynamism and prosperity once more.*

THE PREHISTORIC AND ROMAN CITY

In the 3rd–2nd millennium BC, the area covered by Milan today was inhabited by the Ligurians. It was later settled by Indo-European populations and then, in the 5th century BC, by the Etruscans. Around the lakes, archaeologists have unearthed fascinating pre-Roman objects that reveal the presence of a Celtic civilization in the 9th–6th centuries BC. Milan itself was founded in the early 4th century BC when the Gallic Insuber tribes settled there.

The origins of the city are somewhat obscure, as is its name, which most scholars say derives from *Midland* (or "middle of the plain"), while others say it derives from *scrofa semilanuta* (half-woolly boar), the city emblem in ancient times. In 222 BC the Romans, led by the consuls Cnaeus Cornelius Scipio and Claudius Marcellus, defeated the Celts and conquered the Po river valley and its cities. Milan soon became a flourishing commercial centre and in the Imperial era

Slab with a relief of the half-woolly boar, once the city emblem

attained political and administrative independence. In AD 286 it became the capital of the Western Roman Empire (until 402) and was the residence of Emperor Maximian. By the late Imperial era Milan was the most important city in the West after Rome and it became a leading religious centre after Constantine's Edict of Milan in 313, which officially recognized Christianity as a religion. Sant'Ambrogio (Ambrose) exerted great influence at this time. He was the first great figure in Milan's history: a Doctor of the Church, he built four basilicas (San Simpliciano, Sant'Ambrogio, San Lorenzo, San Nazaro) and was a leading opponent of the Arian heresy (which denied the divinity of Christ). Sant'Ambrogio was the first in a long series of bishops who ran the city's affairs in the early Middle Ages. Roman Milan was a substantial size: the Republican walls, enlarged to the northeast during the Imperial Age, defined an area that was roughly the same size as the present-day city centre.

TIMELINE

4th century BC	191 BC	89 BC	15 BC		Sant'Ambrogio
Foundation of *Mediolanum* by Gallic Insubers	Through an alliance, Milan becomes an integral part of Roman world	Milan becomes Latin colony	Milan capital of IX Augustan region		
			AD 286 Maximian makes Milan Imperial capital		

14th–3rd century BC		2nd–1st century BC	1st–2nd century AD		3rd–4th century AD
222 BC Cnaeus Cornelius Scipio conquers Milan		**55–50 BC** Virgil attends School of Rhetoric in Milan *Virgil*	**49 BC** *Lex Roscia* confers Roman citizenship on Milan	**AD 313** With the Edict of Milan, Constantine grants Christians religious freedom	**AD 374** Sant'Ambrogio (340–397) is made Bishop of Milan

◁ **The *Sforzesca Altarpiece* (1494), now in the Brera art gallery, with portraits of Beatrice d'Este and Lodovico il Moro**

THE EARLY MIDDLE AGES
AND THE COMMUNE OF MILAN

The 5th and 6th centuries marked a period of decline for Milan. In 402 it lost its status as Imperial capital, was sacked by Attila's Huns in 452, conquered by the Germanic Eruli in 476 and then by Ostrogoths in 489. During the war between the Greek Byzantines and Goths, the city, allies of the former, was attacked by the Goths and utterly destroyed. Reconstruction began in 568, when the city was reconquered by the Byzantine general Narses, who was forced to cede it to the Lombards in the following year. Milan was then ruled by the city of Pavia. The few remaining citizens, led by their bishop Honorius, fled to Liguria: what had been one of the most prosperous cities in the Western Roman Empire was reduced to ruins in the 6th and 7th centuries. The Edict of Rothari of 643 describes in detail Lombard administrative structures of the time.

Emperor Frederick Barbarossa at the Battle of Legnano (1176) in a 1308 miniature

In 774, the Franks defeated the Lombards and conquered Northern Italy. The archbishops regained power and there was a revival of the economy with the rise of an artisan and merchant class, which in the 11th century led to the birth of the commune. After centuries in which Monza and Pavia had been the focal points of Lombardy, Milan was once again the political centre of the region. The aristocrats and mercantile classes struggled for power in the 11th century, but then joined forces

King Rothari proclaims his edict (643), miniature, _Codex Legum Longobardorum_

to defend the city against the emperor. Once again the city was led by a series of archbishops, some of whom, such as Ariberto d'Intimiano (1018–45), were both bishops and generals. In 1042 the free commune of Milan was founded and a new city wall built. It was demolished in 1162 when, after a siege, the Milanese were forced to open their gates to Frederick Barbarossa: for the second time the city was burned to the ground. Milan and other northern communes together formed the Lombard League, which defeated Barbarossa's troops at Legnano in 1176. Seven years later the Treaty of Constance sanctioned the freedom of these communes.

TIMELINE

	569 Invasion of Alboin's Lombards	**570** Entire Po river valley under Lombard dominion	**616** Theodolinda, wife of Authari and then of Agilulf, heads regency		*Agilulf and Theodolinda*	
c.491 Invasion of Burgundians						
400	**500**	**600**	**700**	**800**	**900**
452 Milan is sacked by Attila	**539** The Goths exterminate the local population		**643** Edict of Rothari		**824** Milan becomes powerful under its bishops who, defying the Church of Rome, defend the Ambrosian rite
		591 Agilulf is elected King of Italy in the Roman circus			

In the 13th century, Milan created a formidable canal network, the Navigli, which linked the city to Ticino in Switzerland. However, power struggles among the leading families sapped the strength of the entire city and foreshadowed its decline.

THE GREAT DYNASTIES

In 1277 at Desio, the Visconti, under Archbishop Ottone, overthrew the Torriani family. The Visconti then summoned the leading artists of the time, including Giotto, to Milan to embellish the city and its palazzi, and they commissioned new buildings such as the Castello and the Duomo *(see pp46–9)*. The height of Visconti power was achieved under Gian Galeazzo, who became duke in 1395 and undertook an ambitious policy of expansion. Milan soon ruled most of Northern Italy and even controlled some cities in Tuscany, but the duke's dream of a united Italy under his lead came to

Coat of arms of the Visconti family

an end with his death in 1402. The Visconti dynasty died out in 1447 and for three years the city enjoyed self-government under the Ambrosian Republic. In 1450 the *condottiere* Francesco Sforza initiated what was perhaps the most felicitous period in the history of Milan: he abandoned the Visconti expansionist policy and secured lasting peace for the city, which flourished and grew to a population of 100,000. The Visconti castle was rebuilt and became the Castello Sforzesco *(see pp64–7)*, while architects such as Guiniforte Solari and Filarete began work on the Ospedale Maggiore, better known as Ca' Granda *(see p97)*. However, Milan's cultural golden age came with Lodovico Sforza, known as "il Moro" (1479–1508). He was an undisciplined politician but a great patron of the arts. His policy of alliances and strategic decisions marked the end of freedom for Milan, which in 1499 fell under French dominion, yet during his rule Milanese arts and culture were second only to Medici Florence. From 1480 on, great men such as Bramante and Leonardo da Vinci were active in Milan. The former restored numerous churches and designed Santa Maria delle Grazie *(see p71)*, in whose refectory Leonardo painted *The Last Supper (see pp72–3)*, one of his many masterpieces. Leonardo also worked on major city projects such as the Navigli network of canals.

Milan in a 15th-century print

The Visconti and Sforza

T HE PERIOD of the *Signorie*, or family lordships, from the late 13th to the early 16th century, was one of the most successful in the history of Milan. The Visconti dynasty succeeded – especially during Gian Galeazzo's rule – in expanding the city's territories, albeit for a brief span of time. The Sforza dukedom is best known for the cultural and artistic splendour commissioned by Lodovico il Moro, who invited the leading artists and architects of the time to his court.

Gian Galeazzo
imprisoned his uncle Bernabò in 1385 and became sole ruler of Milan. He was made a duke by Emperor Wenceslaus ten years later.

Umberto
† before 1248

| **OTTONE** | **Obizzo** | **Andreotto** |
Archbishop of Milan
Lord of Milan
(1277–8, 1282–5)
† 1295

Tebaldo
† 1276

Ottone
Archbishop of Milan in 1262, he was recognized lord of the city in 1277, after the battle of Desio.

MATTEO
Lord of Milan
(1291–1302, 1311–22)
† 1322

Marco	**GIOVANNI**	**Stefano**	**GALEAZZO I**	**LUCHINO**
† 1329	Archbishop of Milan	Lord of Arona	Lord of Piacenza	**Lord of Milan**
	Lord of Milan	† 1327	**Lord of Milan**	**(1339)**
	(1339)		**(1322–27)**	† 1349
	† 1354		† 1328	

BERNABÒ	**GALEAZZO II**	**MATTEO II**	**AZZONE**
Lord of Milan	**Lord of Milan**	**Lord of Milan**	**Lord of Milan**
(1354–85)	**(1354)**	**(1354)**	**(1329–39)**
	† 1378		

Caterina
Wife of Gian Galeazzo
† 1404

VISCONTI

After defeating the Della Torre (Torriani) family in 1277, the Visconti ruled Milan until 1447, and from 1395 were dukes of the city. Their policy centred around systematic territorial expansion. Under Gian Galeazzo the duchy reached its maximum extent, even conquering Perugia and Siena in central Italy.

GIAN GALEAZZO
Count of Virtue
Lord of Milan (1378)
Duke of Milan (1395–1402)
Married Caterina di Bernabò

GIAN MARIA	**FILIPPO MARIA**
Duke of Milan	*Duke of Milan*
(1402–12)	**(1412–47)**

**Bianca Maria Visconti
and Francesco Sforza**
The sole heir to the duchy, Bianca Maria married Francesco Sforza in 1441 and then helped her husband to take over power in Milan.

Bianca Maria
Wife of Francesco Sforza
Duke of Milan
(1450–66)

SFORZA

After the three-year Ambrosian Republic, the city had a new duke in 1450, Francesco Sforza, the *condottiere* son of Muzio Attendolo, known as "Sforza". The 50 years of Sforza family rule were the most prosperous and splendid Milan had ever enjoyed. Art and commerce flourished, particularly under Lodovico il Moro. However, his unscrupulous foreign policy led to the fall of the dukedom and the end of freedom in Milan.

Francesco I
This great warrior had fought for Filippo Maria Visconti, and married his daughter Bianca Maria. In 1454 he began expanding the duchy through peaceful means until it included Genoa and Corsica.

Muzio Attendolo
Count of Cotignola
† 1424

FRANCESCO I
Natural son of Lucia Terzani,
married Bianca Maria Visconti
Duke of Milan from 1450
† 1466

LODOVICO called IL MORO
Duke of Milan from 1494
† 1508

GALEAZZO MARIA
Duke of Milan from 1466
† 1476

Ascanio
Became cardinal in 1484
† 1505

Lodovico Il Moro
Born in 1452, he usurped power from his nephew Gian Galeazzo Maria in 1480. After being defeated at Novara (1500) he was exiled to France and died there in 1508.

GIAN GALEAZZO MARIA
Duke of Milan from 1476
† 1494

Bianca Maria
wife of Emperor Maximilian
of Habsburg
† 1510

Bona
wife of Sigismund I
King of Poland
† 1557

ERCOLE MASSIMILIANO
Duke of Milan (1512–15)
† 1530

FRANCESCO II
Duke of Milan
(1521–24; 1525; 1529–35) † 1494

The Castello Sforzesco is one of the symbols of the Signoria period in Milan.

WHERE TO SEE
VISCONTI AND SFORZA MILAN

The Milan of the Visconti family is basically Gothic. The main monuments either started or completed under Visconti rule are the Duomo *(see pp46–9)*, San Gottardo *(see p54)* and San Marco (which, however, has been radically altered: *see p112*). Under the Sforza family there was a transition from Gothic to Renaissance architecture, as can be seen in San Pietro in Gessate *(see p99)* and especially in Santa Maria delle Grazie, where Leonardo painted *The Last Supper (see pp71– 3).* The Ospedale Maggiore, or Ca' Granda *(see p97)* was designed by Filarete for Francesco Sforza, and the Castello Sforzesco *(see pp64– 7)* was built by the Visconti but enlarged and embellished by the Sforza, hence the name.

FRANCE AND SPAIN

The Renaissance petered out in the 16th century and was followed by a long period of decline. Milan was greatly affected by the loss of political and military importance on the part of the Italian states, now battlefields for other European powers, and because of its wealth and strategic position the city was a key target. The presence of foreign troops was so common that it gave rise to a bitterly sarcastic proverb: "Franza o Spagna purché se magna" (France or Spain, it doesn't matter, as long as we have something on our platter). When Francesco Sforza died in 1535, Emperor Charles V appointed a governor for Milan and the city thus officially became an Imperial province. However, the city nonetheless con-

Charles V in a portrait by Titian (1532–3)

tinued to thrive and the population grew to 130,000. Its territory expanded and from 1548 to 1560 new city walls were built (called the Spanish walls) corresponding to today's inner ring road. The walls were the most important public works undertaken during Spanish rule. All that is left now is Porta Romana arch, though not in its original position. Many Baroque buildings, such as Palazzo Durini and those facing Corso di Porta Romana, were also built in this period. Among the leading figures in Spanish Milan was San Carlo Borromeo (1538–84), cardinal and archbishop of Milan, patron of the arts and benefactor, who rebuilt many churches and was one of the leading figures in the Counter Reformation. His nephew Federico (1564–1631) was also later archbishop of Milan and was immortalized in Manzoni's novel *I Promessi Sposi (The Betrothed)*, a wide-ranging portrait of Milan under Spanish rule. Economic and social decline reached its lowest point with the 1630 plague, which brought the city's population down to 60,000.

ALESSANDRO MANZONI'S THE BETROTHED

Considered one of the greatest novels in Italian literature and a masterpiece of 19th-century European narrative, *The Betrothed (I Promessi Sposi)* is also a splendid portrait of Milan under Spanish rule in the 1600s. Manzoni rewrote it several times and had three different editions published (1820, with the title *Fermo e Lucia*, 1827 and 1840). The novel is set in 1828–31 and portrays different phases of Milanese life. In chapter 12 the hero Renzo is involved in the bread riots (in Corso Vittorio Emanuele, a plaque marks the site of the bakery), while from chapter 31 onwards there are vivid descriptions of the city devastated by the plague of 1630.

Title page of a rare 1827 edition of Manzoni's novel

I Promessi Sposi
STORIA MILANESE
DEL SECOLO XVII
SCOPERTA E RIFATTA
DA
Alessandro Manzoni
—
TOMO PRIMO
—
LUGANO
Tipografia Veladini e Comp.
1827.

ENLIGHTENMENT MILAN

Spanish rule ended in 1706, when during the War of Spanish Succes-

French troops at the city walls

The leading architect of the time was Giuseppe Piermarini, who designed the Teatro alla Scala *(see pp52–3)*, rebuilt Palazzo Reale in a Neo-Classical style, planned the urban renewal of the historic centre and designed the Corso Venezia gardens. The city's flourishing cultural life did not diminish even when the Austrians had to flee from Napoleon's troops in 1796. As the capital of the short-lived Cisalpine Republic, Milan was the setting for Napoleon's coronation in the Cathedral (1804) and witnessed the con-struction of various new building pro-jects, including the Foro Bonaparte, the Arena and the Arco della Pace. After Napoleon's defeat, the Congress of Vienna handed Milan back to the Habsburgs, whose government, however, was quite different from the one under Maria Theresa.

Maria Theresa of Austria

sion Austrian troops occupied the city. Milan remained part of the Austro-Hungarian Empire until 1859, except for the Napoleonic period and the Cinque Giornate rebellion *(see pp22–3)*. Economic and, in particular, cultural revival marked the 18th century. Milan was one of the capitals of the Enlightenment, encouraged by Maria Theresa's wise administration (1740–80). From June 1764 to May 1766 a group of Milanese intellec-tuals, including Cesare Beccaria and the Verri brothers, published the periodical *Il Caffè*, influencing Italian cultural life by propounding the ideas of the French "Encyclopedists".

There were many abortive revolts, and Milan became one of the focal points of Romanticism and the struggle for Italian independence and unity as propounded in the local periodical *Il Conciliatore*. The publication was repressed by censors and its main exponents (Pellico, Confalonieri and Maroncelli) were imprisoned. The independence movement continued to grow, with the help of the operas of Verdi, and reached its peak with the revolt known as the *Cinque Giornate di Milano*, when the Milanese succeeded, albeit briefly, in driving the Austrian troops out of the city.

Abbé Longo, Alessandro Verri, Giovanni Battista Biffi and Cesare Beccaria, the founders of *Il Caffè*

The Cinque Giornate Revolt

THIS HISTORIC EVENT was preceded by the "smoking strike", held during the first three days of 1848, when the Milanese refused to buy tobacco as a protest against Austrian taxation. The "Five Days" revolt began on 18 March 1848. Clashes initially broke out after a demonstration and continued in a disorderly fashion for two days, during which the Austrians, led by Field Marshal Radetzky, were initially besieged inside the Castello Sforzesco. Then, after the formation of a War Council and a Provisional Government on 22 March at Porta Tosa, the Imperial troops were defeated and driven out of Milan.

The Italian flag in 1848

Carlo Cattaneo (1801–69)
Cattaneo was one of the leaders in the Cinque Giornate, and later went into exile in Switzerland.

Carlo Alberto's Proclamation
With this declaration, Carlo Alberto, king of Sardinia, put himself at the head of the revolt. Yet when the opportune occasion arose he failed to attack the Austrians and in August 1848 he was forced to cede Milan to the Austrian Radetzky.

Behind the barricades were people from all social classes, demonstrating the unity of the Milanese in the battle for independence.

The Austrian Army
Field Marshal Radetzky had some 74,000 men (about a third of them Italians) at his disposal, divided into two army corps. The first and larger one was stationed in Milan.

PORTA TOSA
This painting by Carlo Canella, now in the Museo di Milano, represents the *Battle at Porta Tosa*, when the Milanese dealt the final blow to the Austrian troops on 22 March. After this historic event, the city gate, which is situated in the eastern part of the city, was renamed Porta Vittoria (Victory Gate).

Pasquale Sottocorno
Despite being crippled, this 26-year-old shoemaker managed to set fire to the military engineers' building where the enemy troops were barracked, and capture the hospital of San Marco, which was another Austrian stronghold.

ABITANTI DELLA LOMBARDIA!

Alla testa del prode e vittorioso mio esercito sono entrato sul vostro suolo come il liberatore vostro da una dominazione rivoluzionaria e tirannica. Molti di voi, sedotti da perfide suggestioni, hanno dimenticato i sacri doveri verso il legittimo loro Sovrano. Tornate devoti sotto lo scettro benigno del nostro Imperatore e Re. Io vi offro la mano a sincera conciliazione.

Abitanti la Lombardia, ascoltate il benevolo mio consiglio. Confidenti accogliete le brave mie Truppe. Esse guarentiranno al cittadino pacifico ogni maggior sicurezza della persona e della proprietà, ma contro chi si ostinasse nel cieco delirio della ribellione procederanno irremissibilmente con tutta la severità della legge marziale.

A voi sta la scelta; a me l'impegno di esattamente adempire la mia parola.

Dal Quartier-Generale di Valleggio 27 Luglio 1848.

RADETZKY

The Austrians, forced into retreat

The Austrians Return
After he had defeated King Carlo Alberto at Custoza (25 July), Radetzky returned to Lombardy, as announced in this proclamation of 27 July. He recaptured Milan on 6 August.

Over 1,600 barricades were set up throughout the city during the insurrection.

The Soldier's Widow
In Italy the struggle for independence was closely linked to Romanticism, as can be seen in works dating from this period, such as this 1851 sculpture by Giovanni Pandiani.

THE CINQUE GIORNATE REVOLT

Radetzky

	18 March	19 March	20 March	21 March	22 March
		The revolt spreads throughout the city and barricades are built everywhere		Radetzky proposes an armistice but is rejected	
	Demonstration in the Monforte district for freedom of the press and the establishment of a Civil Guard. Radetzky is besieged in the Castello Sforzesco		Formation of the War Council and Provisional Government	*Guardia Nobile helmet*	The Imperial troops suffer defeat in the last battle at Porta Tosa (renamed Porta Vittoria) and abandon Milan

MILAN AFTER ITALY'S UNIFICATION

In 1861 the population of Milan was 240,000, which shows how much the city had grown under Austrian rule. However, the real demographic explosion was yet to come. Although Milan did not become the political capital after the unification of Italy, it became the economic and cultural capital of the country. Infrastructures created by the Austrians were exploited to the full and by 1920 the city had developed into a thriving industrial metropolis. Business was booming, *Corriere della Sera*, the leading Italian daily newspaper, was founded, the city increased in size and the population exploded (there were 850,000 inhabitants in 1923). This over-rapid growth inevitably brought major social consequences: the first trade union centre was founded, and socialist groups grew in strength. Strikes and demonstrations became more and more frequent, and social tensions exploded in 1898, when a protest against the high cost of living was violently repressed by cannon fire, on the orders of General Bava Beccaris. The early 20th century witnessed the rise of an important avant-garde movement in Milan (the

The 1898 demonstration quelled by Bava Beccaris

A Corriere della Sera poster

second in the city after the Scapigliatura movement of the second half of the 19th century): Futurism, which was founded by Filippo Tommaso Marinetti (a plaque in Corso Venezia commemorates the event). The Futurists were not only important from an artistic standpoint, but also because their ideas and actions fitted in perfectly with the cultural temper of the times, characterized by the pro-intervention attitude regarding World War I and then the rise of Fascism. In fact, Fascism and Mussolini had a very close relationship with Milan. The original nucleus of the movement was founded in Milan in 1919. In 1943, after the fall of the regime and the foundation of the Repubblica Sociale puppet government, Milan – severely damaged by bombing raids – was the last large Italian city to remain under the control of the remaining Fascists and the Germans. On 26 April 1945, the story of Mussolini and Italian Fascism played out its final moments in Milan: the corpses of il Duce, his mistress Claretta Petacci and some party officials were put on display in Piazzale

Milan after the 1943 bombings

Loreto, exactly the same place where some partisans had been executed a few weeks earlier.

THE POSTWAR PERIOD

On 11 May 1946, Arturo Toscanini conducted a concert celebrating the re-opening of the Teatro alla Scala, which had been destroyed by bombs during the war.

Logo of Teatro alla Scala

This historic event demonstrated the desire for recovery and reconstruction that characterized postwar Milan. The linchpin of an industrial triangle with Turin and Genoa, Milan now had 1,800,000 inhabitants. This period of secure growth, disturbed only by student protests in 1968, ended on 12 December 1969, when the explosion of a terrorist bomb in a bank in Piazza Fontana, causing a massacre, began the long, grim period of terrorist activity. The 1980s saw the development of the fashion industry that has made Milan one of the world leaders in this field. The most recent significant event in the city's history was the 1992 anti-corruption investigations which forced many members of the ruling parties to step down from power.

PRESENT-DAY MILAN

Thanks to the dynamism, productivity and inventiveness of its people, today's Milan is a leading European city, but it still has a number of problems: the decline in population, now 1.36 million, is proof of a growing dissatisfaction with a city that is considered, for example, unsuitable for children. The rapid increase in commuter traffic has not been matched by adequate long-distance public transport, which is why the city is frequently blocked by heavy traffic. Last, although Milan is probably the most multicultural city in Italy, clandestine immigration causes its own social problems. Despite this, Milan is an avant-garde city by all standards, a financial, professional and cultural leader in Italian life.

THE GROWTH OF MILAN

This map shows the growth of Milan from the original Roman city to the present-day metropolis.

KEY

- The Roman city
- The medieval city
- Up to the 18th century
- The 19th century
- The early 20th century
- Present-day Milan

1943 The city is heavily bombed	**1950** Creation of Metanopoli, satellite city of San Donato Milanese	*The Pirelli Building*		**1992** Outbreak of political corruption scandal	
			1973 Telemilano (later Canale 5) first private TV station in Italy		

1940	1950	1960	1970	1980	1990	2000
	1946 Toscanini conducts the opening concert of the restored La Scala	**1955–60** The Pirelli Building is constructed		**1973** Bomb in Via Fatebenefratelli	**1997** Dario Fo, actor and playwright, wins Nobel Prize for Literature	**2000** "Needle, Thread and Knot" sculpture erected in Piazza Cadorna
		1969 Bomb at Piazza Fontana				

MILAN AT A GLANCE

ONE OF THE MANY CLICHÉS about Milan is that it is a practical, industrious, even drab city, wholly dedicated to work and the world of commercial gain. In fact, besides being a leading metropolis in Europe from a financial standpoint and in terms of productivity, it is also rich in history and culture, architecture and art. The historic centre has no single dominating architectural style, and the buildings are perhaps more varied than any other city centre in Italy. The museums and galleries are among the finest in Northern Italy, and many of the leading figures in the fields of Italian art, design, culture and politics were either born in Milan or achieved success here. The following eight pages will provide brief descriptions of some of the major aspects of the city, while below is a selection of top attractions that no visitor to Milan should miss.

MILAN'S TOP TEN ATTRACTIONS

Pinacoteca Ambrosiana
See pp56–9

Ca' Granda
See p97

Sant'Ambrogio
See pp84–7

Teatro alla Scala
See pp52–3

San Lorenzo alle Colonne
See pp80–1

Abbazia di Chiaravalle
See pp102–3

Duomo
See pp46–9

Castello Sforzesco
See pp64–7

Pinacoteca di Brera
See pp114–7

The Last Supper
See pp72–3

◁ **Statues decorating the exterior of the Duomo**

Famous Residents and Visitors

MANY LEADING FIGURES in Italian cultural life are connected in some way with Milan, from intellectuals, journalists and politicians to composers, writers and poets. The Italian novelist Alessandro Manzoni was born in Milan, and many other artists have been drawn here, hoping to make their fortune (an illustrious example is Giuseppe Verdi) or, more simply, to find work. One of the most widespread, and perhaps most accurate, sayings about Milan is that it is an open, receptive city ready to give strangers and foreigners a sincere, if brusque, welcome.

Carlo Emilio Gadda (1893–1973)
Milanese by birth, Gadda was one of the great 20th-century authors. One of his major works, L'Adalgisa, celebrates the lives of middle-class Milanese and ends with the hero cleaning the tombs in the Monumental Cemetery.

Giorgio Strehler (1921–97)
In 1947 the great Trieste-born director founded the Piccolo Teatro della Città di Milano with Paolo Grassi. It was the first permanent theatre in Italy.

NORTHWEST
(see pp60–75)

Leonardo da Vinci (1452–1519)
In 1482 Lodovico il Moro invited Leonardo da Vinci to his court in Milan, where he remained for almost 20 years. He left a number of works, including the Codex Atlanticus, *now in the* Biblioteca Ambrosiana *and* The Last Supper, *in Santa Maria delle Grazie (see pp72–3).*

SOUTHWEST
(see pp76–91)

0 metres	700
0 yards	700

Benito Mussolini (1883–1945)
In 1919, in Milan's Piazza San Sepolcro, Mussolini founded the Fasci Nazionali di Combattimento, *the first nucleus of the future Fascist movement. On 16 December 1944 Mussolini gave his last speech at the Teatro Lirico in Milan. A few months later, on 26 April 1945, his corpse was hung upside down in Piazzale Loreto.*

Giuseppe Verdi (1813–1901)
Born in Busseto, in the province of Parma, Verdi moved to Milan at a very early age. His third opera, Nabucco *(1842), brought him fame. He died at the Grand Hotel et de Milan, which he had made his home.*

Alessandro Manzoni (1785–1873)
Manzoni wrote what is considered the greatest Italian novel, The Betrothed, *as well as plays and poetry. His house in Piazza Belgioioso (see p51) is open to the public.*

Cesare Beccaria (1738–94)
A leading exponent of the Enlightenment movement in Milan, Beccaria wrote its most representative work, On Crimes and Punishment. *In the square named after him is a monument in his honour.*

NORTHEAST
(see pp104–23)

STORIC
ENTRE
e pp42–59)

SOUTHEAST
(see pp92–103)

The Verri Brothers
Pietro (1728–97) and Alessandro (1741–1816) Verri met other noted Enlightenment figures at the Caffè Greco, opposite the Duomo, where they conceived the influential periodical Il Caffè.

Carlo Porta (1775–1821)
A poet who wrote in Milanese dialect, Porta offered a vivacious description of the society of his time in his satirical poems. There is a monument in his honour in Piazza Santo Stefano, which was the setting for one of his best-known works, Ninetta del Verzee.

Milan's Best: Churches and Basilicas

Т HE CHURCHES OF MILAN are built in
two basic architectural styles:
Lombard Romanesque, which can be
seen elsewhere in the region, and the
Counter-Reformation Mannerism of
Milan under the Borromeos. The only
exception is the magnificent Duomo, a
splendid example of Lombard Gothic.
There are very few examples of older
styles. This is partly the result of
destructive invasions and time, but is
mostly due to the fact that the city is
built just above the water table, and
older buildings had to be demolished
to make way for new ones.

**Santa Maria
delle Grazie**
*Besides being home
to Leonardo's* Last
Supper, *this church,
designed by Solari
and Bramante, is a
marvellous example
of Renaissance
architecture*
(see pp71–3).

Basilica of Sant'Ambrogio
*The famous church founded by
Sant'Ambrogio has a long architectural
history, culminating in the restoration
carried out to repair damage caused by
the bombs of World War II (see pp84–7).*

NORTHWEST
(see pp60–75)

SOUTHWEST
(see pp76–91)

Basilica of San Lorenzo
*This late 4th-century basilica
still has some original
architectural elements, such
as the columns that surround
the courtyard (see pp80–81).*

**Basilica of
Sant'Eustorgio**
*Inside this 9th-
century basilica are
several aristocratic
chapels, including
the Cappella
Portinari, one of the
great examples of
Renaissance
architecture in Milan*
(see p90).

San Marco
The basic structure is 13th-century Romanesque, while the Neo-Gothic façade was built in 1871. The three statues depicting San Marco between Sant'Ambrogio and Sant'Agostino (above) are works of the Campionese school (see p112).

San Fedele
This typical example of Counter-Reformation architecture was begun in 1569. Pellegrini's original design was completed by Bassi, who built the façade, and by Richini (see p50).

NORTHEAST
(see pp104–23)

**HISTORIC
CENTRE**
*see
pp42–59)*

SOUTHEAST
(see pp92–103)

Duomo
Milan's cathedral is the third largest church in the world (see pp46–9). It was begun by the Visconti family in 1386 and finished by Napoleon in 1805 – over four centuries later.

0 metres	700
0 yards	700

Basilica of San Nazaro Maggiore
Founded by Sant'Ambrogio towards the end of the 4th century, the basilica has been altered many times, but recent restoration work has revived its original austere beauty. Do not miss the Trivulzio Chapel (see p96).

Milan's Best: Buildings and Gardens

CIVIC ARCHITECTURE in Milan suffered the same fate as religious architecture: the sequence of destruction wrought by successive waves of invaders meant constant rebuilding, to the detriment of the works of the past. Nonetheless, the city has emerged enriched, as can be seen in the splendid Baroque buildings in the city centre, the Neo-Classical examples in Corso Venezia, and the late 19th-century Art Nouveau architecture. With all its buildings Milan may seem to have little greenery, but in fact there are landscaped gardens, court-yards and public parks which stand comparison with any northern European city.

Art Nouveau detail, Casa Galimberti *(see p119)*

Castello Sforzesco and Parco Sempione
Behind the fortress built by the Visconti and enlarged by the Sforza (see pp64–7), is the Parco Sempione, the largest park in Milan (see p68).

Casa degli Omenoni
This was the residence of the sculptor Leone Leoni (1509–90), who built it in 1565. The eight telamones, called omenoni *by the Milanese, are by Antonio Abbondio (see p51).*

NORTHWEST
(see pp60–75)

SOUTHWEST
(see pp76–91)

Parco delle Basiliche
This park lies between the basilicas of Sant'Eustorgio and San Lorenzo, hence its name (it is also called Piazza della Vetra). Part of the park was created from land which had been bombed during World War II (see p82).

Palazzo della Ragione
Construction of this splendid example of Romanesque civic architecture began in 1228. Inside is the huge Sala della Ragione (see p54).

Stazione Centrale
The grandiose central railway station was opened in 1931, after almost 20 years of construction work (see p119). Nearby is the Pirelli Building (1955–60), Milan's tallest skyscraper (see p118).

Giardini Pubblici
The public gardens were designed by Piermarini (late 18th century) and house exotic plants, museums and a Planetarium (see pp120–21).

Palazzo Serbelloni
One of the most imposing examples of Milanese Neo-Classical architecture (1793) stands in elegant Corso Venezia (see pp122–3). Napoleon, Metternich and Vittorio Emanuele II were guests here.

NORTHEAST
(see pp104–23)

HISTORIC CENTRE
(see pp42–59)

SOUTHEAST
(see pp92–103)

0 metres	600
0 yards	600

Torre Velasca
A symbol of postwar Milan, this tower was built during the "economic boom" of the late 1950s. It is 106 m (348 ft) high and is based on medieval towers (see p96).

Ca' Granda
Francesco Sforza commissioned this building in the second half of the 15th century as a city hospital (Ospedale Maggiore). It is now the University. Three building phases can be seen: dating from the 15th century, 17th century, and late 18th and early 19th centuries (see p97).

Milan's Best: Museums and Galleries

17th-century clock, Museo della Scienza e della Tecnica

Besides housing priceless works of art, the museums and art galleries of Milan also reflect the history of the city. The Pinacoteca di Brera was founded at the height of the Enlightenment period and the Ambrosiana is the result of patronage of religious art by the Borromeo family. The Castello Sforzesco collections date from the period of the *Signorie*, while the Galleria d'Arte Moderna is a sign of civic commitment to fine arts. Last, the Museo Bagatti Valsecchi and Poldi Pezzoli, private collections, are typical manifestations of the Milanese love of art.

Pinacoteca di Brera
One of Northern Italy's largest art galleries has works from the 14th to the 19th century. Above, Pietà *by Giovanni Bellini (see pp114–7).*

Musei del Castello
The Castello Sforzesco museums are rich in sculpture, furniture and applied arts and also include a gallery with works by great artists, such as this Madonna and Child with the Infant St John the Baptist *by Correggio (see pp64–7).*

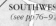

NORTHWEST
(see pp60–75)

Museo Nazionale della Scienza e della Tecnica
The Science and Technology Museum has wooden models of Leonardo's inventions and a section given over to clocks, computers and means of communication and transport (see p88).

SOUTHWEST
(see pp76–9)

Pinacoteca Ambrosiana
This art gallery was founded by Cardinal Federico Borromeo in the 17th century to provide models for the students at the Fine Arts Academy. The collections include works by artists such as Caravaggio and Raphael (see pp56–9), while the Biblioteca Ambrosiana (library) contains the precious Codex Atlanticus *by Leonardo da Vinci.*

Galleria d'Arte Moderna
The imposing Villa Reale (see p121) houses 19th-century Italian art collections, the Museo Marini, the Vismara Collection and the Grassi Collection. Right, Matilda Juva Branca *(1851) by Francesco Hayez.*

Museo Poldi Pezzoli
Together with the many works by Italian artists in this splendid residence-cum-museum (see p108) is Lucas Cranach's Portrait of Martin Luther.

NORTHEAST
(see pp104–123)

Museo Bagatti Valsecchi
This marvellous example of a 19th-century private residence contains 16th-century handicrafts, furniture, arms, ivory pieces, paintings and ceramics (see p109).

Museo del Duomo
The Duomo Museum was founded in 1953 and holds fine sculptures and other objects representing the religious history of Milan. Right, the 16th-century Ambrosian Monstrance, *made of rock crystal and precious stones (see p49).*

ISTORIC
ENTRE
ee pp42–59)

SOUTHEAST
(see pp92–103)

Civico Museo d'Arte Contemporanea
On the second floor of Palazzo Reale, now under restoration (see p54), this museum has a good Futurist collection and works by famous artists such as Picasso and Klee. The sculpture collection is also important, and includes this Woman at the Mirror *by Lucio Fontana (1934).*

0 metres	700
0 yards	700

MILAN THROUGH THE YEAR

MILAN OFFERS a range of different events and attractions at different seasons of the year, from traditional to commercial. The city's citizens are still attached to traditional religious celebrations such as the Carnevale Ambrosiano (Milanese Carnival) and the festivities that take place around 7 December, the Festival of Sant'Ambrogio, the city's patron saint. This is also the date of opening night at La Scala, the world-famous opera house. Such traditional and characteristic festivities alternate with other events that are perhaps more in keeping with the image of a modern, industrial city. Among these are Fashion Week, one of the world's top fashion shows, held twice a year, and SMAU, an important international multimedia and communications technology trade show.

Private courtyards in Milan, open to the public in the spring

SPRING

AFTER THE LONG Milanese winter, local inhabitants welcome the arrival of spring with a sigh of relief. The pleasant spring breezes clear the air of the notorious Milanese smog and the city seems to take on different colours. On very clear days, if you look northwards you will see the peaks of the Alps, which are still covered with snow – one of the finest views the city affords at this time of year.

Towards the end of spring, the clear weather may very well give way to showers and even violent storms, which may blow up in the space of just a few hours, causing problems with city traffic.

This is the season when tourist activity resumes at the lakes. Boat services start up again and the water becomes a major weekend attraction for the Milanese once more.

MARCH

MODIT-Milanovendemoda *(beginning of month)*. The autumn-winter collections of the leading international and Italian fashion designers go on show.
Milano–SanRemo *(third Sat)*. Part of the city centre hosts the start of this prestigious international bicycle race.
Oggi Aperto *(third weekend)*. Monuments and historic buildings usually closed to the public are now open.
BIT. The Fiera (Milan's Exhibition Centre) hosts an international tourist trade show.

APRIL

Fiera dei Fiori *(Mon after Easter)*. In and around Via Moscova, near the Sant'Angelo Franciscan convent, is this fair devoted mainly to flower growing.
Bagutta-Pittori all'Aria Aperta *(third week)*. The famous Via Bagutta plays host to a fascinating outdoor exhibition for artists' work.
Stramilano *(mid-Apr)*. This celebrated marathon is for professionals and amateurs alike and attracts an average of 50,000 competitors every year.

MAY

Milano Cortili Aperti. The courtyards of the city's private residences are open to the public.
Pittori sul Naviglio. Outdoor art display along the Alzaia Naviglio Grande canal *(see p89)*.
Estate all'Idroscalo. Near Linate airport, the Milan seaplane airport inaugurates its summer season with sports events, water entertainment and concerts.
Sagra del Carroccio. At Legnano, 30 km (19 miles) from Milan, there is a commemoration of the battle of 1176, when the Lombard League defeated Emperor Frederick Barbarossa: parades in costume and folk festivities and events.

The Fashion Week, held in March

The March Milan–SanRemo race, opening the Italian cycling season

AVERAGE DAILY HOURS OF SUNSHINE

Hours: 10, 8, 6, 4, 2, 0

Jan Feb Mar Apr May Jun Jul Aug Sep Oct Nov Dec

Sunshine Hours
The hours of sunshine in Milan are in line with the Mediterranean average. However, in autumn and winter the weather can be very foggy, which is a typical feature of the climate in the Po river valley, exacerbated by city pollution. The lakes, surrounded by the Alps, are more shaded in the morning and evening.

Parco Sempione, a major venue for summer entertainment

SUMMER

JUNE IS ONE OF the most pleasant months to visit Milan because the climate is mild and the programme of cultural and sports events is truly packed. In July the torrid, muggy summer heat (the temperature may be as high as 40° C/104° F), together with the heavy traffic, can make sightseeing quite uncomfortable.

In August, most of the factories and offices close for the summer holidays and the empty city is an unusual and, in some respects, quite pleasant sight. The same streets that were crowded a week earlier are now quiet, even restful.

Despite the exodus, many events, both cultural and recreational, are held in Milan during the summer.

This is the busiest season for visiting the lakes of Northern Italy, but also the sunniest. Even at the peak of the summer heat, the water can have a cooling effect.

JUNE

Festa del Naviglio *(first Sun).* You can find everything under the sun at this festival, held in the atmospheric setting of the illuminated Navigli canals: street artists and performers, concerts, sports, an antiques market, handicrafts, regional cooking.
Milano d'Estate *(Jun–Aug).* This marks the beginning of summer entertainment in the city (concerts, exhibits, various cultural events), which takes place in the Parco Sempione.
Sagra di San Cristoforo *(third Sun).* The patron saint of travellers, St Christopher, is celebrated along the Naviglio, in the square facing the church. In the evening decorated barges glide along the canals.
Estate all'Umanitaria.
The Humanitarian Association organizes a festival of cinema, dance, music, theatre and cartoons and shows for children.

Fotoshow. An interesting video, photography and optics show in the Fiera (Exhibition Centre) pavilions.
Orticola. Flower growing and garden furnishings show and market in the Porta Venezia public gardens *(see p120).*
Sagra di San Giovanni.
At Monza, a few miles north of Milan, the patron saint's feast day is celebrated with sports and cultural events, some of which are held at a splendid venue – the park at the Villa Reale.

JULY AND AUGUST

Festival Latino-Americano.
The Forum di Assago hosts this lively festival of Latin-American music, handicrafts and cuisine.
Arianteo. At the Rotonda della Besana *(see p100),* the Anteo motion-picture theatre organizes a series of outdoor showings, which includes all the most important films featured in Milan's cinemas and theatres during the year.

The Festa del Naviglio, marking the beginning of summer events

AVERAGE MONTHLY RAINFALL

mm
200
160
120
80
40
0
Jan Feb Mar Apr May Jun Jul Aug Sep Oct Nov Dec

Rainfall
The average monthly rainfall in the Milan area can vary quite considerably during the year. The wettest season is certainly autumn, when it may rain for several days without a break. In late spring and summer the average rainfall level may increase because of unexpected storms.

AUTUMN

Septentber in Milan really gives you the impression of life beginning anew. In general, by the last week of August the Milanese have returned from holiday, but it is only in September that things get back into full swing.

A Ferrari in action at Monza

As far as the weather is concerned, fog and rain alternate with lovely clear days with that typical "Lombard sky" which Alessandro Manzoni, in *The Betrothed*, described as being "so beautiful when it is beautiful, so blue, so serene".

SEPTEMBER

Premier league football (soccer).
Early September marks the resumption of the Italian football season. Two of the leading Italian teams are based in Milan: Inter and Milan. They are arch-rivals and the local championship is always a major event here.
Panoramica di Venezia *(early Sep)*. Milan cinemas show films from the Venice Film Festival while they are being screened there.
Gran Premio di Monza. Held at one of the top motor racing circuits, the Grand Prix of Italy is often crucial to the outcome of the Formula One competition.

OCTOBER

Fiera di Chiaravalle *(first Mon)*. This famous fair is held in the shade of the *ciribiciaccola* (as the Milanese call the bell tower of the Chiaravalle Cistercian abbey, *see pp102–3*). The fair features music, dancing and an outdoor art exhibition.
SMAU *(first week)*. International multimedia show held in the Fiera

The Fiera, host to both SMAU and fashion shows

Exhibition Centre: IT, from computers for offices to CD-Roms and Virtual Reality.
MODIT-Milanovendemoda *(beginning of month)*. The second major fashion show for leading Italian and international fashion designers. The spring-summer collections in various show-rooms and the Fiera pavilions.

NOVEMBER

Premio Bagutta. Milan's most important literary prize is awarded.

PUBLIC HOLIDAYS

New Year's Day (1 Jan)
Epiphany (6 Jan)
Easter Sunday and Monday
Liberation Day (25 Apr)
Labour Day (1 May)
Ferragosto (15 Aug)
All Saints' Day (1 Nov)
Sant'Ambrogio (Milan's Patron Saint) (7 Dec)
Immaculate Conception (8 Dec)
Christmas (25 Dec)
Santo Stefano (26 Dec)

San Siro stadium, packed with fans at the beginning of the season

AVERAGE MONTHLY TEMPERATURE

C°
25
20
15
10
5
0

Jan Feb Mar Apr May Jun Jul Aug Sep Oct Nov Dec

Temperature
Milan is inland and there are big differences in temperature between winter and summer. The winters can be very cold indeed, particularly in December and January, typical of continental Europe, while there may be torrid heat in summer. The climate is always very humid.

WINTER

CHARACTERIZED by severe cold (heavy snowfall is not rare), the Milanese winter is "warmed up" by a rich and fascinating programme of cultural events, major holidays and special occasions. The city becomes especially lively around the feast day of Sant'Ambrogio (St Ambrose), the local patron saint, and then for Christmas, which is preceded by the usual shopping sprees in the city-centre shops. On the cultural side, the theatres of Milan present a high-quality theatre season, headed by the world-famous Piccolo Teatro.

Typical antiques stalls at the Oh bej Oh bej fair

Christmas decorations in the Galleria Vittorio Emanuele II

DECEMBER

Festa di Sant'Ambrogio
(7 Dec). This is the locals' favourite holiday, just before Immaculate Conception *(8 Dec).* Sant'Ambrogio is celebrated with many events: the jam-packed **Fiera degli Oh bej Oh bej**, a street fair featuring antiques as well as a vast assortment of articles. It is held in the streets around the basilica of Sant'Ambrogio *(see pp84–7).*

La Scala. The season at the world-famous opera house *(see pp52–3)* starts on 7 December. The opening night is a major cultural event, and an important occasion in the Milanese social calendar.

Teatro Grassi (ex Piccolo Teatro). Milan's other famous theatre, founded by Paolo Grassi and world-class director Giorgio Strehler, also inaugurates its programme of plays on 7 December.

JANUARY

Corteo dei Re Magi *(6 Jan).* A traditional procession with a *tableau vivant* of the Nativity goes from the Duomo to Sant'Eustorgio.

Fiera di Senigallia *(every Sat all year long).* Along the Darsena is a colourful market offering ethnic handicrafts, records and bicycles.

Mercato dell'Antiquariato di Brera *(third Sat of month, all year).* Stalls with antiques, books, postcards, jewellery.

FEBRUARY

Carnevale Ambrosiano. The longest carnival in the world ends on the first Saturday of Lent. Floats and stock Milanese characters, such as Meneghin and Cecca, take part in a parade to Piazza del Duomo, which is filled with children throwing confetti everywhere.

Taking part in the Carnevale Ambrosiano in Piazza del Duomo

MILAN AREA
BY AREA

HISTORIC CENTRE

THE AREA AROUND the Duomo was the religious centre of Milan in the 4th century. Up to the 14th century it was the site of the basilicas of Santa Tecla and Santa Maria Maggiore and the Early Christian baptisteries, San Giovanni alle Fonti and Santo Stefano. These were all demolished to make room for the new cathedral. The political and administrative centre of the city was the nearby Palazzo della Ragione. At that time Milan was only slightly larger than the present-day historic centre; in fact, what is today Piazza della Scala was on the edge of town. Piazza del Duomo was the focus of small businesses until the 18th

Leonardo da Vinci, in Piazza della Scala

century, and a stage for the city's major religious and civic ceremonies. In the 19th century it became the nucleus from which avenues radiated. In the 1860s the decaying dwellings and the shops around the Duomo were demolished to make way for the construction of the then futuristic Galleria, the symbol of Milan after the unification of Italy. The damage caused by bombs in World War II created large empty areas later occupied by many modern buildings. The Historic Centre is always thronging with visitors, drawn by the world-famous churches, museums and galleries and also by the excellent shops.

SIGHTS AT A GLANCE

Streets, Squares and Historic Buildings
Casa degli Omenoni **6**
Casa Manzoni and Piazza Belgioioso **7**
Galleria Vittorio Emanuele II **2**
Palazzo Borromeo **14**
Palazzo Marino **4**
Palazzo Reale **10**

Piazza del Liberty and Corso Vittorio Emanuele II **8**
Piazza Mercanti **11**

Churches
Duomo pp46–9 **1**
San Fedele **5**
San Giorgio al Palazzo **15**
San Gottardo in Corte **9**

San Sepolcro **13**
Santa Maria presso San Satiro **16**

Galleries
Pinacoteca Ambrosiana pp56–9 **12**

Theatres
Teatro alla Scala pp52–3 **3**

KEY

◻ Street-by-Street map
  See pp44–5

P Parking

M Metro

i Tourist information

🚖 Taxi

0 metres 400
0 yards 400

GETTING THERE

Underground metro lines 1 (red) and 3 (yellow) have stops in Piazza del Duomo. Trams 1 and 2 stop in front of La Scala and trams 3, 4, 12, 14, 24 and 27 stop in Via Orefici. Bus No. 60, the terminus of which is in Piazza San Babila, goes to the Stazione Centrale (main railway station).

◁ **The Galleria Vittorio Emanuele II, Milan's elegant "drawing room" since 1867**

Street-by-Street: Piazza del Duomo

Sculpture, Casa degli Omenoni

PIAZZA DEL DUOMO, designed by Giuseppe Mengoni and opened in 1865 after protracted difficulties, is the ideal starting point for a visit to Milan's historic centre. The area is packed with visitors fascinated by the "great machine of the Duomo", as Alessandro Manzoni describes the cathedral in *The Betrothed*. There are numerous spots where the Milanese like to meet for an apéritif on Sunday morning. Young people prefer to go to Corso Vittorio Emanuele II, which has most of the cinemas as well as many shops and department stores.

San Fedele
This church, a typical example of Counter-Reformation architecture, is popular with the old Milanese aristocracy ❺

Casa degli Omenoni

PIAZZA MED

VIA MANZONI

PIAZZA SCALA

PIAZZA SAN FEDELE

★ Teatro alla Scala
This was the first monument in Milan to be rebuilt after the 1943 bombings ❸

Palazzo Marino

VIA MENGONI

VIA GROSSI

★ Galleria Vittorio Emanuele II
The Galleria was one of the first iron and glass constructions in Italy ❷

Piazza Mercanti

Zucca in Galleria is a popular café, decorated with mosaics and décor dating from 1921.

0 metres	100
0 yards	100

In the middle of Piazza Meda is a large rotating disc, sculpted by Arnaldo Pomodoro (1980).

San Carlo was built in 1838–47.

Piazza del Liberty was named after the Art Nouveau ("Liberty" in Italian) façade at No. 8. It was restored after the 1943 bombing.

LOCATOR MAP
See Street Finder, maps 3, 4, 7, 8

★ Duomo
The third largest church in the world after St Peter's and Seville Cathedral, the Duomo towers over the large square named after it ❶

Piazza Fontana was the target of terrorism in 1969: a bomb in the Banca dell'Agricoltura killed 16 people. In the centre of the square is a fountain designed by Piermarini in 1783.

STAR SIGHTS

★ **Duomo**

★ **Galleria Vittorio Emanuele II**

★ **Teatro alla Scala**

Palazzo Reale

KEY

— — — Suggested route

Duomo ❶

Statue in the interior

T HE CONSTRUCTION of the Duomo began in 1386, with the city's bishop, Antonio da Saluzzo, as its patron. Duke Gian Galeazzo Visconti invited Lombard, German and French architects to supervise the works and insisted they use Candoglia marble, which was transported along the Navigli canals. The official seal AUF (*ad usum fabricae*), stamped on the slabs, exempted them from customs duty. The cathedral was consecrated in 1418, yet remained unfinished until the 19th century, when Napoleon, who was crowned King of Italy here, had the façade completed.

La Madonnina
The 4.16-m (14-ft) gilded statue of the Madonna was sculpted by Giuseppe Bini in 1774.

Flying buttresses

★ **Stained Glass Windows**
Most of the windows depict scenes from the Bible, and date from the 19th century. The oldest one – the fifth in the right-hand aisle – dates back to 1470–75 and depicts the life of Christ, while the newest one (the seventh) dates from 1988.

★ **Trivulzio Candelabrum**
This masterpiece of medieval goldsmithery was donated in 1562 by Gian Battista Trivulzio. On the pedestal there are fantastic monsters and figures representing arts, crafts and the virtues.

Crypt

THE BUILDING OF MILAN CATHEDRAL

1386 The first stone of the Duomo is laid		**1567** Pellegrino Tibaldi ("il Pellegrini") redesigns the presbytery	**1656** Carlo Buzzi continues façade in Gothic style	**1774** The Madonnina is placed on the tallest spire		**1838–65** The Bertinis make the apse windows
1300	**1400**	**1500**	**1600**	**1700**	**1800**	**1900**
	1418 Pope Martin V consecrates the high altar	**1500** Central spire inaugurated *Martin V*	**1617** Francesco Maria Richini begins work on the façade		**1813** Façade completed with Gothic spires	**1981–4** Presbytery piers restored

★ **Roof Terraces**
*The view of the
city from the roof
terraces is simply
unforgettable.
You can also have
a close-up look at
the central spire.
The roof bristles
with spires, the
oldest of which
dates from 1404.*

About 3,500 statues lend movement to the
massive Duomo. They are typically medieval,
representing saints, animals and monsters.

A plaque confirms that
the Duomo is dedicated
to Maria Nascente.

The Interior
*The five aisles
in the nave are
separated
by 52 piers,
whose capitals
are decorated
with statues.*

**Main
entrance**

STAR FEATURES

★ **Stained Glass Windows**

★ **Trivulzio
Candelabrum**

★ **Roof Terraces**

The Doors
*The five doors were
made from 1840 to
1965. Right,* The
Flagellation *by
Ludovico Pogliaghi,
a bronze relief in the
central door.*

Exploring the Duomo

Statue of Sant'Ambrogio

So that the Duomo could be built, a great Jubilee was proclaimed in 1390 in order to urge the Milanese to contribute money and manual labour to carry out the work. The initial plan was to build it in fired bricks, as the excavations in the northern sacristy have revealed, but in 1387 Duke Gian Galeazzo Visconti, who wanted the cathedral to be seen as a great symbol of his power, demanded that marble should be used instead and that the architectural style should be International Gothic. Building continued over five centuries, resulting in the obvious mixture of styles that characterizes the cathedral.

The presbytery, with the small ciborium dome in the foreground

THE FAÇADE

UP TO THE FIRST level of windows the façade is Baroque. It was completed in the 19th century with Neo-Gothic ogival windows and spires, revealing the difficulties entailed in building the Duomo.

THE INTERIOR

TALL CROSS VAULTS cover the interior and the five aisles in the nave are separated by 52 piers (for the 52 weeks of the year). The capitals on the piers are decorated with statues of saints. Behind the façade, embedded in the floor, is a meridian ①, installed in 1786 by the Brera astronomers. It marked astronomical noon, thanks to a ray of sunlight that enters from the first bay of the south aisle on the right-hand side.

This is a good starting point for a visit to the Duomo. To the right is the sarcophagus of Archbishop Ariberto d'Intimiano ②, bearing a copy of the crucifix that he donated to the San Dionigi monastery (the original is in the Museo del Duomo). Next to this, on the left, is a plaque with the date of the foundation of the cathedral. The corresponding stained-glass window, executed in the old mosaic technique, relates the *Life of St John the Evangelist* (1473–7). The stained-glass windows in the next three bays, showing episodes from the Old Testament, date from the 16th

Stained-glass window, detail

century. In the fifth bay there is a stained-glass window executed between 1470 and 1475 that illustrates the *Life of Christ* ③. Compare this with the other window in the seventh bay – it was made in 1988 and is dedicated to Cardinals Schuster and Ferrari ④. The presbytery ⑤ is constructed in the style imposed in 1567 by Pellegrini who, at the request of San Carlo Borromeo, made this part of the Duomo the Lombard model of a typical Counter-Reformation church. In the middle, under the ciborium behind the altar, is the Tabernacle ⑥, donated by Pius IV to his nephew San Carlo (St Charles). In front of them are two 16th-century gilded copper pulpits ⑦ with

FLOOR PLAN

THE HOLY NAIL OF THE CROSS

In the vault above the choir, a red light marks the location of the niche where a nail from Christ's Cross has been kept since 1461. The nail, which was once kept in the early medieval Santa Maria Maggiore, is in the shape of a horseshoe and was found by St Helena and later given to her son, Emperor Constantine. It was later donated to Sant'Ambrogio and carried by San Carlo in procession during the 1576 plague. It is shown to the public every 14 September, when the Bishop of Milan is raised up to the level of the niche which holds the nail in a kind of decorated balcony, drawn by invisible pulleys.

Tabernacle of the Nail of the Cross

episodes from the Old and New Testaments, surmounted by the organs painted by Giovanni Ambrogio Figino, Camillo Procaccini and Giuseppe Meda.

Behind the altar is an extraordinary wooden choir with the *Life of Sant'Ambrogio* ⑧, carved in 1572–1620. In the right-hand transept is the funerary monument of Gian Giacomo Medici ⑨, the brother of Pope Pius IV, which was once attributed to Michelangelo but is in fact the work of Leone Leoni (1560–63). Past the chapel dedicated to St John the Good, Bishop of Milan in the 7th century, above the side entrance is the splendid stained-glass window of St Catherine of Alexandria ⑩, designed by the Arcimboldi brothers in 1556. A little further on is the strange statue of the flayed St Bartholomew ⑪, signed and dated 1562 by Marco d'Agrate.

At the beginning of the ambulatory there is a *Deposition* on the southern door of the sacristy ⑫ (1393), dedicated to the "Mysteries of the Virgin Mary". Steps ⑬ lead to the crypt (1606), where San Carlo Borromeo is buried, the Duomo Treasury, with its exceptional collection of church vestments and objects, and the Coro Jemale, a small 16th-century room decorated with fine stucco-work (check out the relief sculpture cycle of the *Life of the Virgin Mary*, a 17th-century masterpiece). The apse is illuminated by the

Chalice in the Duomo Treasury

three huge 19th-century stained-glass windows by the Bertini brothers with episodes from the Old ⑯ and New ⑭ Testaments and the Apocalypse ⑮. The ambulatory ends at the northern portal of the sacristy ⑰, with *Christ the Lord and Judge* (1389). The left-hand transept is dominated by the 5-m (16-ft) bronze Trivulzio Candelabrum ⑱, a 12th-century masterpiece by the goldsmith Nicola da Verdun. The candelabrum carries scenes from the Old Testament and the Three Wise Men riding towards the enthroned Virgin. Going down the north aisle, you will see the Chapel of the Crucifix ⑲ carried by San Carlo in procession during the 1576 plague. Behind this is a window with a depiction of the *Discovery of the True Cross by St Helena* (1570–77). To the left of the entrance, steps lead down to the

remains of an Early Christian apse of Santa Tecla and an octagonal baptistery ⑳ where, according to tradition, Sant'Ambrogio (St Ambrose) baptized St Augustine in AD 387. From San Carlo's feast day to Epiphany, the *Quadroni di San Carlo* go on display in the nave. These paintings, the work of leading 17th-century Lombard artists, depict the story of the life and miracles of San Carlo.

ROOF TERRACES

On the way to the lift ㉑ which goes up to the roof, you should go to the apse to admire the central stained-glass window, designed by Filippino degli Organi in 1402. From the roof there is a magnificent view of the city and the mountains to the north, as well as the Duomo spires and statues and even the buttresses below.

MUSEO DEL DUOMO

THE CATHEDRAL MUSEUM, founded in 1953, is at No. 15 Via Arcivescovado. It houses paintings, sculptures, religious objects and stained-glass windows from the Duomo. Among the best works on display are the 15th-century *St Paul the Hermit*, Tintoretto's *Christ among the Doctors* (1530) and a wooden model of the Duomo, begun in 1519. Rooms 18 and 19 document the difficult restoration of the four central piers (1981–4).

One of the exhibition rooms in the Museo del Duomo

Palazzo Marino, the Town Hall since 1860, and the 1872 statue of Leonardo da Vinci on the right

Galleria Vittorio Emanuele II ❷

Piazza della Scala, Piazza del Duomo.
Map 7 C1. **M** *1, 3 Duomo.*

The GALLERIA is an elegant arcade lined with cafés, shops, bookshops and a famous restaurant, Savini *(see p166)*. Work began in 1865, overseen by the architect Giuseppe Mengoni, and it was opened two years later by the king, Vittorio Emanuele II, after whom it was named. The gallery was designed to connect Piazza del Duomo and Piazza della Scala, and formed part of an ambitious urban renewal project. On the floor in the central octagonal area, directly under the 47-m (154-ft) high glass dome, is the heraldic symbol of the Savoy family, a white cross on a red ground. Around it are the arms of four major Italian cities: the bull of Turin, the wolf of Rome, the lily of Florence and the red cross on a white ground (Milan). On the vault are mosaics of Asia, Africa, Europe and America.

Teatro alla Scala ❸

See pp52–3.

Palazzo Marino ❹

Piazza della Scala. **Map** 3 C5.
M *1, 3 Duomo.* 🌑 *to the public.*

This PALAZZO was designed in 1558 by Galeazzo Alessi for the banker Tommaso Marino, but remained un-finished until 1892, when Luca Beltrami completed the façade. From Via Marino on the right you can see the richly decorated, porticoed courtyard of honour.

According to tradition the palazzo, home of Milan Town Hall since 1860, was the birthplace of Marianna de Leyva, the famous nun of Monza described by Alessandro Manzoni in *The Betrothed* as the "Signora".

San Fedele ❺

Piazza San Fedele. **Map** 3 C5. 🚋 *02-72 00 80 27.* **M** *1, 3 Duomo.* 🚎 *1, 2.* 🚌 *61.* 🕐 *8:30am–2:30pm, 4–7pm Mon–Fri.* 🕇 *8, 11am, 12:45, 5:30pm Mon–Fri; 8, 11am, 6.30pm pre-hols; 9:30, 11am, 6:30, 8:30pm hols.* ✉

This CHURCH is the Milanese seat of the Jesuit Order, commissioned by San Carlo Borromeo from Pellegrino Tibaldi in 1569. The work was continued by Martino Bassi and the dome, crypt and choir were designed by Francesco Maria Richini (1633–52). With its austere architecture and nave without aisles, this is a typical model of a Counter-Reformation church. The interior has three interesting paintings. Near the first altar on the right is *St Ignatius's Vision* by Giovan Battista Crespi, known as "il Cerano" (c.1622). A *Transfiguration* by Bernardino Campi (1565) is in the atrium after the second altar on the left; Ciampi also painted the *Blessed Virgin and Child*, by the second altar (left). These last two works came from Santa Maria della Scala, which was demolished to make room for La Scala opera house *(see pp52–3).*

The wooden furniture is also worth a closer look: the confessionals (1596) have scenes from the life of Christ carved by Giovanni Taurini, and the cupboards in Richini's sacristy (1624–28) are by Daniele Ferrari (1639). A statue of the writer Alessandro Manzoni, whose death cert-ificate is kept in San Fedele, stands in the square.

Galleria Vittorio Emanuele II, inaugurated in 1867

Casa degli Omenoni **6**

Via Omenoni 3. **Map** 3 C5. **M** *1, 3 Duomo.* **O** *to the public.*

EIGHT TELAMONES, which the Milanese call *omenoni*, are the most striking feature of this house-cum-studio, built by the sculptor Leone Leoni in 1565. The artist collected many works of art, including paintings by Titian and Correggio and Leonardo da Vinci's famous *Codex Atlanticus (see p59).*

A reference to Leoni can be seen in the relief under the cornice, in which Calumny is torn up by lions *(leoni)*.

The entrance to the Casa degli Omenoni

Casa Manzoni and Piazza Belgioioso **7**

Via Morone 1. **Map** 4 D5. **C** *02-86 46 04 03.* **M** *3 Montenapoleone.* **☐** *1, 2.* **☐** *61.* **O** *9am–noon, 2–4pm Tue–Fri.* **O** *public hols.*

THIS IS THE HOUSE where Italian author Alessandro Manzoni lived from 1814 until his death in 1873 after a fall

Part of the façade of Palazzo Liberty, at No. 8 Piazza del Liberty

on the steps of San Fedele. The perfectly preserved interior includes Manzoni's studio on the ground floor, where he received Garibaldi in 1862 and Verdi in 1868. Next to this is the room where poet and author Tommaso Grossi had his notary office, while on the first floor is Manzoni's bedroom. The house is now the seat of the National Centre for Manzoni Studies, which was founded in 1937. It includes a library with works by Manzoni and critical studies of his oeuvre, as well as the Lombard Historical Society Library with over 40,000 volumes. The brick façade overlooks Piazza Belgioioso, named after the palazzo at No. 2 (closed to the public). This monumental palazzo was designed by Piermarini in 1777–81 for Prince Alberico XII di Belgioioso d'Este. The façade bears heraldic emblems. In the interior a fresco by Martin Knoller represents the apotheosis of Prince Alberico.

Piazza del Liberty and Corso Vittorio Emanuele II **8**

Map 8 D1. **M** *1, 3 Duomo, 1 San Babila.* **☐** *23.* **☐** *61, 65, 73.*

ONCE PAST THE ARCH at the end of Piazza Belgioioso, go through Piazza Meda (1926) and past Corso Matteotti, which was built in 1934 to link Piazza della Scala with Piazza San Babila, and then go down Via San Paolo, which will take you to Piazza del Liberty. This small square owes its name to the Art Nouveau (Liberty) façade on No. 8, restored by Giovanni and Lorenzo Muzio in 1963 with architectural elements from the Trianon café-concert, a building dating from 1905 which was moved from Corso Vittorio Emanuele II.

Go along Via San Paolo to reach Corso Vittorio Emanuele II. This is Milan's main commercial street, and was once called "Corsia dei Servi" (Servants' Lane). It follows the course of an ancient Roman street and in 1628 was the scene of bread riots, described by Manzoni in *The Betrothed.* Near San Carlo al Corso, at No. 13 is the *Omm de preja* (local dialect for *uomo di pietra* or "man of stone") statue, a copy of an ancient Roman work. It is also called "Sciur Carera", a misspelling of the first word of a Latin inscription under the statue *(carere debet omni vitio qui in alterum dicere paratus est).*

The *Omm de preja* statue

Casa Manzoni, now home to the National Centre for Manzoni Studies

Teatro alla Scala ●

**Poster for
Turandot**

BUILT BY Giuseppe Pier-marini in 1776–8, this opera house owes its name to the fact that it stands on the site of Santa Maria della Scala, a church built in 1381 for Regina della Scala, Bernabò Visconti's wife. The theatre opened in 1778; it was badly bombed in 1943, and rebuilt three years later. The traditional opening night of the opera season takes place on 7 December, the feast day of Sant'Ambrogio, Milan's patron saint. La Scala is currently closed for restoration. Until it reopens, in 2004, performances will be held at Teatro degli Arcimboldi.

Teatro alla Scala in 1852, **by Angelo Inganni**

The chandelier, made of Bohemian crystal (1923), holds 383 lightbulbs.

The boxes were like small living rooms where romantic trysts and parlour games were arranged.

★ **Museo del Teatro**
The theatre museum was founded in 1913 and boasts a fine collection of sculpture, original scores, paintings and ceramics related to the history of La Scala as well as of theatre in general.

The façade
was designed by Piermarini so that passers-by in Via Manzoni could catch a glimpse of it.

Entrance

★ **Foyer**
This large, mirror-lined salon was renovated in 1936. There is a bust of the legendary conductor Arturo Toscanini.

STAR FEATURES

★ **Auditorium**

★ **Foyer**

★ **Museo del Teatro**

THE BALLET SCHOOL

La Scala's Ballet School was founded in 1813. Originally there were 48 students who studied dance, mime or specialist disciplines. At the end of an eight-year course, the best students were awarded merits of distinction and became part of the theatre's *corps de ballet* with an annual stipend of 3,000 lire. This rigorously disciplined school has produced such artists as Carla Fracci and Luciana Savignano.

Students at the Ballet School

VISITORS' CHECKLIST

Piazza della Scala. **Map** 3 C5. M 1, 3 Duomo. ⬤ until Dec 2004. **Teatro degli Arcimboldi**: Viale dell'Innovazione. ◖ 02-72 00 37 44. M 1 Precotto, then shuttle bus. w www.teatroallascala.org

A tank filled with water, placed over the wooden vault, was ready for use in case of fire.

Dressing rooms

The orchestra pit was introduced in 1907. Before then the orchestra played behind a balustrade on the same level as the stalls.

Stage
This is one of the largest stages in Italy, measuring 1,200 sq m (13,000 sq ft).

★ **Auditorium**
Made of wood covered with red velvet and decorated with gilded stuccowork, the interior boasts marvellous acoustics and has a seating capacity of 2,015.

The entrance to the church of San Gottardo in Corte

San Gottardo in Corte ❾

Via Pecorari 2. **Map** 8 D1.
▐ 02-86 46 45 00. **Ⓜ** 1, 3 Duomo.
🚋 12, 23, 27. **🚌** 54, 60, 65.
◯ 8am–noon, 2–6pm Mon–Fri (to
5:30 Fri), 2–4pm Sat, 8am–noon Sun.

Aᴢᴢᴏɴᴇ ᴠɪsᴄᴏɴᴛɪ, lord of
Milan, ordered the con-
struction of this church in
1336 as the ducal chapel in
the Broletto Vecchio (Courthouse) courtyard. The interior
was rebuilt in Neo-Classical
style by Piermarini. On the
left-hand wall is a *Crucifixion*
by the school of Giotto.
   Azzone Visconti's funerary
monument, by Giovanni di
Balduccio, is in the apse: the
reclining statue of Visconti is
flanked by the figures of two
women. The octagonal brick
bell tower with small stone
arches and columns is by
Francesco Pecorari (c.1335).

Palazzo Reale ❿

Piazza del Duomo. **Map** 7 C1. **▐** 02-
86 46 13 94. **Ⓜ** 1, 3 Duomo. **🚋** 15,
23, 27. **🚌** 54, 60, 65. **◯** 9:30am–
8pm Sun–Wed (2pm Mon), 9:30am–
11pm Thu–Sat. **CIMAC ⬤** for
restoration. **Palazzo della
Permanente** Via Turati 34. **Map** 4 D3.
▐ 02-659 98 03. **◯** 10am–1pm,
2:30–6:30pm Tue–Fri, 10am–6:30pm
Sat & Sun. **⬤** Mon.

Tʜᴇ sᴇᴀᴛ ᴏғ the commune
administration in the
11th century, this
building was
drastically rebuilt by
Azzone Visconti in
1330–36. At the
height of its impor-
tance it was the head-
quarters of the lords
of Milan. Galeazzo
Maria Sforza's
decision to move
the palace began
the decline of the
Palazzo Reale. In
1598 it housed
the first perma-
nent theatre in
Milan. Made of
wood, it was
rebuilt in 1737
and Mozart
played here as
a child. In 1776 it was
destroyed by a fire.

*Unique Forms of Continuity
in Space (1913) by Umberto
Boccioni*

   The present Neo-Classical
appearance dates from 1778,
when Giuseppe Piermarini
made it into a residence for
Archduke Ferdinand of Austria.
The interior once contained
furniture by cabinet-maker
Maggiolini and was frescoed by
Martin Knoller and Giuliano

Traballesi, becoming a model
for aristocratic Milanese homes.
   In 1920 Vittorio Emanuele III
granted the place temporarily
to the city of Milan, and in
1965 the city purchased it to
use as offices and museums
and for temporary shows. The
**Civico Museo d'Arte Con-
temporanea (CIMAC)** is on
the second floor. There are
two sections. The first begins
with the famous Futurist
sculpture *Unique Forms of
Continuity in Space*, by
Umberto Boccioni, and features 20th-century Italian
art to the post-World War
II period, including
works by Balla, Morandi,
Fontana, Modigliani,
Carrà, and Arturo Martini.
Metaphysical painting is
represented mainly by
De Chirico. A second
section features
Italian art from
the 1950s to the
1980s, and
includes works
by Alberto Burri,
Piero Manzoni,
Vedova and
Tancredi, and the
Jucker Collection,
purchased in
1992. Although CIMAC
is currently closed for
restoration, the Futurist art
collection is on show at the
Palazzo della Permanente.

Piazza Mercanti ⓫

Map 7 C1. **Ⓜ** 1 Cairoli–Cordusio.

Tʜɪs ᴄᴏʀɴᴇʀ of medieval
Milan was the seat of
public and civic activities and
also housed the prison.
Palazzo della Ragione was
built in 1233 by the chief
magistrate (and virtual ruler)
Oldrado da Tresseno, who is
portrayed in a relief by Antelami on the side facing the
square. This courthouse is
also known as "Broletto
Nuovo" to distinguish it from
the older Broletto Vecchio
near Palazzo Reale. Markets
were held under the porticoes, while the Salone dei
Giudici on the first floor was
used as the law court. In 1773
another storey was added to
house the notarial archive.

Palazzo Reale, now used as a venue for temporary exhibitions

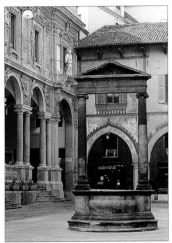

The well in Piazza Mercanti and, on the left, Palazzo delle Scuole Palatine

On one side of the square is the Loggia degli Osii, built by Matteo Visconti in 1316. The façade is decorated with the arms of the districts of Milan and statues of the Virgin Mary and saints (1330). Next is the Palazzo delle Scuole Palatine (1645), the façade of which bears statues of St Augustine and the Latin poet Ausonius. The Palazzo dei Panigarola (to the right), which was rebuilt in the 15th century, was used to register public documents.

In the centre of the square is a 16th-century well. In Via Mercanti is the Palazzo dei Giureconsulti, dominated by the Torre del Comune, built by Napo Torriani in 1272. At the foot of this tower is a statue of Sant'Ambrogio.

Pinacoteca Ambrosiana ⑫

See pp56–9.

San Sepolcro ⑬

Piazza San Sepolcro. **Map** 7 B1.
Ⓜ 1, 3 Duomo. 🚋 2, 3, 12, 14, 19, 24, 27. ⏰ 5pm pre-hols; noon (winter), 5pm hols. ⦸

SAN SEPOLCRO WAS founded in 1030 in the area of the ancient Roman Forum and rebuilt in 1100 at the time of the second Crusade, in which many Milanese took part. The Neo-Romanesque façade was built in 1897, while the interior is basically Baroque. There are two terracotta groups by Agostino De Fondutis (16th century) depicting *Christ Washing His Disciples' Feet* and *The Flagellation of Christ with Caiaphas and St Peter*. The only remaining part of the 1030 church is the Romanesque crypt, with a sculpture group of the *Deposition* by the De Fondutis school in the apse.

Palazzo Borromeo ⑭

Piazza Borromeo 7. **Map** 4 D4.
Ⓜ 1 Cordusio. 🚋 2, 3, 12, 14, 19, 24, 27. 🚌 50, 54.
⏰ courtyard only.

THIS PRESTIGIOUS early 15th-century residence was badly damaged by the 1943 bombings and the only remaining original architectural element is the ogival portal, with leaf decoration and the coat of arms of the Borromeo family. The partly rebuilt second courtyard has porticoes on three sides and on the fourth, between the brick windows, is the original decoration with the family motto *Humilitas*. This courtyard leads to the 15th-century Sala dei Giochi, which is decorated with frescoes of the games played by the aristocracy of the time, including the *Game of Tarot* by a painter known as the Master of the Borromeo Games. The red background is the result of a chemical reaction which changed the original blue of the sky.

The Borromeo family coat of arms with the motto *Humilitas*

San Giorgio al Palazzo ⑮

Piazza San Giorgio 2. **Map** 7 B1.
📞 02-86 08 31. 🚋 2, 3, 14, 20.
⏰ 7:30am–noon, 3:30–7pm daily.
⛪ 6pm pre-hols, 11am, 6pm hols; 8am, 6pm Mon–Fri.

FOUNDED IN 750, this church was named after an ancient Roman *palatium* which stood here. It was radically changed in 1623 and 1800–21 by the architects Richini and Cagnola respectively, and little remains of the original or Romanesque (1129) structures. The third chapel in the right-hand aisle contains paintings by Bernardino Luini (1516) with scenes from the Passion. On the vault there is a fresco of the Crucifixion.

Santa Maria presso San Satiro ⑯

Via Torino 9. **Map** 7 B1.
📞 02-87 46 83. Ⓜ 1, 3 Duomo.
🚋 2, 3, 12, 14, 15, 24.
⏰ 8.30–11.30am, 3.30–5.30pm daily. ⛪ 6pm pre-hols; 11am, 6pm hols; 7:45am, 6pm Mon–Fri.

THE ORIGINAL NUCLEUS of this church, founded by archbishop Ansperto da Biassono, dates from 876. The only remnant is the Sacello della Pietà (chapel of pity), which was altered by Bramante in the 15th century, and the Lombard Romanesque bell tower. In 1478 Bramante was asked to rebuild the church to salvage a 13th-century fresco on the façade, which was said to have miraculous powers. Bramante set it on the high altar, solving the problem of lack of space by creating a sort of *trompe l'oeil* apse of only 97 cm (38 in) with stuccowork and frescoes. The transept leads to the Chapel of San Satiro with a terracotta *Pietà* (c.1482). In the right-hand aisle is the octagonal baptismal font decorated by De Fondutis.

Pinacoteca Ambrosiana ⑫

THE AMBROSIANA ART GALLERY was founded in 1618 by Cardinal Federico Borromeo, the cousin of San Carlo and his successor in charge of the archdiocese of Milan. A true art connoisseur, Borromeo planned the gallery as part of a vast cultural project which included the Ambrosiana Library, opened in 1609, and the Accademia del Disegno (1620) for the training of young Counter-Reformation artists. The gallery, founded to provide inspiration for emerging artists, held 172 paintings – some of which already belonged to Borromeo, while others were purchased later after painstaking research by the cardinal. The collection was then enlarged thanks to private donations.

★ Portrait of a Musician
This is the only Milanese wood panel painting by Leonardo da Vinci. The subject is Franchino Gaffurio, the Sforza court composer.

Adoration of the Magi
Cardinal Borromeo considered this painting by Titian (purchased in 1558) a treasure trove for painters "for the multitude of things therein".

STAR EXHIBITS

★ **Portrait of a Musician**

★ **Cartoon for the School of Athens**

★ **Basket of Fruit**

★ **Madonna del Padiglione**

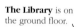

The Library is on the ground floor.

★ Madonna del Padiglione
The recent restoration of this work by Botticelli has revealed its masterful and elegant brushwork.

GALLERY GUIDE

The most famous works are held in the Borromeo Collection, which was subsequently enriched with important 15th–16th-century paintings and sculptures. The Galbiati wing contains 16th–20th-century paintings, a collection of objects, the Sinigaglia Collection of miniature portraits and scientific instruments belonging to the Museo Settala.

Nicolò da Bologna Room

San Sepolcro was annexed to the gallery in 1932.

Centrepiece with Fishing Scene

This is part of the prestigious collection of Neo-Classical gilded bronze objects donated to the Ambrosiana by Edoardo De Pecis in 1827.

KEY

☐ Borromeo Collection and 15th–16th-century paintings

☐ Galbiati Wing

☐ De Pecis Collection & 19th century

☐ Sculpture

☐ Museo Settala

★ Basket of Fruit
Caravaggio painted this extraordinarily realistic work around 1594. The fruit alludes to the symbolism of the Passion of Christ.

★ Cartoon for the School of Athens
This was a preparation for the painting now in the Vatican. Raphael used the faces of contemporary artists – Leonardo, for instance, appears in the guise of Aristotle.

Exploring the Pinacoteca Ambrosiana

Aꜰᴛᴇʀ ꜱᴇᴠᴇɴ ʏᴇᴀʀꜱ of painstaking restoration work, the Pinacoteca was reopened in October 1997. It is housed in a palazzo originally designed by Fabio Mangone in 1611. It was enlarged in the 19th century and again in 1932, when San Sepolcro was added. The new rooms were inaugurated on the third centenary of the death of Federico Borromeo, when about 700 paintings were exhibited, arranged in rows or set on easels. Today the Pinacoteca, whose collections are even larger thanks to donations, has 24 rooms and is one of Milan's finest museums.

18th-century silver stoup

Portrait of a Young Man, a copy of Giorgione's work

Tʜᴇ Bᴏʀʀᴏᴍᴇᴏ Cᴏʟʟᴇᴄᴛɪᴏɴ, 15ᴛʜ–16ᴛʜ-Cᴇɴᴛᴜʀʏ Pᴀɪɴᴛɪɴɢꜱ

Yᴏᴜʀ ᴠɪꜱɪᴛ ʙᴇɢɪɴꜱ in the atrium, which has plaster casts of Trajan's Column, narrating the emperor's victories against the Dacians; on the staircase there are other casts of the *Laocoön* and Michelangelo's *Pietà*. Rooms 1, 4, 5, 6 and 7 house the Borromeo Collection, which boasts many of the best-known works in the gallery. Room 1, which features Venetian and Leonardo-esque painting, opens with the *Holy Family with St Anne and the Young St John the Baptist* by Bernardino Luini (c.1520). Next to this is Titian's *Adoration of the Magi* (1559–60), which is still in its original frame bearing the carved initials of Henry II of France and his wife, who commissioned the work. The main scene is at the far left, while animals and minor figures fill the right-hand half of this original composition. On the opposite wall is a series of portraits, including *Profile of a Lady* by Ambrogio De Predis, and those of *The Young St John the Baptist* and *Benedictory Christ* by Luini, ending with Titian's *Man in Armour*. Rooms 2 and 3 have works acquired after 1618. One is Leonardo da Vinci's *Portrait of a Musician* with its innovative three-quarter profile position and intense expression; it was probably painted in early 1485. Next to this masterpiece is Botticelli's *Madonna del Padiglione*, with its many symbols of the Virgin Mary, and *Sacred Conversation* by Bergognone (c.1485). Another unmissable work is *Adoration of the Child*, by the workshop of Domenico Ghirlandaio. Room 3 features 15th–16th-century Leonardo-esque and Lombard paintings, among which is Salaino's *St John the Baptist*, whose finger pointing upwards alludes to the coming of Christ. Next to this are three works by Bartolomeo Suardi, better known as "il Bramantino". In his *Madonna of the Towers* (which may have had an anti-heretic function), next to the Virgin are an unrecognizable St Ambrose and St Michael Archangel kneeling and offering a soul to the Christ Child. Room 4 has copies from Titian and Giorgione and the *Rest on the Flight into Egypt* by Jacopo Bassano (c.1547). In room 5 is a Raphael masterpiece, a study for *The School of Athens*, the only great Renaissance cartoon that has come down to us. It was purchased by Cardinal Borromeo in 1626. Raphael executed the cartoon in 1510 as a study for the marvellous fresco in the Vatican. The architectonic setting and figure of Heraclitus (portrayed with Michelangelo's face), which were added after the fresco was completed, are not seen in the cartoon.

One of the most famous works in the museum, *Basket of Fruit*, is in room 6. Caravaggio painted it in the late

Adoration of the Child, Domenico Ghirlandaio's workshop

Holy Family with St Anne and the Young St John the Baptist by Bernardino Luini

1500s on a used canvas. The withered leaves represent the vanity of beauty.

The large body of Flemish paintings in the Borromeo Collection is on display in room 7, where you can compare the works of Paul Bril and Jan Brueghel. Interesting works by the latter are *The Mouse with Roses* and *Allegories of Water and Fire*, which Napoleon removed and took back to France. They were later returned.

THE GALBIATI WING

THE SALA DELLA MEDUSA and the Sala delle Colonne feature Renaissance paintings and a collection of objects, the most curious of which are Lucrezia Borgia's blonde hair and Napoleon's gloves.

A short passageway leads to the Spiriti Magni courtyard, decorated with statues of illustrious artists. The three rooms that follow feature 16th-century Italian and Venetian paintings, including an *Annunciation* by Bedoli (room 10), the *Portrait of Michel de l'Hospital* by Giovan Battista Moroni (1554) and Moretto's altarpiece, *Martyrdom of St Peter of Verona* (c.1535, room 12). This latter room, known as the "exedra room", is decorated with a mosaic reproducing a miniature by Simone Martini from the volume of Virgil annotated by Petrarch in the Biblioteca Ambrosiana.

Lucrezia Borgia's hair

Italian and Flemish painting of the 16th and 17th centuries is on display in the Sala Nicolò da Bologna, on the upper floor, along with an unfinished *Penitent Magdalen* (1640–42) by Guido Reni. Seventeenth-century Lombard painting is on display in rooms 14, 15 and 16. Among the interesting works are *Still Life with Musical Instruments* by Evaristo Baschenis (room 14) and Morazzone's *Adoration of the Magi* (room 15), while the following room has

works by Francesco Cairo and Daniele Crespi, as well as *Magdalen* by Giulio Cesare Procaccini. Paintings by Magnasco, Magatti, Fra Galgario and Londonio represent 18th-century Italian art in room 17, but the jewels are two works by Tiepolo on the wall near the entrance.

DE PECIS COLLECTION AND 19TH CENTURY

ROOMS 18 AND 19 form the largest section of the Pinacoteca Ambrosiana, donated by Giovanni Edoardo De Pecis in 1827. This collection consists mostly of Italian and Flemish paintings and includes a series of small Neo-Classical bronze pieces and a *Self Portrait* by sculptor Antonio Canova, inspired by Roman portraiture. The exhibition in this wing ends with a selection of 19th- and early 20th-century canvases, including works by Andrea Appiani *(Portrait of Napoleon)*, Mosè Bianchi and Francesco Hayez. Emilio Longoni is represented with his masterpiece *Locked out of School* (1888). Room 21 has 15th–17th-century German and Flemish art as well as the

Dantesque Stained Glass by Giuseppe Bertini, the Duomo master glassblower. It was executed in 1865 and depicts the author of the *Divine Comedy* surrounded by his characters and with the Virgin Mary above him.

Funerary monument by il Bambaia

SCULPTURE

ROOM 22 IS given over to sculpture. There are ancient Roman, Romanesque and Renaissance pieces as well as the highly elegant bas-reliefs by Agostino Busti – known as "il Bambaia" – sculpted for the tomb of Gaston de Foix around 1516.

MUSEO SETTALA

THE FINAL ROOM contains the rich collection purchased by the Ambrosiana gallery in 1751. It had been collected a century earlier by Manfredo Settala, an eccentric lover of scientific instruments, exotic animals, semi-precious stones, fossils, furniture, paintings and books – forming a sort of "museum of wonders".

BIBLIOTECA AMBROSIANA

Virgil illuminated by Simone Martini

This was one of the first libraries open to the public. It boasts over 750,000 printed volumes, 2,500 of which are incunabulae, and 35,000 manuscripts. Among them is the 5th-century *Ilias Picta*, a copy of Virgil's book annotated by Petrarch and illuminated by Simone Martini; a volume of Aristotle with annotations by Boccaccio; as well as Arab, Syrian, Greek and Latin texts. The Ambrosian Library also has over 1,000 pages of Leonardo da Vinci's *Codex Atlanticus*, purchased in 1637, removed by Napoleon in 1796 and only partly returned in 1815. The Library opened in 1609, already equipped with shelves and wooden footstools to protect readers from the cold floors.

NORTHWEST MILAN

IN THE 14TH CENTURY, when the construction of the Castello Sforzesco began, this district stood outside the city walls and was covered in woods. After the demolition of the Spanish walls around the Castello in the early 19th century, a new plan for the area was drawn up (but only partly realized). The aim was to transform the zone into a monumental quarter by building the Arco della Pace and a number of elegant buildings, which were to be used as offices, luxury residences, markets and theatres. By the end of the century, Via Dante, which leads to the Castello and is lined with fine buildings, was complete, as was the Corso Magenta residential district around Santa Maria delle Grazie. Northwest Milan also hosts two historic theatres: Dal Verme (1872) and the Piccolo Teatro (now called Teatro Grassi), founded in 1947.

The personification of a river, part of the Arco della Pace (Arch of Peace)

GETTING THERE

The Fiera (Amendola, Lotto) and Castello (Cairoli) are served by metro lines 1 and 2. A number of tramlines pass Piazza Cordusio (No. 24 goes to Santa Maria delle Grazie or San Siro stadium).

KEY

- ▨ Street-by-Street map *See pp62–3*
- **P** Parking
- **M** Metro
- ▨ Taxi

0 metres   400
0 yards   400

SIGHTS AT A GLANCE

◁ **The Salone degli Specchi in Palazzo Litta, a fine example of the 18th-century Lombard style**

Street-by-Street: Around the Castello Sforzesco

Visconti coat of arms

THE CASTELLO SFORZESCO and Sempione park today are the result of late 19th-century landscaping and restoration. Architect Luca Beltrami managed to thwart attempts to demolish the castle by converting it into a museum centre. He restored many of its original elements. In the early 1800s, the Arco della Pace and the Arena were built in the Parco Sempione, which was landscaped as an "English" garden by Emilio Alemagna. To mark the 1906 opening of the Galleria del Sempione, an International Exposition was held, featuring new products which later became household names in Italy.

Arena Civica
This amphitheatre, built in 1806, was used for boating displays, when it was filled with water from the Naviglio canals ❹

★ Parco Sempione
The 47-hectare (116-acre) English-style garden was designed by Emilio Alemagna in 1893. It contains a number of historic buildings and monuments ❷

Corso Sempione
Napoleon built this avenue leading to the Castello, modelling it on the Champs-Elysées in Paris ❼

PIAZZALE SEMPIONE

★ Arco della Pace
Modelled on the triumphal arch of Septimius Severus, the Arch of Peace was built to celebrate Napoleon's victories. However, it was inaugurated by Francis I in memory of the peace declared in 1815 ❺

STAR SIGHTS

★ Castello Sforzesco

★ Parco Sempione

★ Arco della Pace

Acquario Civico
The Civic Aquarium was built in 1906 as an exhibition and educational centre. The building still has its original decoration of tiles and reliefs ❸

The Foro Buonaparte
is a semicircular boulevard lined with imposing late 19th-century buildings.

LOCATOR MAP
See Street Finder, maps 2–3

KEY

▬ ▬ ▬ ▬ ▬ Suggested route

Via Dante, one of the city's most elegant streets, is a pedestrian precinct, and one of the few in Milan where you can sit and have a drink outdoors.

★ Castello Sforzesco
The castle, a symbol of Milan, was initially the palace of the Visconti, who built it in 1368 and named it Castello di Porta Giovia, and then of the Sforza, who embellished it, turning it into a magnificent Renaissance residence ❶

Triennale di Milano
The Palazzo dell'Arte holds architecture and design shows. The Triennale show features decorative art, fashion and handicrafts ❻

| 0 metres | 400 |
| 0 yards | 400 |

Castello Sforzesco ●

Umberto I, the Filarete Tower

BUILT IN 1368 BY Galeazzo II Visconti as a fortress, the Sforza castle was enlarged in the 14th century by Gian Galeazzo and then by Filippo Maria, who transformed it into a splendid ducal palace. It was partly demolished in 1447 during the Ambrosian Republic. Francesco Sforza, who became lord of Milan in 1450, and his son Lodovico il Moro made the castle the home of one of the most magnificent courts in Renaissance Italy, graced by Bramante and Leonardo da Vinci. Under Spanish and Austrian domination, the Castello went into gradual decline, as it resumed its original military function. It was saved from demolition by the architect Luca Beltrami, who from 1893 to 1904 restored it and converted it into an important museum centre.

★ Trivulzio Tapestries
The 12 tapestries designed by Bramantino, depicting the months and signs of the zodiac, are masterpieces of Italian textile art.

The Torre Castellana was where Lodovico il Moro kept his treasury. It was "guarded" by a figure of Argus, in a fresco by Bramante at the Sala del Tesoro entrance.

The Cortile della Rocchetta was the last refuge in the event of a siege. Its three porticoes, formerly frescoed, were designed by Filarete, Ferrini and Bramante. The oldest wing (1456–66), opposite the entrance to the Corte Ducale, was the apartment of Lodovico and his wife before he became duke.

The holes in the castle walls, now used by pigeons, were made to anchor the scaffolding used for maintenance work.

Porta Vercellina
Only ruins remain of the great fortified structure that once protected the gate of Santo Spirito.

Cappella Ducale
The Ducal chapel still has the original frescoes painted in 1472 by Stefano de Fedeli and Bonifacio Bembo for Galeazzo Maria Sforza. On the vault is a Resurrection *and on the wall to the left of the entrance is an* Annunciation *with saints looking on.*

VISITORS' CHECKLIST

Piazza Castello. **Map** 3 B5.
📞 02-88 46 37 01.
Ⓜ 1 Cairoli–Cadorna, 2 Lanza–Cadorna. 🚋 1, 3, 4, 12, 14, 27.
🚌 43, 50, 57, 58, 61, 70, 94.
Castello ◯ 9am–5:30pm daily.
Musei Civici ◯ 9am–5:30pm Tue–Sun. ● 1 Jan, Easter, 1 May, 25 Dec. ♿ some rooms only. 🚻 📷

Ducal court

★ Sala delle Asse
This pergola, painted to look like an open air space, was the work of Leonardo (1498). The room owes its name to the planks (asse) *once thought to cover the walls.*

STAR FEATURES

★ **Rondanini Pietà**

★ **Sala delle Asse**

★ **Trivulzio Tapestries**

The Filarete Tower collapsed in 1521 when the gunpowder kept there exploded. It was rebuilt in 1905 by Luca Beltrami, who worked from Filarete's original design for the central castle tower.

★ Rondanini Pietà
Michelangelo's final work was altered at least three times and eventually left unfinished. Christ's arm on the left and a different angle for Mary's face, visible from the right, are part of the first version.

Exploring the Civic Museums in the Castello Sforzesco

SINCE 1896, THE CASTELLO SFORZESCO has housed the
Civic Museums with one of the largest collections of
art in Milan. The Corte Ducale houses the Raccolte di
Arte Antica and the art and sculpture gallery as well as
the furniture collection, while the Rocchetta holds
decorative arts (ceramics, musical instruments and
gold) and the Trivulzio Tapestries. The archaeological
museum, the stamp collections and the Achille Bertarelli Collection, with about 700,000 prints and books,
are also here. Major institutions are also housed here
such as the Art Library, Trivulziana Library, Drawing
Collection and School of Applied Industrial Art.

**Relief of the Three Magi, School
of Antelami (12th century)**

CIVICHE RACCOLTE
D'ARTE ANTICA

THE DISPLAYS making up the
collections of Ancient Art
are arranged in chronological
order (except for Room 6) in
rooms facing the Corte Ducale,
where the 14th-century
Pusterla dei Fabbri postern,
rebuilt after being demolished
in 1900, has 4th–6th-century
sculpture. In room 1 ① is
the Sarcophagus of Lambrate
(late 4th century) and a bust
of the Empress Theodora (6th

century). Room 2 ②
features Romanesque
and Campionese
sculpture, with a fine
early 12th-century tela-
mon. The relief of the
Three Magi is by the
school of Benedetto
Antelami, the great 12th-
century sculptor and
architect. The main
attraction, however, is
the *Mausoleum of
Bernabò Visconti*,
sculpted by Bonino
da Campione in
1363 for the lord
of Milan. He is
portrayed on horse-
back between
Wisdom and
Fortitude, while
on the sarcophagus
are *Scenes from the
Passion*. Room 3 ③
has a window with a
14th-century Tuscan
Benedictory Christ. Room 4 ④
is given over to Giovanni di

Balduccio, with fragments
from the façade of Santa Maria
di Brera (14th century). A
passage leads to the Cappel-
letta ⑤, dominated by a 14th-
century wooden Crucifix.

Room 6 ⑥ features reliefs
from the Porta Romana (1171)
narrating the *Return of the
Milanese after Being Driven
out of Town by Barbarossa*
and *St Ambrose Expelling the
Arians*. In room 7 ⑦ is the
Gonfalone (Standard) of Milan
designed by Giuseppe Meda
in 1566, with scenes from
Sant'Ambrogio's life. On the
walls are 17th-century Flemish
tapestries. The Sala delle
Asse ⑧ is known for its
fine fresco decoration on
the vault, designed by
Leonardo in 1498,
which, despite its poor
condition, is a good
example of Sforza
decoration. From here
you go to the bridge
over the moat ⑨ ⑩,
with important
small sculptures by
Agostino Busti (La
Bambaia). Next is
the Sala dei Ducali
⑪, named after the
arms of Galeazzo
Maria Sforza, with
Lodovico's set above.
Here the early 15th-
century sculpture
is dominated by
Agostino di Duccio's relief of
St Sigismund on a Journey
from the Malatesta Temple in

**The *Mausoleum of
Bernabò Visconti***

PLAN OF THE CASTELLO SFORZESCO

First floor

Second floor

Ground floor

KEY

- ▢ Civiche Raccolte
  d'Arte Antica
- ▢ Applied Art
  collection
- ▢ Furniture;
  art gallery

Sala Castellana �37

Cortile della Rocchetta �

Corte Ducale

Bona Savoia tower

Bertarelli Collection

Piazza d'Armi (main courtyard)

The armour collection in the Sala Verde

Rimini. Left, is the door to the Cappella Ducale ⑫, with a braided Virgin, *Madonna del Coazzone*, a 15th-century work attributed to Pietro Antonio Solari. On the vault is a *Resurrection* painted around 1472 by Bonifacio Bembo and Stefano de' Fedeli. Late 15th-century sculpture is featured in the Sala delle Colombine ⑬, with the Visconti coat of arms and motto, *A Bon Droit*. One of the finest works here is Antonio Mantegazza's *Kneeling Apostles*. The 1463 portal displayed in the Sala Verde ⑭ is attributed to Michelozzo. This room also has some fine armour.

The last room, the Sala degli Scarlioni ⑮, boasts two world-famous sculptures: Gaston de Foix's funerary monument with marvellous reliefs, and Michelangelo's *Rondanini Pietà*. The former is by Agostino Busti, known as "il Bambaia", and commemorates the death on the battlefield of the young captain of the French troops in 1512. Behind a partition is Michelangelo's unfinished masterpiece, which he was working on until a few days before his death in 1564 (he had begun it in 1552–3): the standing Mother of Christ supporting the heavy body of her Son. The exit route goes through the Cortile della Fontana, where the only original window left in the castle can be seen. It was used by Beltrami as a model in his restoration of the Castello.

FURNITURE COLLECTION AND PINACOTECA

FOUR ROOMS on the first floor house 15th–18th-century furniture. Of particular interest are the Torrechiara Choir (15th century) ⑯, the Passalacqua casket ⑱ (1613) and a chest of drawers by Giuseppe Maggiolini ⑲. Room 17 ⑰ has a reconstruction of an interior with frescoes from the Castello di Roccabianca with the *Stories of Griselda* (1460), inspired by a story by Boccaccio. The Belgioioso collection of 17th-century Flemish paintings is on display in room 18.

The art gallery begins at the Sala Nuziale ⑳, with 14th- and 15th-century Italian paintings, including Mantegna's *Madonna in Glory and Saints*

Madonna in Glory and Saints, by Andrea Mantegna

(1497), which you can compare with a *Madonna and Child*, an early work by Giovanni Bellini. Also on show are the two *Saints* by Carlo Crivelli (c.1479).

Fifteenth-century Lombard painting ㉑ is perhaps best represented by Bramantino's *Deposition* (1513). There are also many works by Leonardo-esque painters (Marco d'Oggiono, Cesare da Sesto), together with Correggio *(see pp32–3)* and Romanino.

A room of Mannerist art ㉒ leads to room 23 ㉓, with episodes from the history of the Milanese church by Procaccini, Morazzone, Ambrogio Figino and Cerano. Room 24 ㉔ features 17th-century Lombard art (Giovanni Battista Trotti, Bernardino Campi and Fede Galizia). The permanent collection of portraits (Room 25 ㉕) boasts masterpieces such as *Poet Laureate* (c.1475) attributed to Giovanni Bellini, *Portrait of Giulio Zandemaria* by Correggio (1521), *Young Man* by Lotto and canvases by Titian and Fra Galgario. Room 26 ㉖ has some 17th- and 18th-century works by artists such as Canaletto and Bellotto.

APPLIED ART COLLECTION

RETURN TO THE entrance for access to the first floor to see the collection of old musical instruments ㊱ ㊳, which includes a Flemish double virginal with ottavino. Between these two rooms is the large Sala della Balla (ballroom) ㊲, with Bramantino's splendid Trivulzio Tapestries of the months (1503–09). On the second floor (rooms 28–32) is a large collection of fine Italian and European glass, ceramics, majolica and porcelain, and collections of costumes, ivory works, gold jewellery and scientific instruments. Lastly, in the basement, is the Archaeological Museum: the *Ritrovare Milano* section features Roman objects, a Prehistoric section, and an Egyptian section with funerary cult objects, including a tomb dating from c.640 BC.

Parco Sempione ➋

Piazza Castello–Piazza Sempione
(Eight entrances around perimeter).
Map 2 F3–4, 3 A3–4. **M** *1 Cadorna,
Cairoli, 2 Lanza, Cadorna.* **R** *Ferrovie
Nord, Cadorna.* **🚋** *1, 3, 4, 12, 14,
27, 29, 30.* **🚌** *43, 57, 61, 70, 94.*
◯ *Mar–Apr: 6:30am–9pm;
May: 6:30am–10pm; Jun–Sep:
6:30am–11:30pm; Oct: 6:30am–9pm;
Nov–Feb: 6:30am–8pm.*

ALTHOUGH IT COVERS an area
of about 47 ha (116 acres),
this park occupies only a part
of the old Visconti ducal
garden, enlarged by the Sforza
in the 15th century to make
a 300-ha (740-acre) hunting
reserve. The area was partly
abandoned during Spanish
rule, and in the early 1800s
part of it was used to create a
parade ground extending as
far as the Arco della Pace.
The present-day layout was
the work of Emilio Alemagna,
who in 1890–93 designed it
along the lines of an English
garden. In World War II the
park was used to cultivate
wheat but after the reconstruction period it returned to its
former splendour as a locals'
haunt, especially in spring and
summer, when it plays host
to many entertainment events.
Walking through the park
after dark is not advisable.
   Standing among the trees
are the monuments to
Napoleon III (designed by
Francesco Barzaghi), De

Chirico's Metaphysical construction *Mysterious Baths*,
the sulphur water fountain
near the Arena and the Torre
del Parco, a tower made of
steel tubes in 1932 after a
design by Gio Ponti.

Acquario Civico ➌

Via Gadio 2. **Map** 3 B4. **C** *02-88 46
57 50.* **M** *2 Lanza.* **🚋** *3, 4, 12, 14.*
🚌 *43, 57, 70.* **◯** *9:30am–5:30pm
Tue–Sun.* **🖰** *by appt (02-89 01 07
95).*

THE CIVIC AQUARIUM was built
by Sebastiano Locati for
the 1906 National Exposition,
and it is the only remaining
building. Its 36 tanks
house about 100
species (fish,
crustaceans,
molluscs and
echinoderms)
typical of the
Mediterranean
sea and Italian
freshwater
fauna. There are
also rare kinds
of tropical fish
on display.
   The aquarium
museum is also home to the
Hydrobiological Station,
which has a library
specializing in the subject.
The aquarium building itself
(1906) is a fine example of
Art Nouveau architecture and
is decorated with Richard-

**Sea creature decorating the
façade of the Aquarium**

Ginori ceramic tiles and
statues of aquatic animals,
dominated by Oreste Labò's
statue of Neptune.

Arena Civica ➍

Via Legnano, Viale Elvezia. **Map** 3
A–B3. **M** *2 Lanza.* **🚋** *3, 4, 12, 14.*
🚌 *43, 57, 70.* **◯** *for exhibitions
and events only.*

THIS IMPRESSIVE Neo-Classical
amphitheatre, designed in
1806 by Luigi Canonica, was
– together with the Arco della
Pace, Caselli Daziari and Foro
Buonaparte – part of the project to transform the Castello
Sforzesco area into a monumental civic centre.
Napoleon was
present at the
Arena inaugura-
tion, and it was
the venue for
various cultural
and sports
events, from
horse and mock
Roman chariot races
to hot-air balloon
launchings, mock
naval battles and
festivities. With a
seating capacity of 30,000, it
has also been a football
stadium, but San Siro *(see
p70)* is now the more
important ground. The Arena
is now mainly a venue for
athletics (it has a 500-m,
1,640-ft track) and concerts.

View of the Parco Sempione: in the foreground, the artificial lake and in the background, the Arco della Pace

Arco della Pace ❺

Piazza Sempione. **Map** 2 F3. 🚋 *1, 29, 30*. 🚌 *61*. 🎫 *ascent to the top (Associazione Amici Arco della Pace)*. 📞 *02-669 22 51*.

WORK ON MILAN'S major Neo-Classical monument was begun by Luigi Cagnola in 1807 to celebrate Napoleon's victories. It was originally called the Arch of Victories, but building was interrupted and not resumed until 1826 by Francis I of Austria, who had the subjects of the bas-reliefs changed to commemorate the peace of 1815 instead. The Arch of Peace was inaugurated on 10 September 1838 on the occasion of Ferdinand I's coronation as ruler of the Lombardy–Veneto kingdom. The arch is dressed in Crevola marble and decorated with bas-reliefs depicting episodes of the restoration after Napoleon's fall. On the upper level are personifications of the rivers in the Lombardy–Veneto kingdom: the Po, Ticino, Adda and Tagliamento.

From the top there is a magnificent view of the Castello and Corso Sempione and a close view of the huge bronze Chariot of Peace, by Abbondio Sangiorgio, surrounded by four Victories on horseback. The chariot originally faced France, but when Milan was ceded to Austria, it was turned to face the centre of the city.

Tree-lined Corso Sempione

Triennale di Milano ❻

Viale Alemagna 6. **Map** 3 A4. 📞 *02-72 43 41*. Ⓜ *1–2 Cadorna*. 🚌 *43, 61, 94*. 🚉 *Ferrovie Nord, Cadorna*. 🕐 *10am–8pm Tue–Sun*. ⬤ *1 Jan, Easter, 1 May, 15 Aug, 25 Dec*. 🎫🎫 *(depending on event)*. ♿🚻🛍🖼

THE TRIENNALE Decorative Arts Show is housed in the Palazzo dell'Arte, on the southwestern side of the Parco Sempione. The Palazzo was built by Giovanni Muzio in 1932–3 as a permanent site for the International Exhibition of Decorative Arts. The Triennale show was founded in 1923 to foster the development of Italian arts and handicrafts against a background of their international counterparts. In addition, the Milan Triennale has always played a primary role in promoting architectural development.

Obelisk in front of the Palazzo dell'Arte

Art exhibitions, conferences and occasional lectures on the themes of art and architecture are held in the building. Alongside the exhibition space stands the Teatro dell'Arte, which was redesigned in 1960.

Corso Sempione ❼

Map 2 D1, E2, F3. 🚋 *1, 19, 29, 30, 33*. 🚌 *57, 61, 94*.

MODELLED ON the grand boulevards of Paris, Corso Sempione was the first stage of a road built by Napoleon to link the city with Lake Maggiore, Switzerland and France via the Simplon Pass. The first section, starting at the Arco della Pace, is pedestrianized. The Corso is lined with late 19th-century and early 20th-century houses and is now the main thoroughfare in a vast quarter. The initial stretch (towards the park) is considered an elegant area, with good shops, the headquarters of some Milanese banks and Italian State Radio and TV, RAI (at No. 27). Opposite, at No. 36, is a residence designed by Giuseppe Terragni and Pietro Lingeri in 1935, one of the first examples of Rationalist architecture in Milan.

The semicircular Via Canova and Via Melzi d'Eril cross the Corso, every angle of which offers a different view of the Arco della Pace.

The horses on the Arco della Pace, each cast in one piece

Fiera di Milano ❽

Largo Domodossola 1. **Map** 1 C3.
🅒 02-499 71. ‖FAX‖ 02-49 97 76 05.
Ⓜ 1 Amendola Fiera, Lotto. 🚋 19,
27. 🚌 48, 68, 78. Shuttle from
Linate airport. ATM circle line buses
(free). ◯ for exhibitions only.
🔲 ♿ 🍴 🔲

San Siro Stadium, now named after footballer Giuseppe Meazza

THE FIERA CAMPIONARIA, or Trade Fair, was founded in 1920 to stimulate the domestic market in postwar Italy. It was originally located along the ramparts of Porta Venezia and in 1923 was moved to the parade ground behind the Castello Sforzesco. It was fitted out with permanent pavilions and buildings, many of which were damaged or destroyed in World War II. Some original Art Nouveau buildings have survived at the entrance in Via Domodossola and the Palazzo dello Sport (sports arena, 1925). The Fiera di Milano has become a symbol of Milanese industriousness and spirit of enterprise.

Fiera di Milano logo

In 1985 the Trade Fair became a bona fide Exhibition Centre, and now hosts 78 specialist international shows attracting 2.5 million visitors and 31,000 exhibitors every year. It is now one of the leading exhibition centres in Europe in terms of turnover. The old main entrance to the Fiera faces Piazza Giulio Cesare, which is dominated by a Four Seasons fountain, placed there in 1927.

Meazza (San Siro) Stadium ❾

Via Piccolomini 5. 🅒 02-404 24 32
or 02-48 70 71 23. Ⓜ 1 Lotto
(**Map** 1 A2); shuttle bus. 🚋 24.
🅦 www.sansiro2000.com

NAMED AFTER Giuseppe Meazza, the famous footballer who played for the local teams, Inter and Milan, Italy's top stadium is commonly known as San Siro, after the surrounding district. It was built in 1926, rebuilt in the 1950s with a capacity of 85,000, and then renovated in 1990, when another ring of tiers and a roof were added *(see Entertainment pp194–5)*. In 1999 a gigantic sculpture of a horse, *Il Cavallo*, designed by Leonardo da Vinci but never built, was placed between San Siro stadium and the nearby San Siro racetrack.

Certosa di Garegnano ❿

Via Garegnano 28. 🅒 02-38 00 63
01. 🚋 14. ◯ 7:30am–noon,
3–6pm daily; 🕐 6pm
pre-hols; 7:30, 8:45, 10 &
11:30am, 4:30 & 5:30pm.

THE CHURCH that forms the heart of this important Carthusian monastery, dedicated to Our Lady of the Assumption, was founded in 1349 by Archbishop Giovanni Visconti. Sadly, the Certosa is well-known because the main cloister was ruined by the construction of the A4 motorway. The

courtyard is of impressive size, with the monks' houses, each with a kitchen garden, around the sides. The rules imposed by the semi-closed order required each monk to live independently. The complex was rebuilt in late Renaissance style in 1562; the façade, completed in 1608, was decorated with obelisks and statues, crowned by a statue of Our Lady. A porticoed atrium with an exedra-shaped vestibule provides a harmonious introduction to the complex.

Vincenzo Seregni designed the interior in the 1500s. The aisleless nave is crowned by a barrel vault flanked by blind arcades. The church is famous for the frescoes by Daniele Crespi, a leading 17th-century Lombard artist. He reputedly painted the entire cycle *(The Legend of the Foundation of the Order)* to thank the Carthusian monks for offering refuge after he had been charged with murder. The cycle begins by the first arch on the right, continues on the wall behind the façade, designed by Simone Peterzano, and is resumed in the vault, where there are four medallions. In the first bay on the left Crespi included a self-portrait of himself as a servant blowing a horn and added the date (1629) and his signature in a scroll.

Simone Peterzano painted the frescoes in the presbytery and apse (1578), with scenes from the life of Mary. The chapel on the right has two macabre 17th-century paintings informing novices of the various forms of torture they might encounter while spreading Christianity. On leaving, look at the 14th-century cloister on the right, the only surviving part of the original monastery.

Façade of the Certosa di Garegnano (1608)

Santa Maria delle Grazie ⓫

Piazza Santa Maria delle Grazie.
Map 2 F5. 📞 *02-48 01 42 48.* Ⓜ
1, 2 Cadorna, 1 Conciliazione. 🚋 *24.*
🕐 *7:30am–noon, 3–7pm daily.*
✝ *6:30pm pre-hols; 8, 9:30, 10:30*
& 11:30am, 6:30pm hols.

C ONSTRUCTION OF this famous church was begun in 1463. Designed by Guiniforte Solari, it was completed in 1490. Two years later Lodovico il Moro asked Bramante to change the church into the family mausoleum: Solari's apse section was demolished and then replaced by a Renaissance apse. After il Moro lost power in 1500, the Dominicans continued to decorate the church, later assisted by the court of Inquisition, which had moved here in 1558. Restoration was undertaken only in the late 19th century. In 1943 a bomb destroyed the main cloister, but the apse and the room containing Leonardo's *Last Supper* were miraculously left intact, and restoration work has continued

Frescoed cross vaulting in Santa Maria delle Grazie

since then. On the exterior, Solari's wide brick façade is worthy of note. The doorway was designed by Bramante; it is preceded by a porch supported by Corinthian columns and the lunette has a painting by Leonardo da Vinci with the Madonna between Lodovico and his wife, Beatrice d'Este. The sides and poly-gonal apse are also of interest. As you enter the church you notice the difference between Solari's nave, which echoes Lombard Gothic architecture – entirely covered with frescoes and with ogival arches – and Bramante's design for the apse, which is larger, better lit and is almost bare of decoration. The two parts of the church reflect Bramante's impact on Milanese culture; he introduced the Renaissance style that dominated Tuscany and Umbria in the early 15th century. The all-pervasive painting decoration of the aisle walls is by Bernardino Butinone and Donato Montorfano (1482–6). The Della Torre chapel is the first one in the right-hand aisle: the altar has a 15th-century fresco and to the left is the tomb of Giacomo Della Torre, with bas-relief sculpture by the Cazzaniga brothers (1483). The fourth chapel, dedicated to Santa Corona, has frescoes by Gaudenzio Ferrari. In the next chapel is a *Crucifixion* by Giovanni Demìo (1542).

The apse, decorated only with graffiti to maintain the purity of the architectural

The nave of Santa Maria delle Grazie

volumes, is a perfect cube crowned by a hemisphere. It was built to house the tomb of Lodovico il Moro and Beatrice d'Este, sculpted by Cristoforo Solari, but the work never reached Santa Maria delle Grazie (it is now in the Charterhouse of Pavia). The decoration of the dome is rich in Marian symbols, while the Doctors of the Church appear in the roundels in the pendentives. The carved and inlaid wooden stalls of the choir are lovely; above them on the walls are figures of Dominican saints.

A door on the right leads to the small cloister known as Chiostrino delle Rane because of the frogs *(rane)* in the central basin. The cloister leads to the old sacristy, with its painted wardrobes, one of which conceals a secret underground passageway, used by Lodovico to come from the Castello on horseback. Back in the church, the chapels in the north aisle begin with the Madonna delle Grazie chapel, with Cerano's *Madonna Freeing Milan of the Plague* (1631) on the entrance archway. The altarpiece, *Madonna delle Grazie*, dates from the 15th century. The sixth chapel has a *Holy Family with St Catherine* by Paris Bordone, and the first chapel contains the cloak of St Catherine of Siena.

The façade of Santa Maria delle Grazie, designed by Guiniforte Solari

Leonardo da Vinci's *Last Supper*

THIS MASTERPIECE was painted for Lodovico il Moro in the refectory of Santa Maria delle Grazie in 1495–7. Leonardo depicts the moment just after Christ has uttered the words, "One of you will betray me". The artist captures their amazement in facial expressions and body language in a remarkably realistic and vivid *Last Supper*. It is not a true fresco, but was painted in tempera, allowing Leonardo more time to achieve the subtle nuances typical of his work. The room was used as a stable in the Napoleonic era and was badly damaged by bombs in 1943. Fortunately, the work was saved because it was protected by sandbags.

Lodovico il Moro

Jesus Christ
The isolated, serene figure of Christ contrasts with the agitated Apostles. Half-closed lips show he has just spoken.

The Last Supper is famous for the gesturing hands of the Apostles, which are so harmonious and expressive that critics have said they "speak".

Judas
Unable to find a truly evil face for Judas, Leonardo drew inspiration from that of the prior in the convent, who kept on asking when the work would be finished.

The Apostle Andrew, with his arms upraised, expresses his horror at Christ's words.

The Crucifixion by Montorfano
The Dominicans asked Donato Montorfano to paint a fresco of the Crucifixion on the opposite wall to depict Christ's sacrifice. In this dense composition the despairing Magdalen hugs the cross while the soldiers on the right throw dice for Christ's robe. On either side of the work, under the cross, Leonardo added the portraits – now almost invisible – of Lodovico il Moro, his wife Beatrice and their children, signed and dated (1495).

The Restoration

It was not the humidity but the method used by Leonardo, *tempera forte*, that caused the immediate deterioration of the *Last Supper*. As early as 1550 the art historian Vasari called it "a dazzling blotch" and regarded it as a lost work. There have been many attempts to restore the *Last Supper*, beginning in 1726, but in retouching the picture further damage was done. The seventh and most recent restoration ended in spring 1999: although it lacks the splendour of the original, it is at least authentic.

Material used for restoration

Visitors' Checklist

P. Santa Maria delle Grazie 2. **Map** 2 F5. **☎** 02-498 75 88. *To book: 02-89 42 11 46.* **M** *1, 2 Cadorna.* **🚋** *24.* **◯** *8:15am–6:45pm Tue–Sun (10:15pm Sat).* **●** *public hols, 1 May, 15 Aug.* **♿ 📷 🚫**

The tablecloth, plates and bowls were probably copied from those in the convent to give the impression that Christ was at table with monks.

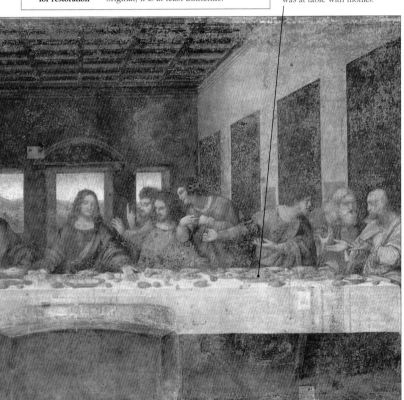

Sketches of the Apostles

Leonardo used to wander around Milan in search of faces to use for the Apostles. Of his many sketches, this one for St James is now in the Royal Library in Windsor.

Christ and the Apostles

1 Christ	**8** John
2 Thomas	**9** Peter
3 James the Greater	**10** Judas
4 Philip	**11** Andrew
5 Matthew	**12** James the Lesser
6 Thaddaeus	**13** Bartholomew
7 Simon	

Corso Magenta 🔟

Map 3 A5. **M** *1 Conciliazione,
1, 2 Cadorna.* 🚊 *18, 19, 24.*

THIS STREET is fascinating,
with its elegant shops and
historic buildings making it
one of the loveliest and most
elegant quarters in Milan. At
No. 65, just past Santa Maria
delle Grazie, is a building
incorporating the remains
of the Atellani residence,
decorated
by Luini,
where
Leonardo da
Vinci stayed
while working
on the *Last
Supper*. Piero
Portaluppi
carried out the
work on No.
65 in 1919.
In the garden
at the back
there are some
vines, said to
be the remains
of the vineyard
that Lodovico il Moro gave to
the great artist. The next
building (No. 61), Palazzo
delle Stelline, originally a
girls' orphanage, is now a
convention centre. At the
corner of Via Carducci, which
was constructed over the
original course of the
Naviglio canal, stands the
Bar Magenta *(see p178)*, a
pleasant café with vintage
décor. The medieval city gate,
the Porta Vercellina, once
stood at this junction.

**Pastry shop
sign in Corso
Magenta**

Palazzo Litta 🔢

Corso Magenta 24. **Map** *3 A5.*
M *1, 2 Cadorna.* 🚊 *18, 19, 24, 27.*
🚌 *50, 54, 58.* 🔘 *during cultural
events only.*

CONSIDERED one of the most
beautiful examples of
18th-century Lombard architecture, this palazzo was first
built in 1648 for Count Bartolomeo Arese by Francesco
Maria Richini. At the end of
the century the interior was
embellished and in 1763 the
pink façade was built at the
request of the heirs, the Litta
Visconti Arese. The façade,

The Sala Rossa in Palazzo Litta, with mementos of Napoleon's visit here

by Bartolomeo Bolli, is late
Baroque, the door flanked by
large telamones. Since 1905
the building has housed the
State Railway offices.
Inside is a number of
sumptuous rooms looking
onto a 17th-century courtyard.
The broad staircase, designed
by Carlo Giuseppe Merlo in
1740 and decorated with
precious marble and the
family coat of arms (a black
and white check), has a
double central flight. It leads
up to the *piano nobile*, where
one of the rooms is named
the Sala Rossa (Red Room)
after the colour of its wallpaper (a copy of the original).
Set in the floor is a pearl,
there to commemorate a tear
said to have been shed
during a meeting between the
Duchess Litta and Napoleon.
The next room is the Salone
degli Specchi, which seems to
be enlarged to infinity by the
large mirrors *(specchi)* on the
walls. The vault decoration is
by Martin Knoller. The Salotto
della Duchessa is
the only room
in the palazzo
which still has
its original 18th-
century wall-
paper. The Teatro
Litta stands to
the left of the
palazzo, the
oldest theatre
in the city.

Civico Museo Archeologico 🔢

Corso Magenta 15. **Map** *3 A5.*
📞 *02-88 46 57 20.* **M** *1, 2
Cadorna.* 🚊 *18, 19, 24, 27.* 🚌 *50,
54, 58.* 🔘 *9am–5:30pm Tue–Sun.*
♿ *(phone ahead).* 🚫

THE ARCHAEOLOGICAL MUSEUM
is well worth a visit for the
finds and to see the only
remaining part of the city's
Roman walls. At the entrance
visitors are greeted by a huge
stone from the Val Camonica
(see p151) with Bronze Age
engravings. Further on is a
model of Milan in Roman
times. The visit begins in a
hall on the right, with clay
objects, including a collection
of oil lamps. This is followed
by Roman sculpture. One of
the most interesting pieces in
the series of portraits dating
from Caesar's era to late
antiquity (1st–4th century
AD), is the *Portrait of Maximin* (mid-3rd century AD). At

**Roman sarcophagus of a lawyer, on display
in the Civico Museo Archeologico**

the end of this room is a huge fragment of a torso of Hercules from the Milanese thermae, dating from the first half of the 2nd century AD. Behind this are some 3rd-century AD floor mosaics found in Milanese houses.

By the window are two of the most important works in the museum: the Parabiago Patera and the Diatreta Cup. The Patera is a gilded silver plate with a relief of the triumph of the goddess Cybele, mother of the gods, on a chariot pulled by lions and surrounded by the Sun and Moon and sea and Zodiac divinities (mid-4th century AD). The marvellous Diatreta Cup, also dating from the 4th century AD, comes from Novara and consists of a single piece of coloured glass, with finely wrought, intricate decoration. Winding around the cup is the inscription *Bibe vivas multis annis* ("Drink and you will live many years"). To the left of the entrance are 6th-century Lombard finds. The entrance hall leads to a second court-yard, where you will see the Torre di Ansperto, a Roman tower from the ancient Maximinian walls. The basement contains a collection of Attic red- and black-figure vases and the museum display ends with a fine collection of Etruscan pieces.

The Roman ruins in Via Brisa

Stela with portraits, Museo Archeologico

San Maurizio **⑮**

Corso Magenta. **Map** 3 A5. **⚏** 02-86 66 60 (Santa Maria alla Porta). **Ⓜ** 1, 2 Cadorna. **🚊** 18, 19, 24, 27. **🚌** 50, 54, 58. **◯** 9am–noon, 2–5pm Tue–Sun. **⛪** 6pm Mon–Fri, 10:15 am (Greek–Albanian) Sun.

I̶N 1503 GIAN GIACOMO Dolcebuono began construction of this church, which was intended for the most powerful closed order of Benedictine nuns in Milan, with one hall for the public and another for the nuns. In the first hall, to the right of the altar, is the opening through which the nuns receive the Body of Christ. Most of the decoration was done by Bernardino Luini. He painted the frescoes in the first hall, including the *Life of St Catherine* (third chapel to the right) and those on the middle wall. The second chapel on the right was decorated by Callisto Piazza, the chapels to the left by pupils of Luini. On the altar is an *Adoration of the Magi* by Antonio Campi. The middle wall of the second hall, occupied by the choir, has frescoes by Foppa, Piazza, an *Annunciation* attributed to Bramantino and *Episodes of the Passion*. Concerts are held here in the winter.

Via Brisa **⑯**

Map 7 B1. **Ⓜ** 1, 2 Cadorna. **🚊** 18, 19, 24, 27. **🚌** 50, 54, 58.

E̶XCAVATIONS CARRIED OUT after the 1943 bombing of this street revealed Roman ruins which were probably part of Maximin's imperial palace: the foundation of a round hall surrounded by apsidal halls and preceded by a narthex. Note the columns that raised the pavement to allow warm air to pass into the palace.

Piazza Cordusio **⑰**

Map 7 C1. **Ⓜ** 1 Cordusio. **🚊** 18, 19, 24, 27. **🚌** 50, 58, 60.

T̶HIS OVAL-SHAPED piazza was named after the *Curtis Ducis*, the main seat of the Lombard duchy. The area, Milan's financial district, was laid out from 1889 to 1901. Buildings include Luca Beltrami's Assicurazioni Generali building, Casa Dario, and the main offices of Credito Italiano, designed by Luigi Broggi.

Piazza Affari **⑱**

Map 7 B1. **Ⓜ** 1 Cordusio. **🚊** 18, 19, 24, 27. **🚌** 50, 58, 60.

T̶HE HEART OF the financial district, this square was laid out in 1928–40 to house the city's markets (especially farm produce). The Borsa Valori, Italy's most important Stock Exchange, stands here. Founded in 1808, it is housed in a building designed by Paolo Mezzanotte in 1931. Ruins of a 1st-century BC Roman theatre were found in the basement area.

The Milan Stock Exchange in Piazza Affari, built in 1931

SOUTHWEST MILAN

RELIGIOUS COMPLEXES once covered this district, preventing further building until the early 19th century. The suppression of the monasteries in the late 18th century paved the way for the urbanization of the area between the medieval and Spanish walls, crossed by two large avenues, Corso Italia and Corso di Porta Ticinese. Beyond Porta Ticinese, which leads to the southern part of Milan, is Corso San Gottardo. The area is bordered by the inner ring

Vault mosaic, Sant'Ambrogio

road, which follows the course of the medieval walls, and the outer ring road, which replaced the Spanish walls. Further on is the Naviglio canals quarter, with the Naviglio Grande and the Pavese, the last vestiges of what was once a major network for communications and commerce. Barges used the Naviglio Grande to transport the Candoglia marble used to build the Duomo and, in the 1950s, the material for postwar reconstruction.

SIGHTS AT A GLANCE

Churches

San Bernardino alle Monache ❺
San Lorenzo alle Colonne pp80–81 ❶
San Paolo Converso ⑪
San Vittore al Corpo ❽
Sant'Alessandro ⑫
Sant'Ambrogio pp84–7 ❻
Sant'Eustorgio ❾
Santa Maria presso San Celso ⑩

Streets, Squares and Historic Buildings

Largo Carrobbio and Via Torino ❸
Piazza della Vetra and medieval Porta Ticinese ❷
Via Circo ❹

Museums and Galleries

Museo Nazionale della Scienza e della Tecnica ❼

San Lorenzo alle Colonne pp80–81; *Sant'Ambrogio pp84–7*

KEY

▢ Street-by-Street map
  See pp78–9
🄿 Parking
Ⓜ Metro
🚖 Taxi

0 metres   200
0 yards   200

GETTING THERE

Sant'Ambrogio is served by bus No. 94 (which continues to San Lorenzo) and by metro line 2. Trams 3, 9, 15, 29 and 30 go to the Navigli, and No. 3 is connected to Via Torino by Nos. 2 and 14. Metro line 3 (Missori stop), tram 15 and bus 65 all stop at Corso di Porta Romana.

◁ **The antiques market, held on the towpath of the Naviglio Grande on the last Sunday of every month**

Street-by-Street: From Sant'Ambrogio to San Lorenzo

SITUATED JUST OUTSIDE the Roman walls, this area was occupied by Early Christian cemeteries and Imperial Age buildings such as the Arena and Circus. Though little remains of this ancient heritage, it is however significant, particularly the columns of the triumphal entrance to the basilica of San Lorenzo. Nine kings of Italy were crowned in Sant'Ambrogio in the 9th–15th centuries and four were buried here. Napoleon came here in 1805, and Ferdinand of Austria in 1838, after their respective coronations in the Duomo. On the feast day of Sant'Ambrogio, 7 December, the *Oh bej Oh bej* fair is held in the streets.

Statue, Università Cattolica

Via Circo
The remains of an ancient Roman circus, used for public spectacles, were found in this street ❹

Cloister of Santa Maria Maddalena al Cerchio

The Università Cattolica (1921) is located in the monastery and cloisters of old Sant'Ambrogio, built by Bramante in 1497.

The Tempio della Vittoria (1930), designed by Giovanni Muzio, commemorates the 10,000 Milanese who perished in World War I.

San Bernardino alle Monache
This church was rebuilt in 1450 for Franciscan nuns. The façade is decorated with majolica bollows ❺

★ Sant'Ambrogio
Founded by Sant'Ambrogio in the 4th century, this church contains masterpieces such as the San Vittore mosaics and the Golden Altar ❻

0 metres	100
0 yards	100

Largo Carrobbio
The name of the crossroads at the end of Via Torino may derive from quadrivium, *meaning a place where four streets converge* ❸

LOCATOR MAP
See Street Finder, map 7, 8

In Largo Carrobbio the small deconsecrated church of San Sisto houses the Museo Messina.

A tower from the Roman Porta Ticinese is hidden in the courtyard of a building between Via del Torchio and Via Medici.

Piazza della Vetra
From this square there are spectacular views of the apses of San Lorenzo and Sant'Eustorgio. Until 1840 the piazza was the scene of executions ❷

VIA TORINO

LARGO CARROBBIO

VIA SAN VITO

VIA CESARE CORRENTI

VIA PIO IV

PORTA TICINESE

VIA MORA

VIA DE AMICIS

VIA MOLINO DELLE ARMI

KEY

━ ━ ━ ━ Suggested route

STAR SIGHTS

★ **San Lorenzo alle Colonne**

★ **Sant'Ambrogio**

Medieval Porta Ticinese

The 16 Corinthian columns may have come from a 2nd–3rd-century AD pagan temple.

★ **San Lorenzo alle Colonne**
This superb 4th-century basilica consists of a main domed section linked to a series of minor buildings, dating from different periods ❶

San Lorenzo alle Colonne ❶

Dating from the 4th century, San Lorenzo is one of the oldest round churches in Western Christendom and may have been the ancient Imperial palatine chapel. The church was built utilizing materials from a nearby Roman amphitheatre. The plan, with exedrae and women's galleries, is unlike Lombard architecture and reveals the hand of Roman architects and masons. Some art historians also see the influence of Byzantine art in the unusual plan. After several fires the church was reconstructed in the 11th and 12th centuries and was again rebuilt after the dome collapsed in 1573, but the original quatrefoil plan has been preserved. The chapel of Sant'Aquilino contains some of the best mosaics in Northern Italy.

Cappella di San Sisto
This chapel was frescoed by Gian Cristoforo Storer in the 17th century.

A bas-relief above the entrance depicts San Lorenzo, who was burnt over live coals in the 3rd century (a recurring symbol in the church).

Main entrance

★ Roman Columns
The 16 Corinthian columns, from the 2nd–3rd century, were part of an unidentified temple and were placed in their present location in the 4th century.

Statue of Constantine
This bronze work is a copy of a Roman statue of the emperor who issued the Edict of Milan in AD 313, bringing persecution of Christians to an end.

The dome, the largest in Milan, is supported by an octagonal tambour lit by eight large windows. It was rebuilt by Martino Bassi after it collapsed in 1573.

An upside-down column symbolizes Christianity rising from the ruins of paganism.

VISITORS' CHECKLIST

Corso di Porta Ticinese 39. **Map** 7 B2. 02-89 40 41 29. 3 Missori. 3. 94. 9am–5:30pm daily. 6pm Mon–Fri; 6pm pre-hols; 9:30, 11:30am, 4pm (in Philippine language), 6pm hols. **Cappella di Sant'Aquilino** 9am–6:30pm daily. (donation).

★ **Cappella di Sant'Aquilino**
This 5th-century chapel has mosaics from the same period: Elijah on the Chariot of Fire and Christ with the Apostles. The entire chapel was once decorated with mosaics.

Byzantine sarcophagus

Behind the altar, steps lead to the crypt, which has stones taken from the amphitheatre and used for compacting the earth.

The 17th-century presbyteries, designed by Trezzi and Richini, were originally designed to join up with the columns so as to revive the pattern of the ancient quadriporticus.

THE STRUCTURE

Most of the walls, towers and three chapels date from the late 4th century. The upper parts of the towers are Romanesque. The dome was built in the late 1500s and the façade in 1894 by Cesare Nava.

KEY

☐ Early Christian

☐ Medieval and modern

☐ Romanesque

STAR FEATURES

★ **Roman Columns**

★ **Cappella di Sant'Aquilino**

Piazza della Vetra, linking San Lorenzo to Sant'Eustorgio

Piazza della Vetra and medieval Porta Ticinese ❷

Map 7 B2. 2, 3, 14. 94.

THE VAST AREA of greenery dominated by a column bearing the statue of San Lazzaro (1728) is also called · Parco delle Basiliche, because it lies between the basilicas of San Lorenzo and Sant'Eustorgio. The name "Vetra" seems to derive from the Latin *castra vetera*, which probably alluded to the Roman military camps positioned here to defend the nearby imperial palace. The name was also given to a canal that was once on the northern side of the square and was lined with tanners' workshops (the tanners were

called *vetraschi*). Until 1840 the square was used for the public hangings of condemned commoners, while nobles were decapitated in front of the law court, the Broletto (*see p54*).

During the Roman era there was a small port here, at the point where the Seveso and Nirone rivers converged in the navigable Vettabbia canal.

This square is worth visiting just for the magnificent view of the apses of the basilicas. In the 12th century, when the city walls were enlarged to include San Lorenzo, the Roman gate at present-day Largo Carrobbio was replaced by the "new" medieval Porta Ticinese. A moat ran around the new walls and along present-day Via Molino delle Armi, which was named after the water mills *(molini)* used mostly to forge weapons.

Porta Ticinese was remodelled after 1329 by Azzone Visconti and decorated with a tabernacle of the *Madonna and Child with St Ambrose Proffering the Model of the City* by the workshop of Giovanni di Balduccio (14th century). This city gate – the only one, along with Porta Nuova on Via Manzoni, still standing – was fortified with two towers in 1865.

Detail of the tabernacle of Porta Ticinese:
Madonna and Child with St Ambrose
by Giovanni di Balduccio's workshop

Largo Carrobbio and Via Torino ❸

Map 7 B2. 2, 3, 14. **Museo Messina** Via San Sisto 4. 02-86 45 30 05. 9:30am–noon, 1:30– 5:30pm Tue–Sun. 1 Jan, Easter, 1 May, 15 Aug, 25 Dec.

THE VAST Carrobbio square, which connects Via Torino and Corso di Porta Ticinese, was either named after the *quadrivium*, a crossroads of four streets, or after *carrubium*, a road reserved for carts. One of the towers flanking the Roman Porta Ticinese is still standing at the corner of Via Medici and Via del Torchio. The name of the gate derived from the fact that it opened onto the road for Pavia, which in ancient times was called *Ticinum*. At the junction with Via San Sisto is the deconsecrated 17th-century church of San Sisto. In 1976 it became the museum-studio of sculptor Francesco Messina (who died in 1990) and now houses a collection of his bronze and

Female nude by Francesco Messina (1967)

coloured plaster sculpture pieces and graphic art.

Largo Carrobbio is at one end of Via Torino, a major commercial street that developed after the merger of the old city districts, which were filled with the workshops of oil merchants, silk weavers, hatters and famous armourers – as can be seen by the names of some streets.

The 16th-century Palazzo Stampa, built by Massimiliano Stampa, stands in Via Soncino. When the Sforza dynasty died out in 1535, Stampa introduced Spanish dominion to the city by hoisting the flag of Charles V on the Castello Sforzesco in exchange for land and privileges. The imperial eagle still stands on the palazzo tower, over the bronze globe representing the dominions of Charles V.

The cloister at Santa Maria Maddalena al Cerchio

Via Circo ❹

Map 7 B1. 🚊 *2, 3, 14.*

THE AREA EXTENDING from Largo Carrobbio to Corso Magenta is very rich in 3rd- and 4th-century ruins, particularly mosaics and masonry, much of it now part of private homes. This was the period when the Roman emperor Maximian lived in Milan: his splendid palace was near Via Brisa. In order to create a proper imperial capital, he built many civic edifices to gain the favour of the Milanese: the Arena, the thermae and the huge Circus used for two-horse chariot races. The Circus, 505 m

(1,656 ft) long, was one of the largest constructions in the Roman Empire. The only remaining parts are the end curve, visible at the junction of Via Cappuccio and Via Circo, and one of the entrance towers, which became the bell tower of San Maurizio in Corso Magenta.

The Circus, active long after the fall of the Roman Empire, was the venue for the coronation of the Lombard king Adaloaldo in 615, while in the Carolingian period it became a vineyard, as the place name of nearby Via Vigna indicates. At No. 7 Via Cappuccio, the 18th-century Palazzo Litta Biumi has incorporated, to the left of the central courtyard, the delightful 15th-century nuns' convent Santa Maria Maddalena al Cerchio, which has been partly rebuilt. Its name, a corruption of the Latin *ad circulum*, refers to the Circus over which it was built. The hood of the nuns' habit *(cappuccio)* is probably the origin of the name of the street where the convent is located. Further along, at No. 13, is Palazzo Radice Fossati (a private house), of medieval origin, with a 13th-century portal and 18th-century frescoes inside.

On Via Sant'Orsola you come to Via Morigi, named after a famous Milanese family who once lived here; all that remains of their residence is a 14th-century tower with a small loggia. The nearby square is dominated by the 14th-century Torre dei Gorani, another tower crowned by a loggia with small stone columns.

Fifteenth-century frescoes by the school of Vincenzo Foppa

San Bernardino alle Monache ❺

Via Lanzone 13. **Map** 7 A1.
📞 *02-645 19 48 (Amici di San Bernardino cultural association).*
🚊 *2, 3, 14.* ⬤ *for restoration.*

THE CHURCH IS the only remaining building in a Franciscan nuns' convent dating from the mid-15th century and attributed to the Lombard architect Pietro Antonio Solari. The church was named after the preacher Bernardino da Siena, whose relics are kept here. It was partly rebuilt in 1922. The narrow, elegant brick façade is decorated with majolica bowls and a fine elaborate cornice with small arches.

The interior houses fine 15th-century frescoes painted by the school of Vincenzo Foppa, and others dating from the early 16th century. The church is under restoration and will be re-opened to the public in the future.

Part of the curve of the Circus built by the Roman emperor Maximian in the late 3rd century AD

Sant'Ambrogio ➏

Detail of the apse mosaic

T HE BASILICA WAS BUILT by Bishop Ambrogio (Ambrose) in AD 379–86 on an Early Christian burial ground as part of a programme to reorganize the Christian face of Milan. The church was dedicated to Ambrogio, a defender of Christianity against Arianism, after his burial here. The Benedictines began to enlarge it in the 8th century, then in the following century Archbishop Anspert built the atrium, which was rebuilt in the 12th century. In the 11th century, reconstruction of the entire church began. The dome collapsed in 1196, and the vaults and pulpit were rebuilt. In 1492 the Sforza family asked Bramante to restructure the rectory and the Benedictine monastery. Sadly, the basilica was badly damaged by bombs in 1943.

The Canons' bell tower was erected in 1124 to surpass in height and beauty the campanile of the nearby Benedictines.

The Capitals
The columns are enlivened by Bible stories and fantastic animals symbolizing the struggle between Good and Evil. Some date from the 11th century.

Anspert's Atrium (11th century) was used by local people as a refuge from danger before the city walls were built.

The Interior
The solemn proportions typical of Lombard Romanesque characterize the interior. The nave is covered by ribbed cross vaulting supported by massive piers.

Apse Mosaic
The mosaic dates from the 4th–8th centuries and was partially restored after the 1943 bombings. It depicts the enthroned Christ and scenes from Sant'Ambrogio's life.

Museum entrance

Apse

VISITORS' CHECKLIST

Piazza Sant'Ambrogio 15.
Map 7 A1. 02-86 45 08 95.
2 Sant'Ambrogio. 50, 54, 58, 94. 7am–noon, 2:30–7pm daily.
6:30pm pre-hols; 9, 10 & 11am (in Latin), 12:15, 6 & 7pm hols; 7:30, 8 & 9am, 6:30pm Mon–Fri.
Museo della Basilica 02-86 45 08 95. Access through presbytery or rear of church.
10am–noon, 3–5pm Wed–Fri & Mon, 3–5pm Sat & Sun.
am pre-hols and hols.

★ Chapel of San Vittore in Ciel d'Oro
The chapel was named after the gold (oro) mosaics on the vault. Sant'Ambrogio is depicted in one of the 5th-century panels.

The ciborium is the small 10th-century baldachin that protects the Golden Altar. It is supported by four Roman porphyry columns and decorated with stuccowork.

★ Golden Altar
This golden altar was made by Volvinius (9th century) for the remains of Sant'-Ambrogio. The reliefs depict the lives of Christ (front) and Ambrogio (to the rear).

★ Sarcophagus of Stilicho
Situated under the pulpit, this 4th-century master-piece has a wealth of relief figures with religious significance. It is tradition-ally referred to as the tomb of the Roman general Stilicho, but probably contained the remains of the emperor Gratian.

STAR FEATURES

★ Golden Altar

★ Chapel of San Vittore in Ciel d'Oro

★ Sarcophagus of Stilicho

Exploring Sant'Ambrogio

THE FACT THAT the church of Sant'Ambrogio houses the remains of the city's patron saint, the church's founder, makes it a special place for the Milanese. Most of its present-day appearance is the result of rebuilding in the 10th and 12th centuries by the Benedictines from the nearby monastery, who made it a model of Lombard Romanesque religious architecture. All that remains of the 4th-century basilica are the triumphal arch and its columns, which became part of the apse. In 1937–40 and in the post-war period the Romanesque structure and delicate colours were restored. From the Pusterla (gate) there is a marvellous view of the church, with its two bell towers and atrium, flanked by the rectory and museum.

Papal statue

PUSTERLA DI SANT'AMBROGIO

THE PUSTERLA di Sant' Ambrogio, one of the minor gates on the medieval walls, is a good starting point for a visit to the church. Rebuilt in 1939, it houses a museum with old weapons and instruments of torture.

A decorated capital in the atrium

ANSPERT'S ATRIUM

JUST BEFORE THE atrium, to the left, is the isolated Roman Colonna del Diavolo (Devil's Column), with two holes halfway up which, according to tradition, were made by the Devil's horns while he was tempting Sant'Ambrogio. The present-day atrium, with its blind arches, dates from the 12th century and replaced one built by Archbishop Anspert in the 9th century. This large courtyard acts as an entrance foyer for the church proper and sets off the façade.

A row of piers (some Roman) with sculpted capitals continues into the basilica. The rhythmic pattern of the arches, half-columns and small suspended arches, as well as the proportions, match those in the church, creating a harmonious continuity between exterior and interior. The atrium houses finds and tombstones from this area, which was once an Early Christian cemetery. The fourth side of the atrium, or narthex, has five bays and is part of the façade, which has an upper loggia with five arches. In the narthex is the main portal (8th–10th centuries), with small columns with figures of animals and the Mystic Lamb, while its wooden wings (1750) have reliefs of the *Life of David*.

The atrium, with finds and tombstones from the surrounding area

THE INTERIOR

THE NAVE PROVIDES the best view of the interior, revealing the basilica in all its splendour. The nave has two side aisles divided by arcades supporting the women's galleries with piers with carved capitals. At the beginning of the nave is the Serpent's Column, said to have been erected by Moses in the desert. Beside it, to the left, excavations show the level of the original 4th-century floor.

The pulpit (or ambo) is made of pieces saved when the dome collapsed in 1196. This magnificent monument is decorated with an eagle and a seated man, symbols of the evangelists John and Matthew. Underneath is the sarcophagus of Stilicho (4th century) with reliefs representing (going clockwise) *Christ Giving the Law to St Peter*, four scenes from the Old Testament, *Christ among the Apostles* and the *Sacrifice of Isaac*. Under the octagonal cupola is the ciborium (10th century), the heart of the basilica, supported by columns taken from the 4th-century ciborium. Its painted stucco sides depict various episodes: on the front is *Christ Giving the Keys to St Peter and the Law to St Paul*. The ciborium acts as a baldachin for the Golden Altar, an embossed work that Archbishop Angilberto commissioned from Volvinius in the 9th century. On the back, a silver relief narrates the *Life of Sant'Ambrogio* and has the artist's signature. On the same side, two small doors allowed the faithful to worship the body of St Ambrose, once kept under the altar. The front is made of gold and jewels, and narrates the *Life of Christ*. Behind the ciborium is the wooden choir with the *Life of Sant'Ambrogio* (15th century) and, in the middle, the bishop's throne (4th and 9th centuries), also used

The Serpent's Column, at the beginning of the nave

by the kings of Italy crowned here. Part of the large mosaic in the apse dates from the 6th and 8th centuries. The scene on the left, a *Benedictory Christ*, is of the same period, while the one on the right is the result of 18th-century and postwar reconstruction.

Next to the presbytery is the stairway to the crypt, decorated with stucco (c.1740). Under the Golden Altar, an urn (1897) has the remains of saints Ambrogio, Gervasio and Protasio. Back upstairs, at the end of the south aisle is the stunning San Vittore in Ciel d'Oro Sacellum, the 4th-century funerary chapel of the martyr, which was later incorporated into the basilica. The 5th-century mosaics on the walls show various saints, including Saints Ambrogio, Gervasio and Protasio.

The Risen Christ by Bergognone (c.1491)

John the Baptist by Bernardo Lanino, who frescoed the *Legend of St George* on the sides (1546). The Baroque chapel of the Holy Sacrament, the fifth, contains the frescoes *The Death of St Benedict* by Carlo Preda and *St Bernard* by Filippo Abbiati (17th and 18th century respectively). In St Bartholomew's chapel (the second) are the *Legends of Saints Vittore and Satiro* (1737) by Tiepolo, detached from the San Vittore Sacellum; they demonstrate the cultural openness of the Cistercians, who commissioned the work. The altarpiece in the second chapel, *The Virgin Mary with St Bartholomew and St John the Baptist*, is attributed to Gaudenzio Ferrari, as is the 1545 *Deposition* in the next chapel, which also has frescoes by Luini on the pillars.

THE SOUTH AISLE

RETURNING TO the entrance in the south aisle, you will see the monks' chapels, built in different eras. St George's chapel – sixth from the entrance – houses an altarpiece of the *Madonna and Child with the Infant St*

THE NORTH AISLE

GO UP THIS aisle from the baptistery (first chapel), which has a porphyry font by Franco Lombardi with the *Conversion of St Augustine* (1940), the saint baptized by Sant'Ambrogio in Milan. It is

dominated symbolically by Bergognone's *The Risen Christ* (c.1491).

In the third chapel is an interesting painting by Luini, a *Madonna with Saints Jerome and Rocco*.

MUSEO DELLA BASILICA

AT THE END OF THE north aisle you come out into the Portico della Canonica, the presbytery portico, which was left unfinished by Bramante (1492–4) and rebuilt after World War II. The columns of the central arch, sculpted to resemble tree trunks, are unusual. The entrance to the Basilica Museum, with six rooms featuring objects and works of art from the church, is here. Among the most interesting pieces are a 12th-century multicoloured tondo of St Ambrose; a cast of Stilicho's sarcophagus; St Ambrose's bed; fragments of the apse mosaics and four wooden panels from the 4th-century portal. The museum also has a *Triptych* by Bernardo Zenale (15th century) and *Christ among the Doctors* by Bergognone. In the garden opposite is St Sigismund's oratory, already famous by 1096, with 15th-century frescoes and Roman columns.

Plaque of the Università Cattolica del Sacro Cuore

UNIVERSITÀ CATTOLICA DEL SACRO CUORE

ON THE RIGHT-HAND side of the church (entrance at No. 1 Largo Gemelli), in the former Benedictine monastery, is the university founded by padre Agostino Gemelli in 1921. Its two cloisters, with Ionic and Doric columns, were two of the four Bramante had designed in 1497. In the refectory is *The Marriage at Cana* by Callisto Piazza (1545).

Old motion picture camera, the Science and Technology Museum

Museo Nazionale della Scienza e della Tecnica **7**

Via San Vittore 21. **Map** 6 F1. **02-48 55 51.** **M** 2 Sant'Ambrogio. 50, 54, 58, 94. 9:30am–4:50pm Tue–Fri; 9.30am–6:20pm Sat, hols. (book at Ufficio Didattico). Library, lecture rooms. **W** www.museoscienza.org

THE SCIENCE and Technology Museum is housed in the former Olivetan monastery of San Vittore (16th century) – partly designed by Vincenzo Seregni – which became a military hospital and then a barracks after monasteries were suppressed in 1804. It was badly damaged in World War II, was restored, and in 1947 became the home of the museum. In the two courtyards surrounded by the old section of the museum, you can see part of the foundation of the San Vittore fortress and that of the octagonal mausoleum of Emperor Valentinian II, both ancient Roman.

The museum boasts one of the world's leading science and technology collections. The vast exhibition space is housed in different buildings. The former monastery contains the technological sections on metallurgy, casting and transport, as well as science sections featuring physics, optics, acoustics and astronomy. Another section shows the development of calculation, from the first mechanical calculating machine, invented by Pascal

in 1642, to IBM computers. There is also a section on time measurement, with a reconstruction of a 1750 watchmaker's workshop. The printing section is also worth a visit: it shows the 1810 automatic inking method by which 800 sheets an hour could be printed, and also has the father of the modern typewriter (1855).

The cinema photography section shows how the claw device, used to make motion-picture film move, grew out of a sewing machine needle conceived by Singer in 1851. In the rooms given over to telephones and television, there is a reconstruction of the 1856 pantelegraph, the ancestor of the fax machine.

The history of trains begins with the first locomotive in Italy, used for the Naples-Portici line in 1839, and ends with 1970s models. A pavilion in Via Olona houses the air and sea transport section, featuring two historic pieces: the bridge of the transatlantic liner *Conte Biancamano* and a naval training ship.

The Leonardo da Vinci Gallery has fascinating wooden models of the machines and apparatus invented by the genius, shown together with his drawings. Some, like the rotating crane and the helical airscrew, which demonstrate principles of physics and applied mechanics, can be operated by the public.

San Vittore al Corpo **8**

Via San Vittore 25. **Map** 6 F1. **02-48 00 53 51.** **M** 2 Sant'Ambrogio. 50, 54, 58, 94. 7:30am–noon, 3:30–7pm daily. 6pm pre-hols; 8:30, 10 & 11:15am; 12:15, 6 & 9 pm hols. (no flash).

THE ORIGINAL basilica on this site was founded in the 4th century, next to the mausoleum of Emperor Valentinian II, who died in 392. The church was rebuilt in the 11th and 12th centuries by Benedictine monks, who arrived here in 1010, and was again altered in 1560 by the Olivetans, who replaced the monks. The architect (either Alessi or Seregni) reversed the orientation and made it one of Milan's most sumptuous churches, with splendid late 16th-century paintings. The Baroque Arese Chapel (1668), designed by Gerolamo Quadrio, and the right-hand apse, with scenes from the life of St Gregory by Camillo Procaccini (1602), are of particular interest. Moncalvo frescoed the angel musicians on the cupola in 1619. The wooden choir stalls, with carvings of episodes from St Benedict's life, date from 1583; above them are three canvases on the same subject by Giovanni Ambrogio Figino. Last, the chapel of Sant'Antonio Abate was entirely frescoed in 1619 by Daniele Crespi.

Façade detail, San Vittore al Corpo

The façade of San Vittore al Corpo

Along the Naviglio Grande

NOW ONE OF THE liveliest quarters in Milan, the Navigli formed the city's port district until the 19th century. Work on the Naviglio Grande canal began in 1177, followed by the Pavia, Bereguardo, Martesana and Paderno canals. A system of locks allowed boats to travel along the canals on different levels (Candoglia marble was taken to the Duomo in the 14th century in this way). Lodovico il Moro

One of the 12 locks

improved this network with the help of Leonardo da Vinci in the 15th century. Barges arrived laden with coal and salt and departed with handmade goods and textiles. Some sections of the canals, which once extended for 150 km (93 miles), were filled in during the 1930s and navigation ceased altogether in 1979. Thanks to the Navigli canals, in 1953 landlocked Milan was ranked the 13th port in Italy.

Typical houses
Along the Naviglio there are typical blocks of flats in "Milan yellow", built with running balconies around courtyards.

San Cristoforo al Naviglio
The church of the patron saint of boatmen is two buildings in one (12th and 14th century).

There are many antiques workshops and shops here.

The big barges have become nightclubs.

On the towpaths, horses or oxen once pulled the barges.

The church of Santa Maria delle Grazie al Naviglio faces the water.

Mercatone dell'Antiquariato
On the last Sunday of the month, from September to June, 400 antique dealers take part in this lively market on the Naviglio Grande.

Vicolo dei Lavandai
On the towpath you can still see the old washing troughs, sheltered by wooden roofs, where women washed clothes in the canal water.

Sant'Eustorgio ⑨

Piazza Sant'Eustorgio 1. **Map** 7 B3.
📞 02-58 10 15 83. 🚋 3, 9, 15, 29,
30. 🚌 59. 🕐 7:30am–noon, 3:30–
6:30pm. 🔔 5pm pre-hols; 9:30, 11am,
12:30, 5pm hols; 5pm Jul, Aug.
Museum 📞 02-89 40 26 71. 🕐
10am–6pm Tue–Sun (10pm Thu).

I N THE 11TH CENTURY work
began on building a basilica
over one founded by St
Eustorgius in the 4th century,
to house the relics of the Magi.
Frederick Barbarossa destroyed
it in 1162 and it was rebuilt in
1190, with the city's tallest bell
tower, the first to carry a
clock, in 1306. At this point
the main body of the present-
day church was built: a three-
aisle nave with cross vaulting
supported by round arches.
On the left-hand side of the
façade, which was rebuilt in
1865, is a small pulpit (1597)
which replaced the wooden
one reputedly used by St Peter
Martyr in the 13th century. On
the right-hand side, chapels
built in different styles date
from the 13th–15th centuries.
   Beyond the apse is the Portinari chapel (1462). In the 19th
century, Baroque elements
were removed from inside and
the original frescoes revealed.
The impressive effect is due to
the slight outward inclination
of the pillars, which have
elegantly sculpted 12th-
century capitals at the top.
   The most interesting art is in
the chapels on the right. The
Brivio chapel houses Tommaso
Cazzaniga's tomb of Giovanni

Stefano Brivio (1486). The
middle bas-relief depicts the
Adoration of the Magi, and the
altarpiece is a triptych by
Bergognone. The next chapel
has Pietro Torelli's tomb. In
the Baroque Crotta-Caimi
chapel is a fine sarcophagus
by Protaso Caimi, the 15th-
century sculptor, and a *St
Ambrose on Horseback*. The
fourth chapel, built
by the Visconti,
has beautiful
14th-century fres-
coes: on the
vault are the
Evangelists;
below left, a
delicate *St
George and
the Dragon*, in
the style of Giovannino de'
Grassi; right, the *Triumph of St
Thomas*, perhaps by Giovanni
da Milano. On the walls are
the sarcophagus of Stefano
Visconti, by Giovanni di Balduccio, and a 13th-century
Crucifix. The Torriani chapel –
the last to be linked to the
aisle by a single vault – is

frescoed with symbols of the
Evangelists, perhaps by Michelino da Besozzo. In the south
transept is the large late-Roman
sarcophagus that once housed
the relics of the Magi, and on
the altar is a Campionese
school marble triptych of the
journey of the Magi (1347).
The Magi are also the subject
of the fresco on the left,
attributed to Luini.
The high altar
houses the remains
of St Eustorgius
and bears a
marble altar-front
depicting the
Passion of
Christ, an
unfinished
work by
various artists, including
Matteo da Campione.
   Behind the altar are the
remains of the 4th-century
apse and a passageway
leading to the Portinari chapel,
commissioned by banker
Pigello Portinari as his tomb,
and to house the body of St
Peter Martyr. Its marvellous
architecture, the first example
of a 15th-century central-plan
church in Milan, exemplifies
the clarity of Bramante's vision
and features typical Lombard
decoration attributed to Vincenzo Foppa, including
masterful frescoes of the
miracles of St Peter and the
life of the Virgin Mary. On the
right-hand lunette, the saint
subdues the Devil in the guise
of Mary. Under the dome,
below dancing angels, is the
tomb of St Peter Martyr (1339)
by Giovanni di Balduccio, held
up by the eight Virtues and
showing scenes of his ministry.
The small chapel on the left
has a silver urn containing the
saint's skull.

**Sculpture on the façade
of Sant'Eustorgio**

The Neo-Romanesque façade of Sant'Eustorgio, built in 1865

The Sanctuary of Santa Maria dei Miracoli and San Celso

Santa Maria presso San Celso ⑩

Corso Italia 37. **Map** 7 C3.
📞 02-58 31 31 87. 🚋 15.
🚌 65, 94. 🕐 7am–noon,
4–6:30pm daily. ✝ 6pm pre-hols;
9 & 11am, 12, 5:30 & 7pm hols.
San Celso ask sacristan.

SAN CELSO was founded in the 11th century over a church built by St Ambrose in the 4th century to mark the spot where he had found the remains of the martyrs Celso and Nazaro. In 1493 construction began on a sanctuary dedicated to Santa Maria dei Miracoli, designed by Gian Giacomo Dolcebuono and subsequently by Vincenzo Seregni and Alessi. The late 16th-century façade is enlivened by sculptures by Stoldo Lorenzi and Annibale Fontana. The late Renaissance interior has a pavement by Martino Bassi and was frescoed by Cerano and Procaccini. There are major works of art in the various chapels: a painting (1606) by Procaccini; the *Holy Family with St Jerome* altarpiece (1548) by Paris Bordone; Antonio Campi's *Resurrection* (1560); *Baptism of Jesus* by Gaudenzio Ferrari; Moretto da Brescia's *Conversion of St Paul* (1539–40); *Martyrdom of St Catherine* by Cerano (1603); an altarpiece by Bergognone.

Under the cupola with terracotta Evangelists by De Fondutis and paintings by Appiani (1795) is the high altar (16th century) in semi-precious stones. The wooden choir is from 1570. Statues by Fontana and Lorenzi adorn the pillars. On the Altar of the Madonna is Fontana's *Our Lady of the Assumption*. Below, a 4th-century fresco lies under two embossed silver doors. By the right-hand transept is the entrance to **San Celso**, with 11th–15th-century frescoes and columns with carved capitals.

San Paolo Converso ⑪

Piazza Sant'Eufemia. **Map** 7 C2.
🚋 15. 🚌 65, 94.
🕐 for exhibitions only.

THIS CHURCH was founded in 1549 for the Angeliche di San Paolo convent and is attributed to Domenico Giunti, while the façade was designed by Cerano in 1611. Now deconsecrated, the church has a front section for the public and another one to the rear, facing the opposite direction, reserved for the nuns. The interior was frescoed in the late 1500s by Giulio and Antonio Campi: in the presbytery are episodes from the life of St Paul, the Ascension of Christ and the Assumption of Mary, framed in an architectural setting with bold foreshortening.

At the end of Corso di Porta Romana is Piazza Missori, with the remains of San Giovanni in Conca (11th cen-tury), once a Visconti mausoleum. The façade was remade for the Waldensian church in Via Francesco Sforza.

Sant'Alessandro ⑫

Piazza Sant'Alessandro. **Map** 7 C2.
📞 02-86 45 30 65. Ⓜ 1 Missori.
🚋 4, 12, 15, 24. 🚌 65.
🕐 7:30am–noon, 4–7pm daily.
✝ 6:30pm pre-hols; 8am (winter),
10:30am (winter), noon, 6:30pm hols.

LORENZO BINAGO built this church in 1601 for the Barnabiti family. The interior has lavish Baroque furnishings and decoration; the frescoes were painted by Moncalvo and by Daniele Crespi. In the presbytery is the *Life of St Alexander* by Filippo Abbiati and Federico Bianchi. The high altar (1741) is decorated with semi-precious stones.

Next to the church are the Scuole Arcimbolde, schools for the poor founded in 1609 by the Barnabiti family, where the poet Giuseppe Parini studied. Opposite is Palazzo Trivulzio, rebuilt by Ruggeri in 1713, with the family coat of arms on the middle window. This family founded the Biblioteca Trivulziana, the library now in the Castello Sforzesco. Nearby Via Palla leads to the Tempio Civico di San Sebastiano, begun by Pellegrino Tibaldi in 1577 and completed in the 1700s. Its round interior has works by Legnanino, Montalto and Federico Bianchi.

The cupola and bell tower of Sant'Alessandro, seen from Corso di Porta Romana

SOUTHEAST MILAN

THE AREA BETWEEN Corso Monforte and Corso di Porta Romana was a typical suburb up to the early 19th century, characterized by aristocratic residences, monasteries and more modest houses typical of the artisans' and commercial districts of Milan. Development of the area began in the 17th century with the construction of Palazzo Durini, one of the most important civic buildings of its time. At the end of the 18th century Corso di Porta Romana and the adjacent streets were changed in keeping with the vast street network renewal plans encouraged by Maria

A statue in the Guastalla gardens

Theresa of Austria. When the empress ordered the suppression of many monasteries, the land where they had stood was purchased by rich nobles. Other areas became available when the Spanish ramparts were demolished. The old atmosphere of Southeast Milan survives above all around the Ca' Granda (now the University), which for almost 500 years was the city hospital, and in the first stretch of Corso di Porta Romana. However, the only vestige of the Verziere, the old vegetable market in Largo Augusto, is the place-name.

SIGHTS AT A GLANCE

Streets, Squares and Historic Buildings

Ca' Granda ④
Conservatorio di Musica
 Giuseppe Verdi ⑫
Corso di Porta Romana ①
Largo Augusto and Via
 Durini ⑦
Palazzo di Giustizia ⑨
Palazzo Isimbardi ⑭
Rotonda della Besana ⑪
Torre Velasca ②

Churches and Abbeys

*Abbazia di Chiaravalle
 see pp102–3* ⑮
San Nazaro Maggiore ③
San Pietro in Gessate ⑩
Santa Maria della Passione ⑬
Santo Stefano Maggiore and
 San Bernardino alle Ossa ⑥

Parks and Gardens

Giardino della Guastalla ⑤

Libraries

Palazzo Sormani Andreani ⑧

0 metres   500
0 yards   500

KEY

Street-by-Street map
See pp94–5

P Parking

M Metro

Taxi

GETTING THERE

The southeastern area of Milan is served by metro line 3 (Crocetta stop). Trams 9, 29 and 30 start from Porta Romana and then continue around the entire outer ring road.

◁ **Detail of *The Legend of St Anthony Abbot*, in San Pietro in Gessate**

Street-by-Street: San Nazaro to Largo Augusto

THERE ARE MANY interesting old buildings in this area, which includes the university quarter, with cafés and specialist bookshops, as well as crafts shops on Via Festa del Perdono. Architectural styles range from the 4th-century San Nazaro, founded by St Ambrose, to the Ca' Granda, the old hospital, a marvellous sight when viewed from Largo Richini because of its sheer size and the beauty of its 15th-century arcade. More changes of style come with the palazzi in Corso di Porta Romana and Via Sant'Antonio and the modern Torre Velasca. The quarter's hospital tradition can be seen in the votive columns at the crossroads, where mass for the sick was celebrated, and the San Bernardino alle Ossa chapel, decorated with the bones of those who died in the hospital.

Sant'Antonio Abate was rebuilt in 1582. It houses paintings by Bernardino Campi, Moncalvo and Ludovico Carracci and is a kind of gallery of early 17th-century painting in Milan.

Torre Velasca
The symbol of modern Milan was built in 1956–8. The tower, 106 m (348 ft) high, houses both offices and flats and is often compared to medieval towers because of the shape of the upper section ❷

Duomo

Corso di Porta Romana
Palazzi with magnificent gardens line this avenue. It follows the route of the ancient Roman road which led from Porta Romana all the way to Rome ❶

KEY

– – – – – Suggested route

★ San Nazaro Maggiore
One of four basilicas founded by Sant'Ambrogio, this church still has some of the original 4th-century masonry. It is preceded by the Trivulzio Chapel, the only Milanese architectural work by Bramantino (1512–50). The view of the back of the church is very striking ❸

STAR SIGHTS

★ San Nazaro Maggiore

★ Ca' Granda

Santo Stefano Maggiore and San Bernardino alle Ossa

The San Bernardino ossuary chapel, rebuilt in the 17th century, is entirely covered with human bones and skulls from the cemeteries that were abolished in the 1600s ⑥

Colonna del Verziere

Santo Stefano

LARGO
AUGUSTO

PIAZZA
SANTO
STEFANO

VIA DELLA SIGNORA

VIA SAN BARNABA

SFORZA

VIA FRANCESCO

VIA LAGHETTO

DEL PERDONO

SAN
RO

LOCATOR MAP
See Street Finder, maps 7, 8

NORTHEAST
MILAN

HISTORIC
CENTRE

SOUTHEAST
MILAN

SOUTHWEST
MILAN

Palazzo Sormani Andreani

The Biblioteca Civica di Milano, housed here, is the largest library in Milan. It includes the private library of the French novelist Stendhal ⑧

Largo Augusto

The Colonna del Verziere here commemorates the end of the 1576 plague ⑦

Giardino della Guastalla

Milan's oldest public garden was laid out in 1555. There are several monuments, including a small Neo-Classical temple designed by Luigi Cagnola ⑤

★ **Ca' Granda**

This was the old city hospital, also known as Ospedale Maggiore. It was built in 1456 to bring all the small hospitals of the city together on a single site. It was in use until 1939. Today it is home to Milan's state university ④

0 metres   300
0 yards   300

Entrance to the Teatro Carcano, in Corso di Porta Romana

Corso di Porta Romana ❶

Map 7 C2. **M** 3 Missori. 🚊 4, 12, 15, 24, 27. 🚌 65, 94.

THIS AVENUE WAS laid out over a porticoed stretch of the ancient Roman road outside the city walls (2nd–3rd century AD) that led to Rome. It ran from Porta Romana – then just beyond present-day Piazza Missori – to a triumphal arch (near the widening in the road known as Crocetta), transformed by Barbarossa into a fortified gate in the walls in 1162. The new gate (1171), further back, was demolished in 1793.

The Corso is lined with many noble palazzi. The 17th-century Palazzo Acerbi at No. 3; Palazzo Annoni at No. 6, designed by Francesco Maria Richini (1631), famous for its art collection which includes works by Rubens and Van Dyck; Palazzo Mellerio at No. 13 and Casa Bettoni (1865) at No. 20, with statues of Bersaglieri flanking the door. Via Santa Sofia crosses the Corso, and over the Naviglio canal close to the Crocetta, whose name derives from a votive cross set there during the 1576 plague.

Opposite is the Teatro Carcano (1803), where the great Italian actress Eleonora Duse performed. The Corso ends at the Porta Romana (in Piazzale Medaglie d'Oro), built in 1598. To the right you can see a fragment of the Spanish walls built by Ferrante Gonzaga (1545); they ran for 11,216 m (37,000 ft) and were demolished in 1889.

Torre Velasca ❷

Piazza Velasca 5. **Map** 7 C2. **M** 3 Missori. 🚊 4, 12, 15, 24, 27. 🚌 65, 94.

THIS TOWER, built in the late 1950s by architects Belgioioso, Nathan Rogers and Peressutti, is one of the best-known monuments in modern-day Milan. The overhang of the upper part of the building and its red colour are reminiscent of Italian medieval towers, but the shape actually grew out of the need to create more office space in a limited area.

Cappella Trivulzio, in San Nazaro Maggiore (16th century)

San Nazaro Maggiore ❸

Piazza San Nazaro. **Map** 8 D2. **C** 02-58 30 77 19. **M** 3 Missori. 🚊 4, 12, 15, 24, 27. 🚌 65, 94. ○ 7:30am–12:15pm, 3:15–6:30pm. ✝ 6pm pre-hols; 8:30, 10, 11:30am, 6pm hols. 🅿 📷 🖐

THE ORIGINAL basilica was built by Sant'Ambrogio in AD 382–6 to house the remains of the Apostles Andrew, John and Thomas, which is why it was known as the *Basilica Apostolorum*. It was dedicated to San Nazaro when his remains – found by Sant'Ambrogio near the basilica – were buried here in 396. The church was built outside the walls in an Early Christian burial ground – as can be seen by the sarcophagi outside and the epitaph in the right-hand transept – and looked onto an ancient Roman porticoed street. It was rebuilt after a fire in 1075 reusing much original material.

The church is preceded by the octagonal Trivulzio Chapel, begun in Renaissance style in 1512 by Bramantino and continued by Cristoforo Lombardo. It houses the tomb of Gian Giacomo Trivulzio and his family.

The nave of the church has a cross vault. Either side of the entrance you will see the remains of the Romanesque doorway covered by the Trivulzio Chapel. On the walls, among fresco fragments, are parts of the original masonry. In the crossing, the dome is supported by the 4th-century piers; two altars in the choir contain the remains of the Apostles and San Nazaro. Left of the altar is the small cruciform chapel of San Lino, with traces of 10th–15th-century frescoes. In the transepts are a fine *Last Supper* by Bernardino Lanino (right) and *Passion of Jesus* by Luini (left). The Chapel of St Catherine (1540) has Lanino's *Martyrdom of St Catherine* and a 16th-century stained-glass window depicting the *Life of St Catherine*.

The remains of San Nazaro, found by Sant'Ambrogio in AD 396

Ca' Granda ❹

17th-century window

THE "CASA GRANDE", or Ospedale Maggiore, was built for Francesco Sforza from 1456 on with the aim of uniting the city's 30 hospitals. The "large house" was designed by Filarete, who built only part of it, and was finished in stages in the 17th and 18th centuries. In 1939 the hospital moved to a new site, and since 1952 the Ca' Granda has housed the liberal arts faculties of the Università Statale, Milan's university. The hospital was modern for its time: there were separate wings for men and women – each with a central infirmary – and a large courtyard between them.

VISITORS' CHECKLIST

Via Festa del Perdono 5. **Map** 8 D2. 📞 02-583 51. Ⓜ 1, 3 Duomo, 3 Missori. 🚊 12, 23, 27. 🚌 54, 60, 65. ◯ 7:30am–7:30pm Mon–Fri; 8am–noon Sat (first 3 weeks of Aug: 7:30am–3:30pm Mon–Fri). ● Sun & hols (open in morning pre-hols). ♿ ⊘ **Chiesa dell'Annunciata** 📞 02-58 30 74 65. ◯ 8am–7pm (when University is open).

The church of the Annunciata (17th-century) contains a 1639 canvas by Guercino.

The Neo-Classical Macchio Wing, seat of the Faculty of Letters, Philosophy and Jurisprudence, housed the benefactors' art gallery, with portraits by leading artists.

★ Fifteenth-century Façade
The brick façade has round arches and is richly decorated. There were workshops and warehouses at ground level.

★ Cortile Maggiore
Francesco Maria Richini designed the courtyard with a Renaissance arcade and Baroque loggia, adding busts in yellow-pink-grey stone.

★ Fifteenth-century Courtyards
These housed the women's bathrooms, the ice-house and the woodshed. The Spezieria is the oldest courtyard.

KEY

▢ 15th-century section

▢ 17th-century section

▢ 18th–19th-century section

1 Entrance to the Faculties of Liberal Arts, Philosophy and Jurisprudence

2 Aula Magna

3 Courtyard entrance

4 Chiesa dell'Annunciata

5 Porticoes, 15th-century wing

6–9 Courtyards, 15th-century wing

10 Crociera, formerly the infirmary

STAR FEATURES

★ **Fifteenth-century Façade**

★ **Cortile Maggiore**

★ **Fifteenth-century Courtyards**

The fish pond in the Giardino della Guastalla, near Via Sforza

Giardino della Guastalla **❺**

Via Francesco Sforza, Via San Barnaba, Via Guastalla. **Map** 8 DE2. 🚃 12, 23, 27. 🚋 37, 60, 73, 77, 84, 94. 🕐 8am–5pm daily.

THIS GARDEN WAS laid out in 1555 by Countess Ludovica Torelli della Guastalla, next to the college of the same name for the daughters of impoverished aristocrats. The garden is Milan's oldest. In the early 1600s it was transformed into an Italian-style garden, and a goldfish pond on two communicating terraces was added. There is also a 17th-century shrine representing Mary Magdalen attended by angels and a Neo-Classical temple designed by Luigi Cagnola. In 1939 the garden was separated from the adjacent Sormani park and opened to the public. At the Via Guastalla exit (No. 19) you can visit the Synagogue, designed by Luca Beltrami (1890–92) and, at the corner of Via San Barnaba, the church of Santi Barnaba e Paolo, which is part of the nearby Chierici Regolari di San Paolo college. It is a prototype of 16th-century Lombard churches, founded in 1558 and then modified by Galeazzo Alessi. Inside are paintings by Aurelio Luini, son of Bernardino, Camillo Procaccini and Moncalvo.

Santo Stefano Maggiore and San Bernardino alle Ossa **❻**

Piazza Santo Stefano. **Map** 8 D1. Ⓜ 1, 3 Duomo. 🚃 12, 23, 27. 🚋 54, 60, 65. **Santo Stefano – Archivio Storico Diocesano (Historic Archive)** 📞 02-76 00 62 22. 🕐 9:15am–12:15pm Mon–Fri (entrance: Via della Signora 1). **San Bernardino alle Ossa** 📞 02-76 02 37 35. 🕐 7:30am–noon, 1–6pm daily. ✝ 8:30am Mon–Sat; 11am hols. 🚫 ♿

SANTO STEFANO dates back to the 5th century. It was rebuilt in 1075 after being destroyed by a fire and was again rebuilt in its present form in 1584 by Giuseppe Meda. The Baroque bell tower was built in 1643–76 by Carlo Buzzi: the pilaster at the base is all that remains of the quadriporticus that once faced the medieval basilica. The church is now used as the Diocesan Archive. Next door are San Bernardino alle Ossa, originally medieval but since rebuilt many times, and the ossuary chapel (with a concave façade) built in 1210 and altered in 1695. The latter is small and entirely covered with human bones and skulls. The dim light and dark walls make a striking contrast to the bright colours of the fresco on the vault by Sebastiano Ricci (1695): *The Triumph of Souls among Angels.*

Statue on the façade of San Bernardino alle Ossa

Largo Augusto and Via Durini **❼**

Map 8 DE1. Ⓜ 1, 3 Duomo. 🚃 12, 23, 27, 37. 🚋 54, 60, 65, 73, 84, 94.

SINCE 1580 the Verziere Column, commissioned by San Carlo Borromeo to celebrate the end of the 1576 plague, has stood in the middle of Largo Augusto. This is one of the few votive columns to survive the late 18th century. Many were lost after the suppression of the monastic orders that owned them, or sacrificed to make room for new building projects. This square marks the beginning of Via Durini, which is dominated by the concave façade of Santa Maria della Sanità (1708). No. 20 is Casa Toscanini, the great conductor's house, and No. 24 is Palazzo Durini, built in 1648 by Francesco Maria Richini. On adjacent Corso Europa is 16th-century Palazzo Litta Modignani, where a Roman mosaic was found. Palazzo Litta was altered in the 1700s.

Palazzo Sormani Andreani **❽**

Corso di Porta Vittoria 6. **Map** 8 E1. 📞 02-884 63 51. 📠 02-76 00 65 88. 🚃 12, 23, 27. 🚋 54, 60, 65, 73, 84, 94. 🕐 9am–7:30pm Mon–Sat. ● public hols, Aug.

THE PALAZZO, constructed in the 18th century, was enlarged in 1736 by Francesco Croce, who made it into one of the most lavish residences

Façade of Palazzo Sormani, the Municipal Library since 1956

of the time. Croce also designed the characteristic late Baroque curved façade. Reconstructed after World War II, the palazzo became the home of the Municipal (or Sormani Andreani) Library, the largest in Milan. It has over 580,000 works, including Stendhal's private library, a newspaper library with about 19,500 Italian and foreign publications, and a record and CD collection. A catalogue of all the Milan libraries is also here, as is the regional periodicals catalogue.

The Neo-Classical back opens onto a garden, part of the larger original one, which is used for small exhibitions. Nearby, at No. 2 Via Visconti di Modrone, is one of Milan's excellent traditional *pasticcerie*, the Taveggia pastry shop *(see p179)*.

Palazzo di Giustizia **9**

Corso di Porta Vittoria. **Map** 8 E1.
🚊 *12, 23, 27.* 🚌 *37, 60, 73, 77, 84.*

THE CENTRE of attention in the early 1990s because of the Mani Pulite (clean hands) corruption inquests and trials which changed much of the face of Italian politics, the Milan Law Courts were designed in typical Fascist style (1932–40) by Marcello Piacentini. The building also houses the Notarial Acts Archive, formerly in the Palazzo della Ragione *(see p54)*. The Palazzo has 1,200 rooms and 65 law courts with works by contemporary artists, including Mario Sironi's fresco in the Assize Court.

The Palazzo di Giustizia (1932–40), a typical example of Fascist architecture

Detail from *The Legend of the Virgin*, **San Pietro in Gessate**

San Pietro in Gessate **10**

Piazza San Pietro in Gessate. **Map** 8 E1. 🛈 *02-545 01 45.* 🚊 *12, 23, 27.* 🚌 *37, 60, 77, 84.* 🕐 *7:30am–6pm daily.* ✝ *8am Mon–Fri; 7pm pre-hols; 9am, 12:15 & 7pm hols.*

THIS CHURCH was built in 1447–75 by the Solari school and financed by the Florentine banker Pigello Portinari, whose emblem is on the outer wall of the apse. In the middle of the façade, rebuilt in 1912, is a portal with an effigy of St Peter, which was added in the 1600s. The Gothic interior has a three-aisle nave with ribbed vaulting and pointed arches and has preserved some original painting. The church was damaged during World War II, in particular the right-hand chapels, where there are traces of frescoes by Antonio Campi, Moncalvo and Bergognone (whose *Funeral of St Martin* is in the fifth chapel). The third and fifth chapels on the left have fine frescoes by Montorfano: *Life of St John the Baptist* (1484) and *The Legend of St Anthony Abbot*. The eight choir stalls were rebuilt with the remains of the 1640 ones by Carlo Garavaglia, damaged in 1943 and partly used as firewood during the war. The left-hand transept (or Cappella Grifi) has frescoes of the *Life of Sant'Ambrogio* (1490) commissioned by the Sforza senator Ambrogio Grifi from Bernardino Butinone and Bernardino Zenale. In the lunettes under the vault, next to *Sant'Ambrogio on Horseback*, you can see the figure of a hanged man whose rope "drops" into the scene below, down to the hangman. These recently restored frescoes were discovered in 1862 under the plaster put on the walls during the plague to disinfect the church.

The arcade in the Rotonda della Besana

Rotonda della Besana ⑪

Via San Barnaba, corner of Via Besana. **Map** 8 F2. ▯ 9, 29, 30. ▭ 77, 84. ○ *for temporary exhibitions and summer cultural events only.*

T HE ROTONDA was the cemetery of the nearby Ca'
Granda Hospital designed in
1695 by Francesco Raffagno
next to the Spanish walls, on
present-day Viale Regina
Margherita. The dead (about
150,000) were buried in the
crypts under the arcades.
When it was closed in 1783,
viceroy Eugène de Beauharnais tried to change it into the
Pantheon of the Regno Italico
(1809), but the project fell
through and the round brick
building first housed patients
with infectious diseases and
then, up to 1940, was the
hospital laundry. It is now
used for temporary exhibitions and as an outdoor
cinema in summer.

In the middle is the deconsecrated San Michele ai Nuovi
Sepolcri, built in 1713. It has
a Greek cross plan with a
central altar, visible from all
sides. The small skulls sculpted on the capitals are a
reminder of the original
function of this complex.

On Via San Barnaba is
Santa Maria della Pace, designed by Pietro Antonio Solari
in 1466, the property of the
Order of Knights of the Holy
Sepulchre. In 1805 the church
was suppressed and the
paintings removed (some are
now in the Brera), but some
17th-century frescoes by
Tanzio da Varallo remain.

The nearby monastery is
the home of the Società
Umanitaria, founded in 1893

to educate and aid
the poor. It has a
library devoted to
labour problems. The
only remaining part
of the monastery is
the refectory, with a
Crucifixion by Marco
d'Oggiono. Returning
to Corso di Porta Vit-
toria, you come to
Piazza Cinque Gior-
nate, with a monu-
ment by Giuseppe
Grandi (1895) commemora-
ting the anti-Austrian insurrection of 1848 *(see p22)*. The
female figures symbolize the
Five Days, whose dead are
buried in the crypt below.

Conservatorio di Musica Giuseppe Verdi ⑫

Via Conservatorio 12. **Map** 8 E1. ▯ 02-762 11 01. ▯ 54, 61, 77. ○ *for concerts only.*

M ILAN'S CONSERVATORY was
founded by viceroy
Eugène de Beauharnais in
1808 in a monastery. Important musicians and composers
have studied here – but the
young Verdi was refused
admission. There is a chamber music hall and a large
auditorium for symphonic
music. The library boasts over
35,000 books and 460,000
pieces of written music,
scores, etc, including works
by Mozart, Rossini, Donizetti,
Bellini and Verdi, as well as
a small museum of precious
stringed instruments.

Santa Maria della Passione ⑬

Via Bellini 2. **Map** 8 EF4. ▯ 02-76 02 13 70. ▯ 54, 61, 77. ▭ 94. ○ *7am–noon, 3–6:15pm daily.* ▮ *7:15, 8:15 am, 5:30pm Mon–Fri; 5:30pm pre-hols; 10, 11am, 3, 5:30pm hols.* ▯
Museum ● *for restoration.*

T HE SECOND LARGEST church
in Milan, after the Duomo,
was built under the patronage
of the prelate Daniele Birago,
who had donated the land to
the Lateran Canons. Work
began in 1486 to a design by
Giovanni Battagio. Originally
the church had a Greek cross
plan but it was lengthened
with a nave and six semi-
circular chapels on each side
in 1573 by Martino Bassi. The
façade of the church – and
the nearby convent, now the
home of the Conservatory –
was added in 1692 by Giu-
seppe Rusnati, who kept it
low so that visitors could
appreciate the majestic octagonal covering of the dome
designed by Cristoforo Lombardo (1530). To enhance this
view and link the church with
the Naviglio, Abbot Gadio
had the Via della Passione
laid out in front of the entrance in 1540. The interior,
with a frescoed barrel vault, is
very atmospheric. Fourteen
early 17th-century portraits of
the saints of the Lateran
Order, attributed to Daniele
Crespi and his school, are on
the piers. In the right-hand
chapels, two works worth
seeing are *Christ at the Pillar*

The Giuseppe Verdi Conservatory, housed in a former monastery

The octagonal dome of Santa Maria della Passione (17th century)

by Giulio Cesare Procaccini, on the altar of the third chapel, and the *Madonna di Caravaggio*, a fresco attributed to Bramantino, in the sixth chapel. The presbytery still has its original Greek cross structure. The paintings hanging from the piers, mostly the work of Crespi, narrate the Passion and include *Christ Nailed to the Cross*. Behind the Baroque high altar is a wooden choir (16th century) with mother of pearl inlay. Either side of the choir are two 16th–17th-century organs, still used for concerts. The doors of the left one have scenes from the Passion painted by Crespi.

There are remarkable Cinquecento paintings in the transepts: the right-hand one has a *Deposition* altarpiece by Bernardino Luini (1510–15) with the *Legend of the Cross* in the predella; and on the altar of the left-hand one is Gaudenzio Ferrari's *Last Supper* (1543), with a *Crucifixion* by Giulio Campi (1560) alongside.

The chapels on the left-hand side of the nave contain fine works by Camillo Procaccini and Duchino and the first chapel is noteworthy because of the impressive realism of Crespi's *St Charles Fasting*. The organ recess to the right leads to the Museum, founded in the old monastery in 1972. It consists of four sections. The Old Sacristy has 17th-century Lombard paintings and ten 18th-century wooden panels with scenes from the Bible.

Santa Maria della Passione: one of the saints of the Lateran Order

The 15th-century Chapter House was designed and painted by Bergognone: saints and doctors are in a false peristyle. On the right-hand wall is Christ with the Apostles. The Gallery has works by Crespi, Procaccini and Nuvolone; the Sala degli Arredi has 17th-century furniture and a vault frescoed by Giulio Campi (1558). In Via Bellini you can see the left side of the church and the dome. At No. 11 is the Art Nouveau Casa Campanini (1904), with wrought iron work by Alessandro Mazzucotelli.

Palazzo Isimbardi

Corso Monforte 35. **Map** 4 E5.
02-77 40 29 73 or 02-77 40 24 16 (Lombardy Province PR Office). **M** 1 San Babila. 9, 23, 29, 30. 54, 61, 94. apply to APT (see p201).

THE SEAT OF the Milan provincial government since 1935, this palazzo dates from the 15th century but was enlarged by the noble families who lived in it, among whom were the Isimbardi, who purchased it in 1775. The 18th-century façade on Corso Monforte leads to the porticoed court of honour (16th century), which still has its original herringbone pattern paving. The garden behind this boasts an admirable Neo-Classical façade designed by Giacomo Tazzini (1826).

The palazzo was recently opened to the public and features many interestingly decorated rooms and fine works of art, such as the wooden 17th-century globe by Giovanni Jacopo de Rossi. The most important room is the Giunta (Council Chamber), which in 1954 became the home of Tiepolo's masterful *Triumph of Doge Morosini*, which came from Palazzo Morosini in Venice. The Sala dell'Antegiunta has a lovely 18th-century Murano glass chandelier, while the Sala degli Affreschi boasts 17th-century frescoes taken from the villa of Cardinal Monti at Vaprio d'Adda. The Studio del Presidente is decorated with a Neo-Classical ceiling, partly in fine gold. In 1940 the Province of Milan enlarged the palazzo. The new façade on Via Vivaio was decorated with bas-reliefs sculpted by Salvatore Saponaro depicting the activities of the Milanese. At No. 31 Corso Monforte is the Palazzo della Prefettura, rebuilt in its present state in 1782. It has frescoes by Andrea Appiani. It is not open to the public.

The 18th-century façade of Palazzo Isimbardi, in Corso Monforte

Abbazia di Chiaravalle ⓯

FRENCH CISTERCIAN MONKS began constructing this church in 1150–60 and it was dedicated to the Virgin Mary in 1221. The complex is a combination of French Gothic and Lombard Romanesque, resulting in a delightful example of Cistercian architecture. The bell tower was added in 1349. The entrance is in the 16th-century tower flanked by two small churches. In 1798 Napoleon suppressed the monastic order, the monks were forced to leave and the abbey deteriorated so much that in 1858 Bramante's 15th-century cloister was demolished to make room for a railway line. Restored and given back to the monks, the abbey has regained its former splendour and is again an oasis of peace.

★ Frescoes
The 14th-century frescoes on the dome narrate The Legend of the Virgin. *Those in the transept (above), represent among other things the genealogical tree of the Benedictine monks.*

★ Wooden Choir
The 44 stalls have carvings of the Life of St Bernard *by Carlo Garavaglia (1645), who according to legend took refuge in the abbey to expiate the murder of his brother.*

The interior had no paintings because this would have distracted the monks from their prayers. The 17th-century frescoes tell the story of the order.

Entrance

The top of the façade, made of brick, is what remains of the original. The porch was added in 1625. The 16th-century main portal has figures of Cistercian saints, including St Bernard holding the church in his hand.

THE MONKS' LAND RECLAMATION

The Cistercian monasteries were based on the rule of *ora et labora* – prayer and labour – and played a crucial role in reclaiming the marshy Milanese terrain, which thanks to the monks became extremely fertile. They used the new water meadow technique, which consisted in flooding the meadows with water from an adjoining stream (kept at a constant temperature of 12° C/54° F) so that the grass would grow quickly and could be harvested even in winter.

A Cistercian monk at work in the garden

★ Bell Tower (*ciribiciaccola*)
Eighty small marble columns adorn the bell tower designed by Francesco Pecorari in 1349. Called ciribiciaccola *(clever contraption) by the Milanese, its bells accompanied the farmers' and monks' working day. The tower bell rope still hangs in the church.*

VISITORS' CHECKLIST

Via Sant'Arialdo 102, Chiaravalle Milanese. 📞 02-57 40 34 04. Ⓜ 3 Corvetto. 🚌 77. ⏰ 9–11:30am, 3–6:30pm Tue–Sat; 3–4:30pm Sun. ⛪ 8, 10 (Gregorian chant), 11:30am, 6pm hols; 8am Mon–Sat. 🅿 📷 (no flash). 💻

The many windows (double, triple and quadruple lancet) lend movement to the tower structure.

Madonna della Buonanotte
Painted in 1512 by Bernardino Luini at the top of the steps leading to the dormitory, this picture is known as the Madonna della Buonanotte *because she "said goodnight" to the monks going to bed.*

The chapter house, designed in the late 15th century by Bramante, has three graffiti from that period depicting Santa Maria delle Grazie, the Duomo and Castello Sforzesco.

Refectory

★ Cloister
Rebuilt in 1952 by using the one surviving side as a model, the cloister has a plaque commemorating the founding of the church, next to which is a stork, the symbol of Chiaravalle.

STAR FEATURES

★ Wooden Choir

★ Cloister

★ Bell Tower (*ciribiciaccola*)

★ Frescoes

NORTHEAST MILAN

ELEGANT VIA MANZONI is the heart of a vast area stretching from the Brera quarter to Via Montenapoleone and Corso Venezia. Brera is known for its characteristic winding streets, some of which still have their 18th-century paving. The fashion district around Via Montenapoleone is the domain of the designer shops. Starting from Piazza San Babila and continuing

Logo of the Museo Bagatti Valsecchi

through Corso Venezia, with its many aristocratic palazzi, you will come to the Giardini Pubblici and the Villa Reale, home of the Modern Art Gallery. The area extending beyond the ramparts, which was undeveloped up to the early 19th century, includes the Cimitero Monumentale, the Stazione Centrale (main railway station) and the Pirelli building, Milan's tallest.

KEY

- ▨ Street-by-Street map *See pp106–107*
- ▨ Street-by-Street map *See pp110–111*
- **P** Parking
- **M** Metro
- 🚖 Taxi

GETTING THERE

Metro line 3 (Montenapoleone) and trams 1 and 2 go to the fashion area and Brera quarter, which is also served by metro line 2 (Lanza), bus 61 and trams 3, 4, 12, 14 and 27. The Cimitero Monumentale is served by trams 3, 4, 12, 14, 29, 30 and 33, while metro lines 2 and 3 stop at the Stazione Centrale.

SIGHTS AT A GLANCE

Streets and Squares
Archi di Porta Nuova **4**
Bastioni di Porta Venezia **15**
Corso Venezia, see pp122–3 **21**
Via Manzoni **1**

Historic Buildings
Palazzo Cusani **7**
Palazzo Dugnani **19**
Pirelli Building **13**
Stazione Centrale **14**

Museums and Galleries
Museo Bagatti Valsecchi **3**
Museo di Storia Naturale **17**
Museo Poldi Pezzoli **2**
Pinacoteca di Brera see pp114–17 **6**
Planetarium **16**
Villa Reale and Galleria d'Arte Moderna **20**

Gardens and Cemeteries
Cimitero Monumentale **12**
Giardini Pubblici **18**

Churches
San Marco **5**
San Simpliciano **9**
Sant'Angelo **10**
Santa Maria del Carmine **8**
Santa Maria Incoronata **11**

◁ **Statue of Napoleon by Canova (1809), in the middle of the Brera art gallery courtyard**

Street-by-Street: the Fashion District

Versace logo

VIA MONTENAPOLEONE represents the elegant heart of Milan and is one of the four sides of the so-called *quadrilatero* or fashion district (the other three sides are Via Manzoni, Via Sant'Andrea and Via della Spiga). When strolling through this district, besides the shops of some of the top Italian and international fashion designers, you will see grand Neo-Classical aristocratic residences such as Palazzo Melzi di Cusano, at No. 18 Via Montenapoleone, built in 1830. Via Bigli, on the other hand, is lined with 16th- and 17th-century palazzi with porticoed courtyards.

Archi di Porta Nuova
This city gate, once part of the medieval walls, is decorated with copies of 1st-century AD Roman tombstones. Left, a stele representing a family ❹

Via Manzoni
This broad street is lined with aristocratic palazzi ❶

Grand Hotel et de Milan

Under the Portico del Lattèe (milkman's arcade) is the wall of the demolished church of San Donnino alla Mazza.

★ **Museo Poldi Pezzoli**
The Portrait of a Young Lady (15th century), attributed to Antonio Pollaiolo, is the symbol of this museum created by Gian Giacomo Poldi Pezzoli. Besides paintings by Mantegna, Piero della Francesca and Bellini, it has rugs, armour and precious ceramics ❷

STAR SIGHTS

★ **Museo Poldi Pezzoli**

★ **Museo Bagatti Valsecchi**

0 metres	50
0 yards	50

★ Museo Bagatti Valsecchi

This Neo-Renaissance palazzo was built as the family residence by the Bagatti Valsecchi brothers. It still has 16 rooms with their original 19th-century furnishings and many works of art belonging to the owners, who were art collectors ❸

LOCATOR MAP
See Street Finder, map 4

GIORGIO ARMANI

DOLCE & GABBANA

Via Montenapoleone follows the course of the ancient Roman walls. It gets its name from a bank that once stood here called "Monte Napoleone". Designer shops line the street.

KEY

━ ━ ━ ━ Suggested route

A Renaissance portal with a bas-relief *Annunciation* leads to the courtyard of Palazzo Bigli, decorated with frescoes by the school of Luini.

GUCCI

GIANNI VERSACE

TOP FASHION DESIGNERS

① **Byblos** Via della Spiga 42.
② **Cerruti 1881** Via della Spiga 20.
③ **Chanel** Via Sant'Andrea 10a.
④ **Etro** Via Montenapoleone 5.
⑤ **Fendi** Via Sant'Andrea 16.
⑥ **Genny** Via della Spiga 4.
⑦ **Gianfranco Ferrè** Via Sant'Andrea 15.
⑧ **Hermès** Via Sant'Andrea 21.
⑨ **Jil Sander** Via P Verri 6.
⑩ **Krizia** Via della Spiga 23.
⑪ **Laura Biagiotti** Via Borgospesso 19.
⑫ **Mila Schön** Via Montenapoleone 2.
⑬ **Moschino** Via Sant'Andrea 12.
⑭ **Prada** Via Sant'Andrea 21.
⑮ **Romeo Gigli** Via della Spiga 30.

The inner garden of a palazzo in Via Manzoni

Via Manzoni ❶

Map 3 C4. Ⓜ *1 Duomo, 3 Montenapoleone.* 🚋 *1, 2.* 🚌 *61, 94. Palazzi not open for visitors.*

Once known as "Corsia del Giardino" (Garden Lane) because of its many parks, this street acquired its present name in 1865, when the great Italian novelist Manzoni died. Its aristocratic appearance is created by the patrician palazzi and Teatro alla Scala *(see pp52–3)*, which stimulated the opening of chic cafés attracting a smart clientele. At No. 6 is 19th-century Palazzo Brentani, decorated with medallions with busts of illustrious persons, and No. 10 is Palazzo Anguissola (1775–8), which now houses the historic archive of the Banca Commerciale Italiana. No. 12, another 19th-century building, is the home of the famous Museo Poldi Pezzoli, and No. 29 is the Grand Hotel et de Milan (1865), where Giuseppe Verdi died in 1901.

Near the end of Via Montenapoleone stands Aldo Rossi's monument to former Italian President Sandro Pertini (1990) and, next to this, Palazzo Gallarati Scotti (No. 30), built in the early 1700s. Opposite, Via Pisoni takes you to the remains of the 15th-century cloister of the Umiliate di Sant'Erasmo monastery, now part of a modern building. In the last stretch is 18th-century Palazzo Borromeo d'Adda, which was a haunt for literati and artists, including Stendhal.

Museo Poldi Pezzoli ❷

Via Manzoni 12. **Map** 4 D5. 📞 *02-79 48 89.* Ⓜ *3 Montenapoleone.* 🚋 *1, 2.* 🚌 *61, 94.* 🕙 *10am–6pm Tue–Sun.* 🔴 *1 Jan, Easter, 1 May, 15 Aug, 25 Dec.* 📷 *(no flash).* ♿ *ground floor only.* 🎫 *Lecture hall, Library.*

This private museum was established by nobleman Gian Giacomo Poldi Pezzoli and opened to the public in 1881. The building, a singular example of a late 19th-century aristocratic Milanese residence, contains Poldi Pezzoli's fine collection of paintings, sculpture, armour, rugs, watches, glass and textiles. The ground floor houses arms and armour from ancient Roman times to the 18th century. The Salone dell'Affresco, named after *The Apotheosis of Bartolomeo Colleoni* frescoed by Carlo Innocenzo Carloni, boasts a Tabriz carpet with hunting scenes (Persia, 1522–3), made of wool and silver on silk. In the adjoining room is the museum's collection of textiles, including a 15th-century cope with Florentine embroidery representing *The Coronation of the Virgin*, after a drawing by Botticelli.

The staircase, decorated with landscapes by Magnasco, leads to the first floor. In the Salette dei Lombardi is 15th–16th-century Lombard painting, with canvases by Bergognone, Luini, the Leonardo-esque painters, a *Polyptych* by Cristoforo Moretti, and Vincenzo Foppa's *Portrait of Giovanni Francesco Brivio*. The portraits of Martin Luther and his wife by Lucas Cranach (1529) are in the Sala degli

Poldi Pezzoli Museum logo

Stranieri. A display case with precious porcelain separates the next room from the Salone Dorato. Designed by Poldi Pezzoli and destroyed by bombs in 1943, this hall was restored in 1974 by Luigi Caccia Dominioni. On display are fine works such as *St Nicholas of Tolentino* by Piero della Francesca, Botticelli's *Madonna and Child* and *Pietà*, a *Madonna and Child* by Andrea Mantegna, Giovanni Bellini's *Pietà* and a *Portrait of a Young Woman* attributed to Antonio Pollaiolo. Three small rooms house the Visconti Venosta collection of portraits by Fra Galgario, including *Gentleman with Tricorn*, and interesting 16th–18th-century clocks. The Saletta dei Vetri Antichi di Murano has fine specimens of glasswork, and the Gabinetto Dantesco features two stained-glass windows narrating episodes from Dante's life. The last rooms house a collection of small bronzes, paintings by Tiepolo, a *Sacred Conversation* by Lotto, and Giovanni Bellini's *Crucifixion*. Lastly, the Gabinetto degli Ori has a collection of precious ancient jewellery and goldsmithery.

Botticelli's *Pietà* (1495), Museo Poldi Pezzoli

A cradle from the Camera Rossa in the Museo Bagatti Valsecchi

Museo Bagatti Valsecchi ❸

Via Gesù 5. **Map** 4 D4. ☎ 02-76 00 61 32. Ⓜ 3 Montenapoleone. ☷ 1, 2. ◷ 1–6pm Tue–Sun. ● 1 Jan, Easter, 1 May, 15 Aug, 25 Dec. ♿ ground floor only. ◲ by appt. ⬜ Ⓦ www.museobagattivalsecchi.org

OPENED IN 1994 in the prestigious late 19th-century residence of the two Bagatti Valsecchi brothers, Fausto and Giuseppe, this fascinating museum is an important record of art collectors' taste in that period. The building was designed in Neo-Renaissance style, with an elegant façade and two well proportioned courtyards, and was furnished with works of art and imitation Renaissance furniture. It was seen as a private house and not a museum, and was furnished with every possible comfort. The rooms feature tapestries, ceramics, ivory work and arms, as well as important paintings such as the elegant *Santa*

Giustina by Giovanni Bellini (c.1475; kept in what was Giuseppe Bagatti Valsecchi's bedroom), Bernardo Zenale's panels and a *Polyptych* by Giampietrino. The library, with its valuable 15th-century parchments and a series of 16th–17th-century porcelain pharmacy vases, is also worth a look.

The intriguing Valtellinese bedroom has a magnificent 16th-century bed with Christ ascending Calvary and scenes from the Old Testament carved in the bedstead. The Sala della Stufa Valtellinese is also interesting, with its marvellous 16th-century wood panelling with an elegant sculpted frieze and a piece of furniture ingeniously concealing a piano. The Camera Rossa contains a delightful small collection of 15th–17th-century furniture for children that includes a high chair, a baby walker and a cradle. The dining room has a collection of kitchenware, tapestries and sideboards.

Archi di Porta Nuova ❹

Map 4 D4. Ⓜ 3 Montenapoleone. ☷ 1, 2. ☷ 61, 94.

THIS CITY GATE, restored in 1861, is one of two surviving ones forming part of the medieval wall system. Construction began in 1171, and the gate was probably modelled on the corresponding Porta Romana, some of whose building materials it used. The inner side on Via Manzoni is decorated with copies of 1st-century AD Roman tombstones, while the outside facing Piazza Cavour bears a tabernacle decorated with a *Madonna and Child with Saints Ambrose, Gervase and Protasius* (1330–39).

Facing the piazza is Palazzo dei Giornali (No. 2), built in 1942 as the main office of the newspaper *Il Popolo d'Italia* and decorated with bas-reliefs by Mario Sironi. The square is framed by the Giardini Pubblici, in front of which is a monument to Cavour by Odoardo Tabacchi (1865).

The Porta Nuova arches seen from Via Manzoni

MUSEUMS DEVOTED TO THE HISTORY OF MILAN

Several museums, collectively the Civiche Raccolte Storiche, are devoted to the history of Milan. Palazzo Morando Attendolo Bolognini (No. 6 Via Sant'Andrea) houses the Museo di Milano and the Museo di Storia Contemporanea. The former features documents and paintings about old Milan and its illustrious citizens, and the latter has mementoes from the period of the two world wars. The palazzo is also home to the Civico Museo Marinaro Ugo Mursia, a nautical museum. The Museo del Risorgimento in Palazzo Moriggia (No. 23 Via Borgonuovo) covers the history of the Italian unification movement, from the late 1700s to the annexation of Rome (1870).

Sign for the entrance to a chocolate factory, now in the Museo di Milano

Street-by-Street: the Brera Quarter

T HE NAME OF MILAN'S traditional Bohemian
quarter derives from the Germanic word
braida, which denoted a grassy area. The
presence of art students at the Accademia di
Belle Arti and the world-famous Brera art
gallery has contributed to the lively feel of this
quarter, which is reinforced by the many cafés,
restaurants, galleries, antique shops and nightclubs established here. In summer the
narrow streets are enlivened even more
by street stalls and fortune tellers.
An antiques market is held on
the third Saturday of each
month in Via Brera.

**The Indian
Café** is one of
the most popular
spots in the area.

**The Museo
Minguzzi** has
100 pieces
by the
Bolognese
sculptor.

The Naviglio della Martesana canal
flowed from the Adda river and along
present-day Via San Marco. It was used
for transporting foodstuffs and building
materials. At the end of the street is the
Tombone di San Marco, a wooden canal
lock that regulated the water flow.

★ **San
Simpliciano**
*This church
was one of the
four basilicas
founded by
Sant'Ambrogio
and has pre-
served most
of its original
Early Christian
architecture* **9**

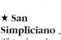

CAFÉ LIFE IN THE BRERA

The cafés and bars of the Brera
quarter are lively and atmospheric.
The Tombon de San Marc (Via San
Marco) was once the haunt of the
stevedores from the nearby Naviglio
and now welcomes customers of all
kinds. The famous Jamaica café (Via
Brera) has jazz sessions on Mondays.
Other atmospheric spots are the Louisiana Bistrò (Via Fiori
Chiari), Sans Égal, in the pedestrian precinct of Via Fiori
Chiari, the Indian Café (Corso Garibaldi) and the ethnic
Soul to Soul (Via San Marco) *(see pp178–9, pp190–91).*

**Inside the Jamaica
café, in Via Brera**

0 metres   100

0 yards   100

STAR SIGHTS

★ **Pinacoteca di Brera**

★ **San Simpliciano**

★ **San Marco**

★ San Marco
The façade of this church, founded in 1254, was rebuilt in 1871 in Neo-Gothic style. The only remaining part of the original is the stone doorway, which has a relief of Christ between two saints and among symbols of the Evangelists **5**

LOCATOR MAP
See Street Finder, maps 3, 4

The Civico Museo del Risorgimento, opened in 1896, is in Neo-Classical Palazzo Moriggia.

★ Pinacoteca di Brera
The nucleus of one of Italy's top art galleries consists of works taken from churches that were suppressed in the late 1700s. The Brera boasts masterpieces by great artists such as Piero della Francesca, Mantegna, Raphael and Caravaggio **6**

Palazzo Cusani
This building with a late Baroque façade (1719) is the headquarters of the Third Army Corps. On the first floor is the Officers' Club **7**

Santa Maria del Carmine
The 15th-century church was built with material taken from the nearby Castello Sforzesco when it was partly demolished **8**

KEY

– – – – Suggested route

The lunette over the entrance to San Marco

San Marco ❺

Piazza San Marco 2. **Map** 3 C4. 📞 02-29 00 25 98. 🚌 41, 43. ⏰ 7:30am–noon, 4–7:30pm daily. ✝ 7:45, 9:30am, 6:30pm Mon–Fri; 6:30pm pre-hols; 9:30, 11am, 12:15, 6:30pm hols.

T HIS CHURCH WAS BEGUN in 1254 by the Augustine monk Lanfranco Settala. It was built on the site of an older church, dedicated by the Milanese to St Mark, patron saint of Venice, to thank the Venetians for help in the struggle against Emperor Frederick Barbarossa. In 1871 Carlo Maciachini built a new, Neo-Gothic façade around the Camionese school ogival portal and tabernacle.

The church has a Latin cross plan and nine patrician chapels, which were added to the right-hand aisle in the 14th–19th century. They contain 16th–17th-century paintings, including some by Paolo Lomazzo. In the right-hand transept is the *Foundation of the Augustine Order* by the Fiammenghino brothers, Settala's sarcophagus by Giovanni Balduccio (1317–49), and fragments of late Gothic frescoes found during the 1956 restoration. The presbytery is decorated with large canvases by Camillo Procaccini and Cerano depicting the Legend of St Augustine, and the *Genealogical Tree of the Order* by Genovesino (17th century), who also painted the *Angels' Backs* on the cupola. The left-hand transept leads to the Chapel of the Pietà, with *The Ascent to Calvary* by Ercole Procaccini. The left-hand aisle has canvases by Camillo and Giulio Cesare Procaccini and Palma

il Giovane, and a Leonardo-esque fresco found in 1975. From outside the Romanesque transept the 13th-century bell tower is visible.

Pinacoteca di Brera ❻

See pp114–7.

Palazzo Cusani ❼

Via Brera 15. **Map** 3 C4. Ⓜ *2 Lanza*. 🚊 3, 4, 12, 14. 🚌 61. ⚫ *to the public.*

O RIGINALLY BUILT in the 1500s, this palazzo was rebuilt in 1719 by Giovanni Ruggeri, who designed the late Baroque façade with its ornate windows and balconies, while the Neo-Classical façade facing the garden was designed by Piermarini. Tradition has it that the Cusani brothers ordered two main entrances so that each could have independent yet equal access. In the drawing room is an allegorical Tiepolo-like fresco (1740). The palazzo was the seat of the Ministry of War in the 19th century.

Santa Maria del Carmine ❽

Piazza del Carmine 2. **Map** 3 B4. 📞 02-86 46 33 65. 🚊 1, 3, 4, 12, 14, 27. 🚌 61. ⏰ 7:15–11:30am, 3:30–7pm daily. ✝ 7:55, 9:45am, 6:30pm Mon–Sat; 9:45, 10:45 (English) & 11:45am, 4:45 (English) & 6:30pm hols.

S ANTA MARIA DEL CARMINE was built in Gothic style in 1447 over a Romanesque church and was then rebuilt in the

Baroque period, while the present-day façade was designed by Carlo Maciachini in 1880. The spacious interior has a three-aisle nave covered by cross vaulting. The inclination of the first piers is due to the absence of a façade for a long period and the subsequent gradual settling of the building.

The right-hand transept contains part of the tomb of the Ducal Councillor Angelo Simonetta, above which are two paintings by Carlo Francesco Nuvolone and Fiammenghino; the opposite transept is decorated with a painting by Camillo Landriani.

The statues in the wooden choir (1579–85) are the original plaster models created for the spires of the Duomo by 19th-century artists. The Cappella del Rosario, built on the right of the choir (1673) by Gerolamo Quadrio, has marble

A statue in the choir

dressing and is decorated with canvases by Camillo Procaccini depicting *The Legend of Mary*.

On the left-hand side of the church is the monastery cloister, with remains of noble tombs and ancient tombstones, and a Baroque sacristy, with furniture made by Quadrio in 1692.

Part of the Baroque sacristy, Santa Maria del Carmine

Angel Musicians by Aurelio Luini (16th century), in the church of San Simpliciano

San Simpliciano **9**

Piazza San Simpliciano 7. **Map** 3 B4.
C 02-86 22 74. **M** 2 Lanza.
T 3, 4, 12, 14. **B** 43, 57, 70.
O 9:30–11:30am, 3–6pm daily
(4–7pm Sun). **T** 6pm Mon–Fri; 6pm
pre-hols; 8, 10 & 11:30am, 6pm hols.

THE CHURCH WAS founded by
Sant'Ambrogio in the 4th
century as the *Basilica Virginum* and completed in 401. It
is preceded by a porch and
once had open galleries on
either side where penitents
and new converts could take
part in Mass. The façade,
decorated with glazed plates,
was added in 1870 by Maciachini, who retained the main
portal. The capitals have 12th-
century carvings of the pro-
cessions of the Wise and
Foolish Virgins. Fourteenth-
century frescoes have been
discovered in the first chapel
on the right, and in the fourth
is Enea Salmeggia's *Miracle of
St Benedict* (1619). The apse
is frescoed with the
Coronation of the Virgin by
Bergognone (1508). The Neo-
Classical altar covers the
wooden choir (1588), and on
either side
are two

organ pedestals frescoed by
Aurelio Luini in the 1500s. The
transept leads to the Early
Christian Sacellum of San
Simpliciano (closed), built to
house the remains of San
Simpliciano and of martyrs.

Sant'Angelo **10**

Piazza Sant'Angelo 2. **Map** 4 D3.
C 02-65 45 51. **T** 41, 43. **B** 94.
O 6:30am–8pm daily. **T** 7pm
Mon–Fri; 7pm pre-hols; 9, 10 & 11
am, 12:15 & 7pm hols.

BUILT IN 1552 by Domenico
Giunti to replace the
older Franciscan church outside the Porta Nuova gate,
which had been demolished
to make room for the Spanish
ramparts, Sant'Angelo is an
important example of 16th-
century Milanese architecture.
The nave is separated from
the presbytery by a triumphal
arch with the *Assumption of
Mary* by Legnanino (17th
century). There are many
16th- and 17th-century paintings in the chapels. The first
one on the right has canvases
by Antonio Campi (1584) and
a copy of the *Martyrdom of St
Catherine of Alexandria* by

Gaudenzio Ferrari (the original is in the Brera); the second
has Morazzone's *St Charles in
Glory* and in the apse is Procaccini's *Legend of the Virgin*.

Santa Maria Incoronata **11**

Corso Garibaldi 116. **Map** 3 C2.
C 02-65 48 55. **M** 2 Garibaldi.
B 94. **O** 7:15am–1:30pm,
4–7pm Mon–Sat; 8am–12:30pm,
4–7:30pm Sun. **T** 7:30 &
9:30am, 4:30pm Mon–Sat;
8:30, 10 & 11:30am,
6:30pm hols.

THIS CHURCH consists of two
buildings designed by
Guiniforte Solari, which were
merged in 1468. The left one
was built for Francesco Sforza
in 1451 and the other was
built soon afterwards for his
wife. The brick façade is
double, as is the nave, which
has two apses with 15th- and
17th-century frescoes. In the
right-hand chapels are plaques
in memory of Sforzesco court
personages. The chapels opposite have frescoes by Montalto and Bernardino Zenale
(the fresco in the first chapel
is attributed to Zenale).

**Lunette over one of the doors
of San Simpliciano**

SAN SIMPLICIANO, THE THREE MARTYRS AND THE CARROCCIO

St Ambrose asked the young Sisinius, Martirius and
Alexander to go to Anaunia (today Val di Non) in
northern Italy to spread Christianity. In 397 they were
martyred and the bodies were given to Bishop Simpliciano, who buried them in the *Basilica Virginum.*
According to legend, the martyrs were decisive in leading the Milanese to victory in the
battle of Legnano against Barbarossa (1176). On that occasion three white doves flew out of
the basilica and landed on the Carroccio (cart), the symbol of Milan, waiting to be blessed
before the battle. On 29 May the city commemorates this event with a solemn ceremony.

Pinacoteca di Brera ⑥

THE BRERA ART GALLERY holds one of Italy's most important art collections, featuring masterpieces by leading Italian artists from the 13th to the 20th centuries, including Raphael, Mantegna, Piero della Francesca and Caravaggio. The Pinacoteca is housed in the late 16th–early 17th-century palazzo built for the Jesuits in place of the Santa Maria di Brera Humiliati monastery. The Jesuits made this into a cultural centre by establishing a prestigious school, a library and the astronomical observatory – all activities supported by Empress Maria Theresa of Austria, who founded the Accademia di Belle Arti after the Jesuit order was suppressed (1773).

Portrait of Moisè Kisling
Amedeo Modigliani painted this work in 1915, reflecting his interest in African sculpture.

Finding the Body of St Mark
The bold perspective and almost super-natural light in the room where the saint's body is found make this canvas (1562–6) one of Tintoretto's masterpieces.

KEY

- ☐ Jesi Collection (20th-century art)
- ☐ 13th–15th-century Italian painting
- ☐ 15th–16th-century Venetian painting
- ☐ 15th–16th-century Lombard painting
- ☐ 15th–16th-century Central Italian painting
- ☐ 17th–18th-century Italian, Flemish and Dutch painting
- ☐ 18th–19th-century Italian painting

Mocchirolo Chapel

Twin staircases
lead to the entrance to the gallery on the first floor.

The Kiss
This canvas by Francesco Hayez (1859) is one of the most reproduced 19th-century Italian paintings – a patriotic and sentimental work epitomizing the optimism that prevailed after the unification of Italy.

★ **Dead Christ**
This masterpiece by Mantegna (c.1480) is striking for its intense light and bold fore-shortening. The work was among the artist's posses-sions at the time of his death.

This room has works by painters active in Lombardy from the late 15th to the mid-16th century, including Bergognone, Luini, Bramantino and Vincenzo Foppa.

★ **Montefeltro Altarpiece**
Piero della Francesca painted this great work in 1475 for Federico da Montefeltro, the Duke of Urbino, who is portrayed dressed in a Milanese suit of armour.

The courtyard with twin columns is the work of Richini (17th century).

GALLERY GUIDE
The Brera Gallery has 31 rooms, with works arranged in chronological order. The only exception is Room 1, where the Jesi Collection is on display. It includes 20th-century works which will be exhibited elsewhere in future. The paintings are also grouped together by schools of painting (Venetian, Tuscan, Lombard, etc.). The Sala della Passione on the ground floor is used for temporary exhibitions.

STAR EXHIBITS

★ **Dead Christ**

★ **The Marriage of the Virgin**

★ **Montefeltro Altarpiece**

Entrance

★ **The Marriage of the Virgin**
Raphael signed and dated (1504) his masterful altarpiece on the temple in the background. Some scholars say the young man breaking the staff is a self-portrait of the artist.

Exploring the Pinacoteca di Brera

THE ORIGINAL NUCLEUS of the Brera Gallery consisted mainly of plaster casts and drawings used as models for the art students of the Accademia di Belle Arti (founded in 1776). This collection was augmented with works from suppressed churches in Northern Italy and was officially opened in 1809, the paintings being arranged in rows on the wall, from floor to ceiling. The Pinacoteca became independent from the Accademia in 1882, and its fine collection further expanded through 19th- and 20th-century donations. The gallery has always suffered from lack of space, but there are plans to use the adjacent Palazzo Citterio.

The City Rises (c.1910) by Umberto Boccioni

JESI COLLECTION

THE 72 works donated by Emilio and Maria Jesi in 1976 and 1984 are at the beginning. The collection, mostly by Italian artists, covers the 1910–40 period. Key works include *Portrait of Moisè Kisling* by Modigliani, Umberto Boccioni's *Brawl in the Galleria* (1911) and *The City Rises* (a study for the canvas now in the New York MOMA), Carlo Carrà's *The Metaphysical Muse* (1917) and still lifes by Giorgio Morandi, as well as sculpture by Medardo Rosso, Arturo Martini and Marino Marini.

13TH–15TH-CENTURY ITALIAN PAINTING

THE SECTION given over to 13th–15th-century Italian art (rooms 2–4) includes frescoes from the Oratory at Mocchirolo, painted by an unknown Lombard master in around 1365–70. Among the gold-background works are the *Santa Maria della Celestia*

Polyptych by Lorenzo Veneziano (14th century), Ambrogio Lorenzetti's *Madonna and Child* and *Christ the Judge* by Giovanni da Milano. A fine example of the International Gothic style is the *Valle Romita Polyptych* by Gentile da Fabriano, flanked by Stefano da Verona's *Adoration of the Magi* (1435), in which the viola and carnation at the feet of Jesus symbolize his humility and the Passion.

15TH–16TH-CENTURY VENETIAN PAINTING

ROOMS 5 AND 6 feature works by 15th–16th-century artists active in the Veneto such as Giovanni d'Alemagna and Antonio Vivarini, who painted the *Praglia Polyptych* (1448). Room 6 also has

Mantegna's masterpieces *Dead Christ* and *St Luke Altarpiece* (1453–4). Giovanni Bellini is represented by two Madonnas with Child and a *Pietà* (c.1470), and Carpaccio by *Legend of the Virgin*. There are portraits by Titian, Lotto and Tintoretto in room 7. *St Mark Preaching in Alexandria* (room 8) was painted for the Scuola Grande in St Mark's in Venice by Giovanni and Gentile Bellini.

The following room has works by Titian and Paolo Veronese, as well as the *Finding of the Body of St Mark*, which Tintoretto painted for Tommaso Rangone, who is portrayed as the kneeling man in the the middle of the scene.

15TH–16TH-CENTURY LOMBARD PAINTING

A LARGE COLLECTION of 15th–16th-century Lombard paintings is exhibited in rooms 15, 18 and 19. The leading figure, Vincenzo Foppa, is represented by the *Polittico delle Grazie* (c.1483). An unknown master contributed the *Sforzesca Altarpiece* (1494), showing Lodovico il Moro and his family worshipping the Madonna. This room also has works by Bergognone, Gaudenzio Ferrari – an artist with a marked narrative vein, as can be seen in *Martyrdom of St Catherine* – and Bramantino's *Crucifixion*. Works influenced by Leonardo da Vinci include

Gentile da Fabriano's *Valle Romita Polyptych*

Supper at Emmaus, painted by Caravaggio in 1606

the small paintings for private chapels by De Predis and Luini (*Madonna del Roseto*), while the Cremona area is represented by names such as Boccaccino, Campi and Piazza.

15TH–16TH-CENTURY CENTRAL ITALIAN PAINTING

Rooms 20–23 illustrate artistic movements in the regions of Emilia and Le Marche. The Ferrara school is represented by its leading artists, Cosmè Tura, Francesco del Cossa and Ercole de' Roberti (whose *Madonna and Child among Saints* was painted around 1480). Correggio's *Nativity* is a major Emilian school work, while painting in Le Marche is documented by the works of Carlo Crivelli, including his *Madonna della Candeletta* (1490–91), rich in symbols.

Room 24 houses the two best-known masterpieces in the Brera. Piero della Francesca's *Montefeltro Altarpiece* (c.1475), was commissioned by Federico da Montefeltro. The egg suspended from its shell is a symbol of the Creation and of the Immaculate Conception. Next is Raphael's splendid *Marriage of the Virgin (see p115).*

Christ at the Pillar is a rare painting by Bramante, while works by Bronzino and Genga represent Mannerism.

17TH–18TH-CENTURY ITALIAN AND FLEMISH PAINTING

Room 28 features works by the Bolognese school, founded by the Carracci, including Guido Reni and Guercino. The next room boasts a masterpiece by Caravaggio, *Supper at Emmaus* (1606), in which the appearance of Christ occurs in a setting illuminated only by the light emanating from Jesus's face. Lombard artists shown here are Cerano, Morazzone and Giulio Cesare Procaccini, who painted the *Martyrdom of Saints Rufina and Seconda* together. Baroque painting is represented by Pietro da Cortona and the still lifes of Baschenis. Among the non-Italian artists are Rubens (*Last Supper,* 1631–32), Van Dyck, Rembrandt (*Portrait of the Artist's Sister,* 1632), El Greco and Brueghel the Elder (*The Village).*

Madonna della Candeletta by Crivelli

18TH–19TH-CENTURY ITALIAN PAINTING

The following rooms cover various genres in 18th-century Italian art. Large-scale religious paintings are in room 34 with works by the Neapolitan Luca Giordano and two Venetians: Giovan Battista Tiepolo's *Madonna del Carmelo* (1721–7), intended to be viewed from the side, and Piazzetta's *Rebecca at the Well.*

Giacomo Ceruti (Il Pitochetto) represents "genre painting", which was popular in the 18th century. This is followed by Venetian *vedutismo*, views by Bernardo Bellotto, Guardi and Canaletto. The works of Bellotto and Canaletto are characterized by their bright light and precision of detail (the latter even used a camera obscura to help him render this "photographic" effect).

Portraiture is best exemplified by Fra Galgario (*Portrait of a Gentleman).*

A representative 19th-century painting is Andrea Appiani's Neo-Classical *Olympus*, while the Macchiaioli movement is on display with works by Silvestro Lega and Giovanni Fattori, among others. The Brera also has paintings by the leading exponent of Lombard Romanticism, Francesco Hayez: his famous *The Kiss* and several portraits. The gallery closes with Divisionist Giuseppe Pelizza da Volpedo's *The Flood* (1895–97), a hymn to the struggle of the working class, and an early version of his *Fourth Estate,* now on display at the Villa Reale *(see p121).*

Cimitero Monumentale ⑫

Piazzale Cimitero Monumentale.
Map 3 A1. ⓒ 02-88 46 56 00.
🚋 3, 4, 11, 12, 14, 29, 30, 33.
🚌 41, 51, 70, 94. ⏱
8:30am–5:15pm Tue–Sun;
8:30am–1pm hols. Free
map of the cemetery
available at the entrance.

Extending over an area of 250,000 sq m (300,000 sq yds), the Cimitero Monumentale was begun by Carlo Maciachini in 1866. The eclectic taste of the time dictated the use of various styles for the cemetery, from mock-Lombard Romanesque to Neo-Gothic, with touches of Tuscan thrown in. The linchpin of the structure is the Famedio *(Famae Aedes)*, or House of Fame, a sort of pantheon of illustrious Milanese and non-Milanese buried here. Author Alessandro Manzoni, Luca Beltrami, the architect who oversaw restoration of the Castello Sforzesco, the patriot Carlo Cattaneo and the Nobel Prize-winning poet Salvatore Quasimodo all have tombs in this cemetery. There are also busts of Garibaldi, Verdi and Cavour. The Romantic painter Hayez lies in the crypt. A visit

Sculpture by Fontana, Cimitero Monumentale

to the Cimitero Monumentale, which is a kind of open-air museum of art from the late 19th century to the present, begins at the large square inside, which contains the tombs of important Milanese figures. Around the square are monumental shrines and the Civico Mausoleo Palanti, an enormous mausoleum with a crypt, used as an air raid shelter in 1943. Among its tombs are those of comic actor Walter Chiari and Hermann Einstein, Albert's father. On the terraces, to the left are the Elisi (sculpted by Francesco Penna, 1916) and Morgagni tombs, and an epigraph by Mussolini commemorating a disastrous aeroplane crash. In the central avenue are two tombs designed and sculpted by Enrico Butti: that of Isabella Casati, *Young Woman Enraptured by a Dream*, a typical Lombard realist work (1890), and the Besenzanica shrine with *Work* (1912). On your right, you will come to the monumental Toscanini tomb (Bistolfi, 1909–11), built for the conductor's son.

Among other monumental tombs for major figures in Milanese life are those of Carlo Erba, Bocconi, Campari and Falck. Many famous sculptors made pieces for this place: Leonardo Bistolfi, Giacomo Manzù, Odoardo Tabacchi, Adolfo Wildt and Lucio Fontana. The two enclosures beside the Famedio are for Jews and Catholics, with the remains of sculptor Medardo Rosso, publishers Arnoldo Mondadori and Ulrico Hoepli and Jules Richard, founder of the Richard-Ginori ceramics industry.

The Cimitero Monumentale, with tombs and shrines produced by famous sculptors

The Pirelli Building, symbol of Milan's postwar reconstruction

Pirelli Building ⑬

Piazzale Duca d'Aosta–Via Pirelli.
Map 4 E1. Ⓜ 2, 3 Centrale.
🚋 2, 5, 9, 33. 🚌 42, 60, 82.
⬤ to the public.

The symbol of postwar reconstruction in Milan, the Pirelli Building, affectionately called "Pirellone" (big Pirelli) by the Milanese, was built in 1955–60. It was designed by a group of leading architects and engineers: Gio Ponti, Antonio Fornaroli, Alberto Rosselli, Giuseppe Valtolina, Egidio Dell'Orto, Pier Luigi Nervi and Arturo Danusso. At 127.10 m (417 ft) high, it was the largest reinforced concrete skyscraper in the world until the 1960s. The slender, elegant edifice occupies only 1,000 sq m (1,200 sq yds) and stands on the site where, in 1872, Giovan Battista Pirelli built his first tyre factory. The skyscraper was constructed as the Pirelli company's main offices. Among the many records established by the "Pirellone" was that it was the first building in Milan taller than the Madonnina on the Duomo (108.50 m, 356 ft). As a token of respect, a small statue of the Virgin Mary was placed on the Pirelli roof. Since 1979 the building has been the headquarters of the regional government of Lombardy. Next door is the luxurious Excelsior Hotel Gallia, opened in the 1930s.

The Stazione Centrale, with its spectacular iron and glass roof

Stazione Centrale ⓮

Piazzale Duca d'Aosta. **Map** 4 E1.
Ⓜ 2, 3 Centrale. 🚊 2, 5, 9, 33.
🚌 42, 53, 60, 82, 90, 91, 92.

MILAN'S MAIN RAILWAY station is one of the largest and perhaps the most monumental in Europe. Ulisse Stacchini's project design was approved and ready in 1912, but construction work proved so slow that the building was not opened until 1931. The new railway station replaced one located in present-day Piazza della Repubblica.

The building is dressed in Aurisina stone, and was clearly inspired by the late Art Nouveau style in vogue in the early 20th century, in marked contrast with the austere 1930s architecture of the surrounding buildings.

The façade is 207 m (679 ft) wide and 36 m (118 ft) tall and is crowned by two winged horses. The large arcades link up with the Galleria dei Transiti, a gallery decorated with four medallions by Giannino Castiglioni representing Labour, Commerce, Science and Agriculture. In the large ticket office hall, flights of steps lead up to the huge departures and arrivals lobby, with tile panels representing the cities of Milan, Rome, Turin and Florence.

The massive building is a landmark in Milan and second only to the cathedral in size. There are numerous shops inside, and some are open 24 hours a day.

Bastioni di Porta Venezia ⓯

Map 4 E3. Ⓜ 1 Porta Venezia, 3 Repubblica. 🚊 1, 2, 9, 11, 29, 30.

WHAT IS TODAY a major road was once part of the walls built to defend the city in 1549–61 by the Spanish governor Ferrante Gonzaga. In 1789 the walls became a tree-lined avenue for walking and coach parking. The Porta Venezia ramparts, flanked by the Giardini Pubblici, link Piazza della Repubblica and Piazza Oberdan. The former was laid out in 1931 when the 19th-century railway station was demolished and rebuilt 800 m (2,624 ft) away and greatly

Plaque commemorating
the *lazzaretto*

enlarged to cope with increasing traffic resulting from the opening of the St Gotthard (1882) and Simplon (1906) passes through the Alps.

Not far from the piazza, in Via Turati, is the Palazzo della Permanente, designed by Luca Beltrami in 1885 as the home of the Permanent Fine Arts Exhibition and now used for temporary exhibitions.

Piazza Oberdan is dominated by Porta Venezia, the city gate rebuilt in 1828 on the site of the Spanish gate of the same name and used as a customs toll station. The two buildings are decorated with statues and reliefs concerning the history of Milan. Porta Venezia separates Corso Venezia and Corso Buenos Aires, a major commercial thoroughfare.

In 1488–1513, Lazzaro Palazzi chose a site beyond the gate to build the *lazzaretto*, a hospital for plague victims commissioned by Lodovico il Moro. The few remains from the 1880 demolition can be seen in Via San Gregorio. A slight detour from Piazza Oberdan towards Viale Piave will take you past some interesting Art Nouveau style buildings: Casa Galimberti, designed by Giovan Battista Bossi in 1903–4, decorated with wrought iron and panels of ceramic tiles, and the Hotel Diana Majestic.

Casa Galimberti, decorated with wrought iron and tile panels

Planetarium ⓰

Corso Venezia 57. **Map** 4 E4.
[02-295 31 18. M 1 Porta
Venezia–Palestro. 9, 29, 30.
3 & 4:30pm Sat & Sun.

Donated to the city by the publisher Ulrico Hoepli, the Planetarium was built in 1930 in Classical style by Piero Portaluppi. The projection hall has a large hemispherical dome (the technology was updated in 1955) and 600 swivelling seats to enable you to gaze at the movements of the stars.

The Planetarium offers guided tours (including tours for students of the subject) and scientific or popular-level lectures on astronomy.

Museo di Storia Naturale ⓱

Corso Venezia 55. **Map** 4 E4.
[02-88 46 32 80. M 1 Porta
Venezia–Palestro. 9, 29, 30.
9am–6pm daily. 1 Jan, Easter,
1 May, 15 Aug, 25 Dec. (tel.
02-78 35 28). Lecture hall,
Library.

The museum of Natural History was founded in 1838 with the donation of the Giuseppe de Cristoforis and Giorgio Jan collections. The building was constructed in Neo-Romanesque style and with terracotta decoration in 1893 by Giovanni Ceruti. The museum has a specialist library holding over 30,000 volumes, including sections on mineralogy and zoology. On the ground floor are the mineralogy and entomology

The Giardini Pubblici, a rare area of greenery in Milan

collections, and part of the Museo Settala, which was created by a canon named Manfredo. It features scientific instruments and natural history specimens of varied provenance. In the palaeontology halls there are reconstructions of dinosaurs such as the Triceratops and a large Allosaurus skeleton. The ground floor also has displays of molluscs and insects. The upper floor is reserved for reptiles, cetaceans and mammals. There are also several reconstructions of animal habitats.

Giardini Pubblici ⓲

Corso Venezia, Via Palestro, Via Manin,
Bastioni di Porta Venezia. **Map** 4 E4.
M 1 Porta Venezia–Palestro, 3
Repubblica–Turati. 1, 9, 11, 29,
30. 94. 6:30am–sunset daily.

The public gardens extend for about 160,000 sq m (192,000 sq yds) and form the largest city park in Milan. They were designed by Piermarini

Reconstruction of a dinosaur skeleton, Museo di Storia Naturale

in 1786 and enlarged in 1857 by Giuseppe Balzaretto, who annexed Palazzo Dugnani and its garden. Further changes were made by Emilio Alemagna after the international exhibitions held in the 1871–81 period.

The park is also home to the Padiglione del Caffè (1863), now a nursery school, and the Museo di Storia Naturale.

Palazzo Dugnani ⓳

Via Manin 2. **Map** 4 D3.
M 3 Turati. 1, 2. 61, 94.
Tiepolo rooms only.
Museo del Cinema [02-655 49
77. 3–6pm Fri–Sun.

Palazzo Dugnani was built in the late 1600s and renovated a century later. Since 1846 it has belonged to Milan city council. A monumental staircase leads up to a magnificent two-storey salon with a gallery for musicians. Here, in 1731, the great Giambattista Tiepolo painted the frescoes *The Allegory of the Dugnani Family* and *The Legends of Scipio and Massinissa*. Both were damaged by the 1943 bombings and by the terrorist bomb that exploded in Via Palestro in 1993.

The palazzo houses the Museo del Cinema which documents the evolution of motion-picture cameras from the 18th-century magic lanterns to those used by the Lumière brothers, as well as apparatus that became obsolete when talking pictures were invented. There are also movie posters from 1905 to 1930.

Villa Reale and Galleria d'Arte Moderna ⓴

MILAN'S MODERN ART GALLERY is housed in a Neo-Classical villa built by Leopold Pollack in 1790 for Count Ludovico Barbiano di Belgioioso. It was lived in by Napoleon in 1802 and later by Marshal Radetzky. The gallery is devoted to 19th-century art movements in Italy, from Hayez to Piccio, the Scapigliatura, Divisionism and the Macchiaioli artists Fattori and Lega. The villa also houses the Grassi and Vismara collections of 19th- and 20th-century Italian and foreign artists (including Impressionists, Matisse, Picasso, Morandi) as well as the Marino Marini Museum.

VISITORS' CHECKLIST

Via Palestro 16. **Map** 4 E4.
🄲 02-76 00 28 19. Ⓜ 1
Palestro. 🚆 1, 2. 🚌 61, 94.
◻ 9am–5:30pm Tue–Sun.
⬤ 1 Jan, Easter, 1 May, 15 Aug,
25 Dec. 🅰 🗗 Many rooms
closed for restoration.
**Giardini di Villa Reale
(Villa Gardens)** ◻ Nov–Feb:
9am–noon, 2–4pm; Mar, Oct:
9am–noon, 2–6pm; Apr–Sep:
9am–noon, 2–7pm.

KEY

☐	Cineteca Italiana
☐	Vismara Collection
☐	Modern Art Gallery
☐	Marino Marini Museum
☐	Grassi Collection

Grassi Collection
In 1956 Nedda Grassi donated this fine collection to the city in memory of her son Gino. It comprises rugs, Oriental objets d'art and 135 paintings, including foreign and Italian 19th- and 20th-century artists such as Van Gogh, Cézanne, Corot and Gauguin, Fattori, Lega, Balla, Boccioni and Morandi.

Antonio Canova's bronze of Napoleon and plaster sculpture of Hebe are displayed here.

Furnishings and frescoes
decorate the main floor; the top attraction is the dining room, with a *Parnassus* by Appiani.

This room is used for civil weddings.

STAR EXHIBIT

★ **Fourth Estate**

Marino Marini Museum
This section opened in 1973. It holds paintings and sculptures donated by Marini himself, including portraits of people he admired, such as Arp, De Pisis, Carrà, Chagall and Stravinsky.

★ **Fourth Estate**
In this fine 1901 canvas, Quarto Stato, *Giuseppe Pelizza da Volpedo expresses solidarity with the struggles and suffering of the lower classes.*

Corso Venezia ㉑

Formerly called corso di porta orientale, this famous and popular street was named after the gate in the medieval walls corresponding to present-day Via Senato. The same name was given to the quarter, whose emblem is the lion on the column in front of the church of San Babila. Corso Venezia was lined with relatively few buildings and bordered by kitchen gardens and orchards until the mid-18th century, when the reforms carried out by Maria Theresa of Austria led to the construction of the numerous patrician palazzi that make this one of Milan's most elegant streets.

Locator Map
See Street Finder, map 4

Three inner courtyards lead to the garden.

On the balustrade are statues of the *Dei Consenti* (the 12 chief Roman gods) by Pompeo Marchesi and Grazioso Rusca.

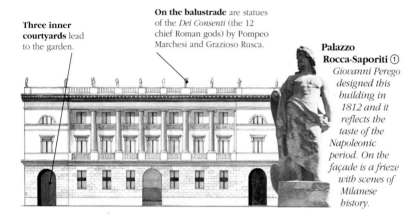

Palazzo Rocca-Saporiti ①
Giovanni Perego designed this building in 1812 and it reflects the taste of the Napoleonic period. On the façade is a frieze with scenes of Milanese history.

Palazzo Castiglioni ②
This palazzo was built by Giuseppe Sommaruga in 1904. There were once two female nudes on the façade (later removed), hence its name Ca' di Ciapp (House of Buttocks).

On the first floor is a lovely three-flight staircase and the Sala dei Pavoni.

A loggia with Ionic columns emphasizes the central section.

The side facing Via San Damiano has retained its original 17th-century features.

Palazzo Serbelloni ③
Completed in 1793 by Simone Cantoni, this palazzo played host to Napoleon and Vittorio Emanuele.

★ **Casa Fontana-Silvestri** ④
*This rare example of a Renaissance
residence in Milan was built in the late
15th century by Angelo Fontana.
The windows on the façade are
framed in brick and the portal by
candelabrum columns.*

Bramante is thought
by a number of
scholars to have
worked on the
decoration of
the façade.

Above the portal is
San Carlo's motto,
Humilitas.

**Seminario
Arcivescovile** ⑤
*This seminary was begun in
1565 by Seregni for San
Carlo Borromeo. The portal
was added in 1652 by
Francesco Maria Richini.*

The campanile was built in 1820,
after the original collapsed.

**The present-day Neo-Romanesque
façade** was designed in 1906 by
Paolo Cesa Bianchi, who also built
the high altar.

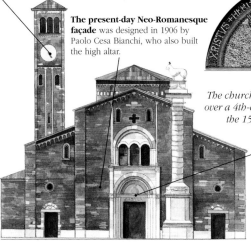

★ **San Babila** ⑥
*The church was built in the 11th century
over a 4th-century basilica and rebuilt in
the 1500s. The rather heavy-handed
restoration of the Romanesque
original began in 1853.*

STAR SIGHTS

★ **San Babila**

★ **Casa
Fontana-Silvestri**

THE LAKES OF
NORTHERN ITALY

THE LAKES OF NORTHERN ITALY

APPRECIATED BY THE ANCIENT ROMANS *for their beautiful location and mild climate, the lakes of Northern Italy – most of which are in Lombardy – are deservedly renowned for the fascinating and unique combination of magnificent scenery and historic and artistic heritage that characterizes the lakeside towns.*

Besides Lake Maggiore, Lake Como and Lake Garda, there are smaller and less well-known bodies of water such as the lakes of Orta, Varese, Iseo and Idro. All these lovely lakes are the result of glaciation in the Pleistocene era, which enlarged clefts already in the terrain. The lake shores were inhabited during the prehistoric period – traces of ancient civilizations have been found almost everywhere – and for the most part were colonized by the Romans, as can be seen in the grid street plans of many towns and in the villas at Lake Garda. Churches, sanctuaries and castles were built here in the Middle Ages. In the winter the shores of the lakes can be battered by winds from Central Europe, but the climate remains quite mild thanks to the water. Typical Mediterranean vegetation can be seen everywhere: vineyards, olive trees, oleanders and palm trees. The many splendid villa gardens along the lakes' shores enhance the environment, and nature reserves have been established to protect some stretches.

In the 18th century a visit to the lake region was one of the accepted stages on the Grand Tour, the trip to Europe considered essential for the education of young people of good birth. These shores were also favourites with writers, musicians and artists such as Goethe, Hesse, Klee, Toscanini, Hemingway, Stendhal, Byron and Nietzsche. The numerous vantage points, connected to the shore by funiculars, narrow-gauge trains and cable cars, offer truly spectacular views over the landscape.

The peaceful shores of Lake Como, southwest of Bellagio

◁ **Torre di San Marco at Gardone Riviera, on the western shore of Lake Garda**

Exploring the Lakes

T HE LARGER LAKES offer the best facilities for visitors,
with hotels, restaurants and cafés lining the lake
front. The lake shores are dotted with pretty villages,
castles (Sirmione sul Garda), villas and gardens such
as Villa Taranto or the Vittoriale, the residence of the
poet D'Annunzio at Lake Garda, as well as a number
of small local museums. In summer, you may be able
to participate in cultural events such as the famous
Settimane Musicali di Stresa music festival at Lake
Maggiore. Although the smaller lakes offer fewer
facilities, they are very peaceful, unspoilt places.

Cannobio, Lake Maggiore

GETTING THERE

The lakes of Northern Italy can be
reached via Malpensa and Linate
airports in Milan and Catullo airport
in Verona. There are also good
connections by motorway from
Milan: the A8 autostrada goes to
lakes Maggiore and Varese, the A9
to Lake Como, and the A4 to Iseo
and Garda. Traffic on the major and
minor roads is often heavy, so
make allowances when planning.
Boat services on the three major
lakes are quite efficient; they go to
the islands and are an enjoyable
way of getting about.

0 kilometres   10

0 miles   10

THE LAKES

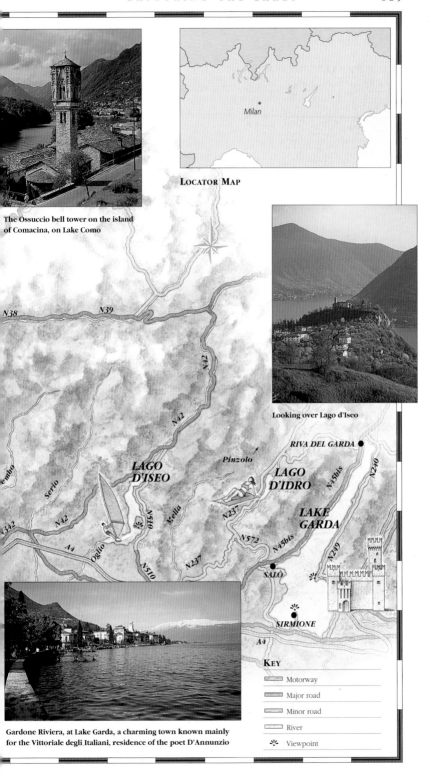

The Ossuccio bell tower on the island of Comacina, on Lake Como

LOCATOR MAP

Milan

Looking over Lago d'Iseo

N38 N39

N42

N42

RIVA DEL GARDA

Pinzolo

LAGO D'ISEO

LAGO D'IDRO

embo

Serio

N42

N42

Oglio

A4

N510

Mella

N237

N237

N572

N45bis

N45bis

LAKE GARDA

N249

N240

SALO

SIRMIONE

A4

1342

N510

KEY

Motorway

Major road

Minor road

River

Viewpoint

Gardone Riviera, at Lake Garda, a charming town known mainly for the Vittoriale degli Italiani, residence of the poet D'Annunzio

Lake Maggiore

Villa statue, Isola Madre

WITH BORDERS IN PIEDMONT, LOMBARDY and the Ticino canton in Switzerland, Lake Maggiore, or Verbano, is the second largest lake in Italy (212 sq km, 82 sq miles) and has a maximum depth of 372 m (1,220 ft). For the most part it is fed and drained by the Ticino river, and is also fed by the Toce. The towns were embellished with churches and paintings from 1449 on, thanks to the wealthy Borromeo family, and with villas and gardens in the 18th–19th centuries. The opening of the Simplon pass and the introduction of ferry services (1826) helped trade to develop in the area.

★ Isole Borromee
Of the three islands, the best known is Isola Bella, named after Isabella d'Adda, wife of Charles III Borromeo ❺

The two castles of Malpaga, built in the 13th–14th century on two islets at the foot of Mount Carza, belonged to the Mazzardites, the pirates who raided the lake.

Stresa
This old fishermen's village began to become a tourist attraction thanks to the descriptions of famous writers such as Stendhal, Byron and Dickens ❹

★ Villa Taranto
One of Italy's best-known botanic gardens was founded here in 1931 by an Englishman called McEacharn in an area of about 16 ha (40 acres). Many examples of species of plants from all over the world, including Victoria amazonica, are grown here (see p134).

Map labels:
Magaduno
Vira
Locarno
San Nazzaro
Gerra-Gambarogno
Ascona
Sant'Abbondio
Porto Ronco
Isola di Brissago
Brissago
Maccagno
Cannobio ❽
Gannero Riviera
Lu
❾
Pieggio
Po Veltrava
Ghiffa
Intra
Verbania ❼
Isola Madre
Ba

★ Santa Caterina del Sasso Ballaro
Perched on a rocky spur near Laveno, this monastery is one of the most enchanting sights on Lake Maggiore. It was built by a local merchant in the 12th century to fulfil a vow made when he was saved from a storm ⑪

Visitors' Checklist

ℹ️ Local tourist bureau.
🚉 FS Milan–Domodossola or Milan–Bellinzona line (848-88 80 88); Ferrovie Nord Milano, to Laveno (02-202 22). 🚌 to Sesto Calende and Angera, Autol. Zani (02-86 46 48 54); to Luino, Autol. Baldioli (02-869 05 00).
⛴️ Navigazione Lago Maggiore (800-55 18 01).

Sights at a Glance

Arona ②
Baveno ⑥
Cannobio ⑧
Isole Borromee ⑤
Laveno ⑩
Lesa and Belgirate ③
Luino ⑨
Rocca di Angera ⑫
Santa Caterina
   del Sasso Ballaro ⑪
Sesto Calende ①
Stresa ④
Verbania ⑦

★ Rocca di Angera
The imposing medieval fortress of the Borromeo family has 14th- and 15th-century frescoes. It now houses the Doll Museum ⑫

Arona
The huge 17th-century statue of San Carlo Borromeo was placed in Arona in honour of its illustrious citizen. A 35-m (115-ft) stairway leads to the top, from where there is a fine panoramic view ②

Sesto Calende
The town museum in Piazza Mazzini contains objects found in nearby Bronze Age sites.

🚉⑩ Laveno

⑪ Santa Caterina del Sasso Ballaro

Isola Bella

⑤ Isole Borromee
④ Stresa

Belgirate

③

Lesa

Méina

Angera
⑫

② Arona

Key

- - - - Ferry routes
🚉 Ferry service
☼ Viewpoint

0 kilometres   2
0 miles   2

Star Sights

★ **Santa Caterina del Sasso Ballaro**

★ **Rocca di Angera**

★ **Villa Taranto**

★ **Isole Borromee**

Sesto Calende ❶

Varese. 🚇 9,500. 🛈 APT, Via Carrobbio 2, Varese (0332-28 36 04). 🛒 antiques, 3rd Sat of month.

THE TOWN AT the southern tip of Lake Maggiore marks the end of two motorways leading to the Verbano region. The road to Arona goes to **San Donato**, known as "La Badia" or abbey, a 9th-century basilica rebuilt in the 11th–12th century. The capitals have sculpted figures of animals and humans. There are frescoes from the 15th and 16th centuries in the nave and from the 18th century in the crypt. South of Sesto, near Golasecca, are Iron Age tombs (9th–5th century BC), part of the civilization named after the place. State road 33 to Arona will take you to the **Lagoni di Mercurago Regional Park**, with varied bird species and the remains of ancient villages.

🛕 **Abbazia San Donato**
Via Sandonato 6. 📞 0331-92 46 92.
🕐 8am–noon, 4–7pm daily.
🏞 **Lagoni di Mercurago Regional Park**
Via Gattico 6, Mercurago.
📞 0322-24 02 39.
🌐 www.parchilagomaggiore.it

Arona ❷

Novara. 🚇 16,000. 🛈 Piazzale Duca d'Aosta (0322-24 36 01). 🛒 antiques, 3rd Sun of month.

ARONA ONCE OCCUPIED an important trading position between Milan and the lake and mountain regions of Northern Italy.

Looking over the lakeside town of Arona

Because of its strategic location, a Rocca or fortress (the twin of the one at Angera; *see p135*), was built here; it was enlarged by the Borromeo and dismantled by Napoleon. Corso Marconi has a view of the Rocca at Angera, and leads to Piazza del Popolo. Here are the 15th-century Casa del Podestà, with an arched portico, and the 16th-century Madonna di Piazza church. Santi Martiri has 15th-century paintings by Bergognone, and Santa Maria Nascente has an altarpiece by Gaudenzio Ferrari (1511).

Just north of the centre is a massive **statue of San Carlo**. It was designed by Cerano in 1614 and finished in 1697. In the church of San Carlo there is a reconstruction of the room where San Carlo was born, which was taken from the demolished Rocca.

Villa Ponti is a mid-17th-century villa with Baroque and Art Deco decoration. It stands in a garden with a nympheum and a fountain.

🛕 **Statue of San Carlo**
Piazza San Carlo. 📞 0322-24 96 69.
🕐 22 Mar–10 Nov: 8:30am–12:30pm, 2–6:30pm daily (5pm from 4 Oct); 11 Nov–21 Mar: 9am–12:30pm, 2–5pm Sat, Sun, hols. 🎟 **San Carlo and Birthplace of San Carlo**.
Collegio De Filippi; 🛈 Piazzale San Carlo (0322-24 24 88).
🏛 **Villa Ponti**
Via San Carlo 57. 📞 0322-444 22.
⬤ to the public.

The square in Arona with the huge statue of San Carlo Borromeo

Lesa and Belgirate ❸

Lesa (Novara). 🚇 2,400. Belgirate (Verbania). 🚇 500. 🛈 Via Principe Tommaso 70, Stresa (0323-304 16).

LESA LIES ON A PARTICULARLY charming stretch of the lake between Arona and Stresa, and has been a resort for noble Lombard families since the 18th century. The **Museo Manzoniano di Villa Stampa** has mementos of author Alessandro Manzoni, who was a guest here. The hamlet of Villa boasts the Romanesque church of San Sebastiano. Once past Lesa, continue to Belgirate and its charming historic centre, whose houses have porticoes and porches. This village also commands a panoramic view of the lake. It was a haunt of philosopher Antonio Rosmini and poet Guido Gozzano. On the hills 4 km (2 miles) from Belgirate is the 13th-century **Castello Visconti di San Vito**, decorated with frescoes of the period. Nearby is the Romanesque church of San Michele, with a leaning bell tower.

🏛 **Museo Manzoniano di Villa Stampa**
Via alla Fontana, Lesa.
📞 0322-764 21.
🕐 Jul–Sep: 5–7pm Sat, 9:30am–noon Sun; Aug: also 10am–noon Thu.
🏰 **Castello Visconti di San Vito**
Via Visconti 1, Massino Visconti.
📞 0322-21 97 13. ⬤ to the public.

Stresa ❹

Verbania. 🏠 *4,800.* ℹ IAT,
Piazza Marconi 16 *(0323-301 50)*.

THE ORIGINS OF MEDIEVAL
Strixia, dating from before
1000, are partially hidden by
the palazzi and villas built for
the aristocracy in the late
19th–early 20th century,
partly because of the opening
of an electric rack-railway
(the first in Italy), which goes
to the top of Mount Mottarone. The town is now a
centre for conferences and
tour groups, attracted by the
easy access to the Borromean
islands. On the lakefront are
19th-century villas, Sant'
Ambrogio (18th century) and
the **Villa Ducale** (1770), with
mementos of 19th-century
philosopher Antonio Rosmini,
who died here (the villa is
now the Rosmini Study
Centre). Mount Mottarone
(1,491 m, 4,890 ft), a ski
resort, has a view from the
Alps to the plain.

🏛 **Villa Ducale**
Centro di Studi Rosminiani
Corso Umberto I 15.
🎧 *0323-300 91.*
⬤ *to the public.*

ENVIRONS
🌿 **Parco
di Villa
Pallavicino**
State road 33. 🎧 *0323-
324 07.* ⬤ *Mar–Oct:
9am–6pm daily.* 📷 ♿
🚻 🍴
This villa near Stresa is
famous for its gardens. The
luxuriant English garden has
centuries-old plants as well
as exotic creatures such as
llamas and pelicans.

The garden of the 18th-century palazzo on Isola Madre

Isole Borromee ❺

Verbania. ⛴ *from Arona, Laveno,
Stresa, Baveno, Pallanza. To Isola
Madre: tel. 0323-312 61; to Isola Bella:
tel. 0323-305 56 Apr–Oct.* ⬤ *27 Mar–
24 Oct: 9am–noon, 1:30–5:30pm daily.*
⬤ *Oct–Mar.* 📷 🎫 *by appt.* 🍴

THESE THREE ISLANDS, which
can be reached easily
from Stresa, became famous
thanks to the Borromeo
family, who built elegant
palazzi and magnificent
gardens there. The loveliest
is **Isola Bella**, an old fishing
village transformed
from 1632 to
1671 by the
Borromeo
family into a
lovely complex
consisting of a
Baroque palazzo
and a terraced
Italian-style garden with rare
plants. Inside are a music
room (where Mussolini met
British and French officials in
1935), the Sala di Napoleone
(where Napoleon stayed in

**A fountain
at Villa Pallavicino**

1797), a ballroom, throne
room and bedroom with
17th-century decoration and
furnishings and paintings by
Carracci, Cerano and Tiepolo.
The six grottoes are decorated
with shells and pebbles.
  Isola Madre, the largest
island, boasts an 18th-century
villa with a garden where
white peacocks roam freely;
it has rare plants as well as
azaleas, rhododendrons,
magnolias and camellias. The
villa has period furnishings
and a collection of 18th- and
19th-century puppet theatres.
  Tiny **Isola dei Pescatori**,
once the leading fishing
village, has retained its quaint
atmosphere and architecture.

Baveno ❻

Verbania. 🏠 *4,500.* ℹ IAT, Piazza
Dante Alighieri 14 *(0323-92 46 32)*.

MADE FAMOUS by its pink
granite quarries, which
among other things supplied
the stone for the Galleria in
Milan *(see p50)*, Baveno
became a fashionable resort
in the mid-19th century,
entertaining guests such as
Queen Victoria, who stayed
in the Villa Clara (now Villa
Branca) in 1879. A major
attraction is Santi Gervasio e
Protasio, with its 12th-century
façade and 15th-century
octagonal baptistery with
Renaissance frescoes. Going
towards Verbania, take the
turn-off for San Giovanni at
Montorfano, one of the
loveliest churches in the area.

The garden at Villa Pallavicino, the home of many species of animals

Verbania ❼

🏠 *31,000.* ℹ️ *IAT, Corso Zanitello 6–8 (0323-50 32 49).* 🛍️ *antiques, 3 Jul–4 Sep: from 5pm on Fri.*

PALLANZA AND INTRA were merged in 1939 to create the town of Verbania (capital of the Verbano-Cusio-Ossola province established in 1992). The former, facing the Borromeo gulf, is the seat of the municipal government and has retained its medieval aspect and atmosphere. The latter dominates the promontory of Castagnola and has a decidedly Baroque and Neo-Classical flavour. Intra, the most important port of call on the lake and one of its major industrial centres, was the regional leader in textile manufacturing in the 18th century. Pallanza was the only town in Lake Maggiore not under Borromeo dominion, and it has some of the most important monuments. These include Romanesque Santo Stefano, the parish church of San Leonardo and 18th-century Palazzo Dugnani, home to the **Museo del Paesaggio**, which has on exhibit 16th–20th-century landscape paintings, sculpture by Arturo Martini and Giulio Branca and a plaster cast gallery. Isolino di San Giovanni was a favourite refuge of Arturo Toscanini. In the environs is 16th-century Madonna di

Effigy of McEacharn, who created the Villa Taranto gardens

Campagna, with a small Romanesque campanile and frescoes by Gerolamo Lanino and Camillo Procaccini (16th–17th centuries).

🏛️ Museo del Paesaggio
Via Ruga 44. 📞 *0323-50 24 18.* 🕐 *Apr–Oct: 10am–noon, 3:30–6:30pm Tue–Sun.*

ENVIRONS
🌿 Giardini di Villa Taranto
Via Rossano 22, Pallanza. 📞 *0323-55 66 67.* 🕐 *Apr–Oct: 8:30am–7:30pm daily.* 🅿️ 🎁 ♿ 🚻

In 1931 a British captain named McEacharn created one of the outstanding botanic gardens in Europe on the Castagnola promontory, using the lake water for irrigation. He is buried in the small park church. McEacharn exploited the valley terrain, creating terraced gardens, a winter garden and a marsh garden among small falls and water lily ponds. He donated the Villa Taranto garden to the Italian state and it was opened to the public in 1952. It has a range of exotic plants, including *Victoria amazonica* in the glasshouses. Azaleas, dahlias and rhododendrons (over 300 varieties) look wonderful in full flower.

Cannobio ❽

Verbania. 🏠 *5,300.* ℹ️ *IAT, Viale Vittorio Veneto 4 (0323-713 93).*

THIS PLEASANT TOURIST resort is the last Italian town on the Piedmontese side of the lake. It still retains its old medieval character, exemplified in the Palazzo della Ragione or Palazzo Parrasio, the town hall with a 12th-century Commune Tower. The Santuario della Pietà, which was rebuilt by San Carlo Borromeo in 1583, contains a fine altarpiece by Gaudenzio Ferrari.

The Orrido di Sant'Anna, in Val Cannobina

In nearby Val Cannobina, the Orrido di Sant'Anna is worth a visit. This deep gorge was carved out of the rock by the Cannobino river.

Luino ❾

Varese. 🏠 *15,300.* ℹ️ *APT, Via Chiara 1 (0332-53 00 19).*

LUINO, WHICH occupies a cove on the eastern side of the lake, is a town dating from ancient Roman times. Its name may have derived from the Luina torrent or perhaps from the local term *luina* (landslide). In the Middle Ages it was contested by the leading Como and Milanese families and became famous when Garibaldi landed here in 1848 with a group of volunteers and routed an entire Austrian detachment.

The large railway station (1882) shows how important the town was when it linked Italy with Central Europe, a position that declined when railway traffic shifted to Chiasso. Luino's market was founded by an edict of Charles V in 1541 and is still a tourist attraction. San Pietro in Campagna has frescoes by Bernardino Luini and a lovely Romanesque bell tower; the oratory of the Chiesa del Carmine dates back to 1477. A must is a visit to the town's symbol, the 17th-century oratory of San Giuseppe.

Laveno ⓾

Varese. 🚂 8,800.
ℹ️ c/o Comune Mombello-Laveno,
Villa Frua (0332-66 66 66).

**The natural harbour of Laveno,
once an Austrian naval base**

THE NAME OF this town goes back to Titus Labienus, the Roman general who was Caesar's legate in Cisalpine Gaul. Laveno was important strategically because of its port, the only natural harbour on Lake Maggiore. During their period of rule, the Austrians moored the gunboats controlling the lake here. Today the town is the main ferry point to the Piedmontese shores. The Ferrovie Nord railway linked Laveno to Varese and Milan, fostering commercial development, especially in the field of ceramics with the founding of well-known Società Ceramica Italiana Richard-Ginori, in 1856. In the town centre, the garden in the Villa Frua (18th century) is worth visiting.

A cable car goes up to Sasso del Ferro, at 1,062 m (3,483 ft), behind Laveno with fine views of the lake, Monte Mottarone and Monte Rosa.

Santa Caterina del Sasso Ballaro ⓫

📞 0332-64 71 72. 🕐 17 Oct–Easter: 8:30am–noon, 2–5pm Sat & Sun.
🔒 4:30pm hols. 🚫

TO GET TO THIS small monastery – one of the most enchanting in Northern Italy – perched on a steep rock 18 m (59 ft) above the lake, you can either climb the steps near Leggiuno or take the boat and enjoy the lovely views. The place was founded in the mid-12th century by a local merchant. The Dominicans arrived in 1230 and after numerous changes in fortune have since returned here. Over the centuries the original building was enlarged and rebuilt, as can be seen by the different architectural styles. The chapter at the entrance has important 14th–15th-century frescoes, including a *Crucifixion with Armigers* (14th century). The 17th-century fresco in the second portico, only partly preserved, represents a *Dance of Death*. The frescoes inside the church were executed in the 16th century, and the *Madonna and Child with Saints* on the high altar dates from 1612. By the entrance porticoes there is a large wine press made in 1759.

**14th–15th-century frescoes,
Rocca di Angera**

Rocca di Angera ⓬

Fortress and museum Via Rocca, Angera. 📞 0331-93 13 00. 🕐 Apr–Oct: 9:30am–6pm daily.
📷 ♿ 🚫 ℹ️

A MAJESTIC FORTRESS, probably built over the ruins of an ancient Roman fortification, the Rocca once belonged to the archbishops of Milan. In the 13th century it was taken over by the Visconti family and in 1449 was granted as a fief to the Borromeo family, who still own it. The Visconti building has single and double lancet windows and partly lies against the earlier castle tower. The frescoes in the halls are well worth a look, especially those in the Salone Gotico, with a cycle of the *Battles of Ottone Visconti against the Torriani* (14th century). The vaults in this hall are decorated with the Visconti coat of arms, while those in the other rooms have geometric patterns and signs of the Zodiac. The Borromeo wing has frescoes removed from Palazzo Borromeo in Milan in 1946, with *Aesop's Fables* by the school of Michelino da Besozzo (15th century). The Rocca is used for art shows and is also home to the **Museo della Bambola** (Doll Museum) in the Visconti wing, one of the best of its kind in Europe, created with the collection of Princess Bona Borromeo. Besides dolls and doll's houses, it contains books, games and children's clothing.

Santa Caterina del Sasso Ballaro, built on a cliff overlooking the lake

Lake Como

THE LAKE, ALSO KNOWN AS LARIO, is the third largest in Italy and the deepest (410 m, 1,345 ft). It is shaped like a sprawling upside-down Y, with the arms of Como, Lecco and Colico. The Como shore is the most developed, with restaurants and hotels and a scenic road that follows the ancient Strada Regina, lined with elegant villas and aristocratic gardens. The Lecco area has more stark scenery and small coves. The lake is known for sudden gusts of wind that make navigation difficult. You may spot the typical "Lucia" boats, named after the heroine in Manzoni's *The Betrothed*, which was partly set here.

Decoration in Villa d'Este, at Cernobbio

★ **Bellagio**
Its position at the junction of the arms of the lake and the spectacular view from the Spartivento point make this one of the most popular spots on Lake Como 12

★ **Como**
Construction of Como's Duomo began in 1396 and ended in 1740 with the huge dome. Next to it is the elegant 13th-century Broletto, the old town hall 1

The bell tower on Santa Maria Maddalena at Ossuccio is one of the symbols of the lake.

Menaggio 6

Lenno 4   Tremezzo 5   Cadenat
Colonno   Isola 3
Argegno   Comacina
Lake Como
Bezzeno
Nesso
Careno

STAR SIGHTS
★ Bellagio
★ Como
★ Tremezzo

0 kilometres   5
0 miles

Torrigia
Urio   Carate
Moltrasio   Pognana Lario
Cernobbio 2   13   Torno
Belvio   Faggeto Lario
Tavernola
Como 1   Brunate

KEY

- - - Ferry routes

🚢 Ferry service

🔆 Viewpoint

Cernobbio
The 16th-century Villa d'Este in Cernobbio, now a famous hotel, is surrounded by beautiful landscaped gardens with many fountains 2

Gravedona

Santa Maria del Tiglio in Gravedona is the most famous Lombard Romanesque construction in the Alto Lario region. Its main features are the layers of black and white stone and the unusual octagonal bell tower set into the façade **7**

VISITORS' CHECKLIST

ℹ️ Local information bureaus.
🚉 FS: Milan–Chiasso line (848-88 80 88); Ferrovie Nord Milano: (031-30 48 00 or 02-202 22).
🚌 SPT: Como–Colico line (031-24 72 47).
⛴️ Navigazione Lago di Como (800-55 18 01 (freefone) or 031-57 92 11).

Lake Mezzola, separated from the Lario region by silt from the Adda river, is a natural reserve inhabited by grey herons.

The "crotti" are typical mountain caves in the upper Lario region, used as wine cellars since the 19th century.

The medieval Vezio castle, built on the site of a Roman tower, is a ten-minute walk from Varenna and offers a stunning panoramic view.

Varenna

Some of the paths in this village, one of the best preserved on the lake, consist of steps and raised boardwalks perched over the water **10**

★ Tremezzo

The Villa Carlotta in Tremezzo was a wedding gift for Carlotta of Prussia (1843). Inside there is a copy of Canova's Cupid and Psyche **5**

Como ●

👤 *86,000.* 🛈 APT, Piazza Cavour
17 *(031-330 01 11).*

C OMUM WAS founded by the
Romans in 196 BC and
in the 12th century fought
against Milan as an ally of
Barbarossa, who built the
medieval walls. In 1335 Como
came under Visconti rule and
in 1451 under Sforza rule.
The town shared Milan's fate
under Spanish and Austrian
domination, becoming part of
the Kingdom of Italy in 1859.

Como's many Romanesque
churches include the 12th-
century San Fedele and the
jewel of the Comacine masters, 11th-century Lombard–
Romanesque Sant'Abbondio.

The **Duomo**, begun in
1396, is dominated by Filippo
Juvarra's Baroque dome. The
sculpture on the Gothic façade
and the Porta della Rana door
were executed by Tommaso
and Jacopo Rodari (c.1500).
The nave and side altars are
decorated with 16th-century
tapestries and canvases by
Ferrari and Luini. Next to the
Duomo is the Romanesque-
Gothic Broletto (1215).

The **Tempio Voltiano**
(1927) contains relics of
Alessandro Volta, the great
physicist from Como, who
gave his name to "voltage".

The Casa del Fascio (1936)
exemplifies Italian Rationalist
architecture. **Villa Olmo**,

Piazza del Duomo in Como, the birthplace of Pliny the Elder

designed by Simone Cantoni in
1797, has frescoed rooms and
a park, open to the public. A
funicular goes up to Brunate.

🏛 Duomo
Piazza Duomo. 📞 *031-26 52 44.*
🕐 *7am–noon, 3–7pm daily.*

⚱ Tempio Voltiano
Viale Marconi. 📞 *031-57 47 05.*
🕐 *Apr–Sep: 10am–noon, 3–6pm
Tue–Sun; Oct–Mar: 10am–noon,
2–4pm Tue–Sun.* 📷

⚱ Villa Olmo
Via Cantoni 1. 📞 *031-25 24 43.*
🕐 *9am–noon, 3–6pm Tue–Sun.*
⬤ *hols.* 📷 📹

Cernobbio ●

Como. 👤 *7,200.* 🛈 Via Regina 33b
(031-51 01 98).

C ERNOBBIO marks the
beginning of the series
of splendid villas
surrounded by
parks that have
made the western
side of the lake
famous. **Villa
d'Este**, built by
Pellegrino Tibaldi
in 1570 for the
Gallio family,
became a luxury
hotel in 1873,
frequented by
princes and actors.
The rooms have
period furnishings
and are used for
conferences. The
villa stands in an
Italianate garden
with a nympheum.
18th-century **Villa
Erba** (now an
exhibition centre)

is known for its interior (visits
by request): the Salone da
Ballo, chapel and Sala delle
Nozze, decorated by Gio-
condo Albertolli, are lovely.

⚱ Hotel Villa d'Este
Via Regina 40. 📞 *031-34 81.*
🎭 Villa Erba
Largo Visconti 4. 📞 *031-34 91.*
🕐 *May–Oct: 2–6pm Sat, 10am–6pm
Sun.* ⬤ *Nov–Apr.*

Lenno ●

Como. 👤 *1,600.* 🛈 APT, Piazza
Cavour 17, Como *(031-330 01 11).*

T HIS TOWN IS FAMOUS for the
Villa del Balbianello, built
by Cardinal Durini in the 17th
century onto a 16th-century
building attributed to Pellegrini. The magnificent garden

FROM MULBERRY TO SILK

Como produces
about 80 per cent
of Europe's silk.
Silk worms were
imported in the
14th century and
production thrived
in the 17th century with
the large-scale cultivation
of mulberries, the worms'
food. Silk thread was
woven and sent on the
"silk route" in Austria and
Bavaria. Competition from
Chinese silk now forces
Como to concentrate on
quality silk, as shown in
the Museo della Seta (Silk
Museum) in Como.

Cocoons

**The Villa d'Este in Cernobbio, once host to the
Duke of Windsor and Mrs Simpson**

with candelabrum plane trees has a loggia with a view of Isola Comacina on one side and the Tremezzina bay on the other. Access to the villa is by boat from Sala Comacina.

Also worth a visit are the octagonal baptistery and church of Santo Stefano, built in the 11th century over a Roman building and decorated with frescoes by Luini. Just above the town is the Cistercian abbey of Acquafredda, rebuilt in the 17th century, with frescoes by Fiammenghino. At nearby Giulino di Mezzegra, the Fascist dictator Benito Mussolini and his mistress Claretta Petacci were executed on 28 April 1945, following their capture on the previous day.

⊞ Villa del Balbianello
Balbianello. **☎** *0344-561 10 (FAI).*
Garden ◯ *Apr–Oct: 10am–12:30pm, 3:30–6:30pm Tue, Thu–Sun.*
Villa ◯ *by appointment only.*

Isola Comacina ❹

Como. **🚹** APT, Piazza Cavour 17, Como *(031-330 01 11).* **🚢** *(as far as Sala Comacina, then by boat).*

THE ONLY ISLAND on Lake Como has been inhabited since Roman times. It was fortified by the Byzantines and enjoyed a period of splendour in the Middle Ages. The people of Como conquered the fortress in 1169 and destroyed the seven churches on the island. The ruins, together with those of a mosaic-decorated baptistery,

Villa Carlotta, built in the 18th century by Marchese Giorgio Clerici

were found after World War II and are now being studied. Sala Comacina, where boats depart for the island, has an 18th-century church with a fresco by Carlo Carloni, and the villa of Cesare Beccaria, where Manzoni was a guest.

Tremezzo ❺

Como. **👥** *1,300.* **🚹** APT, Piazza Cavour 17, Como *(031-330 01 11).*

THIS LAKESIDE town is a major tourist resort and its main claim to fame is the 18th-century **Villa Carlotta**. The residence, surrounded by a terraced garden with landscaped staircases, was converted in the 19th century into a Neo-Classical villa. It houses paintings by Hayez, furniture by Maggiolini and sculpture pieces by Canova, including a copy of *Cupid and Psyche* and *Terpsichore*.

Among the many rooms decorated with stuccowork is one with Appiani's frescoes taken from the Palazzo Reale in Milan. The villa is also famous for its garden.

⊞ Villa Carlotta
Via Regina 2b. **☎** *0344-404 05.* **◯**
15 Mar–31 Oct: 9–11:30am, 2–4:30pm daily; Apr–Sep: 9am–6pm daily.

Menaggio ❻

Como. **👥** *3,200.* **🚹** APT, Piazza Garibaldi 3 *(0344-329 24).*

THE NAME MENAGGIO supposedly derives from two Indo-European words: *men* (mountain) and *uigg* (water), referring to the mouth of the Sanagra river on which the town lies. Menaggio is the leading commercial centre in the upper Lario region and a popular tourist resort as well. It is dominated by the ruins of a castle and has preserved some of its medieval layout. Sights worth visiting are the parish church of Santo Stefano – whose Baroque architecture conceals its Romanesque origin – and 17th-century San Carlo, with a good painting by Giuseppe Vermiglio (1625). The lakeside promenade, with its arcaded houses and villas, is a must. Past Menaggio, at Loveno, is the Neo-Classical Milyus-Vigoni villa with family portraits by Francesco Hayez. Around it is a lovely park, designed by Balzaretto in 1840, with many rare trees.

Menaggio, a lakeside town especially popular with British visitors

Gravedona **7**

Como. 🏠 *2,800.* 🛈 Pro Loco, Piazza Cavour 7 *(0344-896 37).*

A FORTIFIED TOWN of some importance in ancient Roman times, Gravedona was destroyed by the people of Como in the 13th century because it was allied with Milan. It later became capital of the small Tre Pievi republic. The town then declined and was ceded to Cardinal Tolomeo Gallio, who in 1583 asked Tibaldi to build Palazzo Gallio. Gravedona is known for the church of **Santa Maria del Tiglio** (12th century). The aisled nave with tall galleries houses a 12th-century wooden Crucifix, a floor mosaic dating from the 6th century and various 12th–14th-century frescoes. Santi Gusmeo e Matteo was frescoed by Fiammenghino, while Santa Maria delle Grazie (1467) contains 16th-century frescoes. Nearby Dongo is an ancient village known for the Falck steelworks, which was responsible for building the metal parts of the *Italia* and *Norge* airships. Above Gravedona, at Peglio, is the Sant'Eusebio complex, with fine 17th-century frescoes in the church. The Spanish fort in the outskirts was built in 1604 to guard the Adda river plain.

Santa Maria del Tiglio
Piazza XI Febbraio. 📞 *0344-852 61.* 🕐 *9am–6pm daily.*

Palazzo Gallio, designed by architect Pellegrino Tibaldi in 1583

The Cluniac Piona abbey, founded in the 11th century

Abbazia di Piona **8**

Via Santa Maria di Piona 1, Colico. 📞 *0341-94 03 31.* 🕐 *8:30–11:45am, 2:30–5:30pm daily.* 🔒

A PROMONTORY on the northeastern shore of the lake conceals this extraordinary abbey built by Cluniac monks in the 11th century. The exterior of Romanesque San Nicolao is adorned with small arches and pilasters. There are 13th-century frescoes in the apse. The bell tower dates from 1700 and the cloister (1252–7) has sculpted capitals with fantastic figures and 13th-century frescoes.

Bellano **9**

Lecco 🏠 *3,400.* 🛈 APT, Via Nazario Sauro 6, Lecco *(0341-36 93 90).*

I N THE MIDDLE AGES Bellano was the summer residence of Milanese bishops and it has preserved its medieval character. Among houses with wrought-iron coats of arms is the church of Santi Nazaro, Celso e Giorgio, the work of Campionese masters (14th century). Santa Marta houses a *Pietà* executed in 1518. However, the main appeal of Bellano is the Orrido, a deep gorge created by the Pioverna torrent.

🏔 Orrido
🕐 *Jun–Sep: 10am–10:30pm daily; Oct–May: 10am–1pm, 3–6pm Tue–Sat; 10am–6pm Sun & Mon.* 🅿

Varenna **10**

Lecco. 🏠 *800.* 🛈 Pro Loco, Piazza Venini 1 *(0341-83 03 67).*

T HIS SPLENDID VILLAGE of ancient Roman origin, with a perfectly intact medieval layout, was a haven for the inhabitants of Isola Comacina when the citizens of Como burned the island (1169). In the town centre, 14th-century San Giorgio has an altarpiece by Pietro Brentani (1467), while Santa Marta houses the parish art gallery. Varenna is famous for **Villa Cipressi**, with its terraced garden, and **Villa Monastero**, built over a Cistercian monastery. Now a conference centre, the villa has preserved some of its original furnishings and has an elegant garden. All around the town were quarries for black Varenna marble – used for the flooring in the Milan Duomo. Since 1921 Mandello del Lario has been the home of the **Moto Guzzi factory**, with a Motorcycle Museum.

🏛 Villa Cipressi
Via IV Novembre 18. 📞 *0341-83 01 13.* 🕐 *(garden) Mar–Sep: 9am–7pm (6pm Mar–Jun) daily.* ⬤ *Oct–Feb.* 🅿

🏛 Villa Monastero
Via Polvani 2. 📞 *0341-83 01 29.* 🕐 *(garden) Mar–Sep: 9am–7pm (6pm Mar–Jun) daily.* ⬤ *Oct–Feb.* 🅿

🏛 Museo Moto Guzzi della Motocicletta
Via Parodi 57, Mandello del Lario.
📞 0341-70 91 11. 🕐 3–4pm
Mon–Fri. ⬤ hols.

Lecco ⓫

🚹 46,000. 🛈 APT, Via Nazario
Sauro 6 (0341-36 93 90).

L ECCO LIES ON the southern
tip of the arm of the lake
of the same name. It was
inhabited in prehistoric times
and fortified in the 6th century
AD. In the 1300s it was taken
over by Azzone Visconti, who
built the Ponte Vecchio.

Manzoni set his novel
*I Promessi Sposi (The Betroth-
ed)* here. Mementos of his life
can be found in his childhood
home, the **Casa Natale di
Manzoni** at Caleotto, which
also houses the Galleria Com-
unale d'Arte. In the centre are
the Teatro della Società (1844)
and San Nicolò, whose baptistery chapel has 14th–15th-
century frescoes. The **Museo
di Storia Naturale** in the
18th-century **Palazzo
Belgioioso** is also of interest.
Sites described by Manzoni
in his novel have been identified, including the castle of
the Unnamed at Vercurago,
and Lucia's home at Olate.
Near Civate is Romanesque
San Pietro al Monte (12th
century), with 11th–12th-
century frescoes and reliefs
with scenes from the Passion.
A turn-off on the road to
Bellagio leads to the Madonna
del Ghisallo sanctuary.

**The Italian writer Manzoni,
author of *The Betrothed***

A drawing room in Villa Serbelloni overlooking the lake

🏛 Casa Natale di Manzoni
Via Guanella 1. 📞 0341-48 12 47.
🕐 9:30am–5:30pm Tue–Sun. 🏷 ♿
🏛 Palazzo Belgioioso and Museo di Storia Naturale
Corso Matteotti 32. 📞 0341-48
12 48. 🕐 9:30am–2pm
Tue–Sun. ⬤ 1 Jan, Easter,
15 Aug, 1 May, 25 Dec. 🏷 ♿
🔒 San Pietro al Monte
Civate. 📞 0341-55 15 76.
🕐 9am–3pm Sun
(booking necessary
Mon–Fri).

Bellagio ⓬

Como. 🚹 3,050.
🛈 Piazza G Mazzini
12 (031-95 02 04).

K NOWN SINCE
antiquity for its fine
climate and scenery, Bellagio
still has its medieval layout,
with stepped alleyways. It
became the site of splendid
noble villas in the 18th century
and then became a famous
resort town with numerous
hotels in the 19th century.
Among the attractive residences, the loveliest are **Villa
Serbelloni** and **Villa Melzi
d'Eril**. The former was set
in the middle of a park with
woods and rose gardens by
the Serbelloni, and in 1870
became a hotel which
numbered Winston Churchill
and J F Kennedy among its
famous guests. The Neo-
Classical Villa Melzi was
built in 1810 by Giocondo
Albertolli. The interior is not

open to the public, but the
Museo Archeologico, the
chapel and the gardens are.
Near the town are
the 18th-century
Trivulzio and Trotti
villas. Do not miss the
12th-century San Gia-
como, with its pulpit
decorated with symbols
of the Evangelists.

**One of the statues
at Villa Melzi d'Eril**

🏛 Villa Serbelloni
Piazza Garibaldi (book at
IAT). 🕐 11am–4pm
Tue–Sun Apr–Oct. 🏷
🏛 Villa Melzi d'Eril
Lungolario Marconi.
📞 031-95 03 18.
🕐 9am–6:30pm
Apr–Oct. 🏷

Torno ⓭

Como. 🚹 1,100. 🛈 APT, Piazza
Cavour 17, Como (031-26 97 12).

T HE VILLAGE OF TORNO boasts
the churches of Santa
Tecla, which has a beautiful
marble portal dating from
1480, and the 14th-century
San Giovanni, with its
remarkable Renaissance door.
However, Torno is known
most of all for the Villa
Pliniana, built in 1573 (and
attributed to Tibaldi) for
Count Anguissola, the
governor of Como. The villa
is surrounded by a park and
stands right by the lake. The
writers Foscolo, Stendhal and
Byron, and composer Rossini
were all guests here.

Lake Garda

ITALY'S LARGEST LAKE was created by glaciation. The scenery is varied, with steep, rugged cliffs at the northern end and softer hills southwards, where the basin widens and Mediterranean flora prevails. Over the centuries the praises of Lake Garda have been sung by such greats as Catullus, Dante and Goethe, and today it caters for luxury holidays and tour groups alike. Garda is an ideal spot for windsurfing and sailing, and it hosts famous regattas such as the Centomiglia.

Remains of mosaics in the Roman villa at Desenzano del Garda

★ Desenzano del Garda
This is one of the liveliest and most popular towns on Lake Garda. Above, one of the frescoes in the Roman villa, built in the 4th century and discovered in 1921 ❷

Villa Bettoni near Bogliaco (1756) has elegant frescoed rooms with masterpieces by Reni and Canaletto, as well as a garden with a nympheum.

★ Gardone Riviera
Near this pleasant tourist resort is the Vittoriale degli Italiani, where the writer Gabriele D'Annunzio lived from 1921 to 1938. It embodies the decadence of which this poet and novelist was the last exponent ❺

Bog

Toscolano Maderno ❻

Gardone Riviera ❺ · Fasano

Salò ❹

The Valtènesi and San Felice del Benaco ❸ · Isola di Garda

Manerba

Sirmione ❶

San Pietro in Mavino

Castelletto di Brenzone ❷

★ Sirmione
This Roman villa, which extends over a large area and was once thought to be the residence of the Latin poet Catullus, is one of the most impressive examples of an ancient Roman dwelling in Northern Italy ❶

KEY

- - - Ferry routes

⛴ Ferry service

☀ Viewpoint

0 kilometres 5

0 miles 5

Limone sul Garda
The abundance of citrus trees grown here is supposedly the reason why the locals have the longest life expectancy in Italy **7**

8 Riva del Garda

Torbole

Limone sul Garda 7

9 Malcésine

Campione del Garda
Tignale

Isola di Trimelone

Argnano

Brenzone

Castelletto di Brenzone

Pai

At Torbole, now a surfers' paradise, Venetian ships – which defeated the Visconti in 1440 – were reassembled after being transported along the Val d'Adige.

Punta San Vigilio was named after the bishop from Trent who brought Christianity to the area in the 4th century.

10 Torri del Benáco

The Camaldolite Hermitage
(16th century), which only recently allowed women visitors, has a splendid panoramic view.

Punta San Vigilio

11 Garda

Bardolino 12

Lazise

14 Gardaland

13 Peschiera del Garda

SIGHTS AT A GLANCE

Bardolino and Lazise **12**
Desenzano del Garda **2**
Garda **11**
Gardaland **14**
Gardone Riviera **5**
Limone sul Garda **7**
Malcesine **9**
Peschiera del Garda **13**
Riva del Garda **8**
Salò **4**
Sirmione **1**
Torri del Benaco **10**
Toscolano Maderno **6**
The Valtènesi and San Felice del Benaco **3**

Torri del Benaco
The economy of this small town, which thanks to its strategic position controls access to the upper lake region, is based on tourism and fishing. The townspeople have enjoyed special fishing privileges since the 1400s **10**

STAR SIGHTS

★ **Sirmione**

★ **Gardone Riviera**

★ **Desenzano del Garda**

Sirmione ❶

Brescia. 🏠 *5,100.*
ℹ️ Viale Marconi 2 *(030-91 61 14).*

ROMAN SIRMIO lay in the
hinterland and only the
villa quarter faced the lake. In
the 13th century the Scaligeri
lords of Verona turned it into
a fortress to defend Lake
Garda. In 1405 Sirmione was
taken over by Venice, which
then ruled until the 18th century. The main focus of the
town is the **Rocca Scaligera**,
a castle built by Mastino I
della Scala (13th century), the
inner basin of which served as
shelter for the Veronese boats.
Roman and medieval plaques
are in the entrance arcade.
 Fifteenth-century Santa
Maria Maggiore, built over a
pagan temple, has a Roman
column in its porch, while the
campanile was a Scaligera
tower. The interior has 15th-
and 16th-century frescoes and
a 15th-century Madonna.
 The famous **spas** use the
water from the Boiola spring,
known since 1546. San Pietro
in Mavino, rebuilt in 1320,
boasts fine 13th–16th-century
frescoes. Sirmione is also
famous for the so-called
Grotte di Catullo, a huge
Roman residence built in the
1st centuries BC–AD. The
most evocative rooms are
the Grotta del Cavallo, the
Cryptoporticus and the pool.
The Sala della Trifora del
Paradiso and Sala dei Giganti
overlook the lake. The Antiquarium has finds from the
villa, including a mosaic of
a seascape and a portrait of
Catullus (1st century BC).

🏰 **Rocca Scaligera**
Piazza Castello. 📞 *030-91 64 68.*
🕐 *8:30am–4:30pm Tue–Sun
(until 6pm Sun from Apr).*
⬤ *hols.* 📷
Terme Catullo (Spa)
Piazza Castello 12.
📞 *030-990 49 33.*
🏛 **Grotte di Catullo**
Via Catullo 📞 *030-91 61 57.*
🕐 *Mar–14 Oct: 9am–7pm Tue–
Sun; 15 Oct–Feb: 8:30am–4:30pm
Tue–Sun.* ⬤ *Mon (Tue if Mon is
hol).* 📷

***Christ Enthroned with Angels
and Saints**, San Pietro in Mavino*

Desenzano
del Garda ❷

Brescia. 🏠 *21,000.* ℹ️ Via Porto
Vecchio 34 *(030-914 15 10).*
🏷 *antiques, 1st Sun of month
(except for Jan & Aug).*

PROBABLY FOUNDED by the
Romans on a site inhabited
since prehistoric times, Desenzano was taken over by
Venice in the 15th century,
when it became the leading

lakeside town. Since the 19th
century it has been a tourist
resort. The heart of the town
centre is Piazza Malvezzi,
home to an antiques market
known for its silverware and
prints. The 16th-century town
hall and Provveditore Veneto
buildings are also here. In the
Duomo (16th century) is a
fine *Last Supper* by Tiepolo.
The **Museo Civico Archeologico**, in the cloister of Santa
Maria de Senioribus, contains
displays of Bronze Age finds
and the oldest known
wooden plough (2000 BC).
 The **Villa Romana** was
built in the 4th century AD
and rediscovered in 1921.
It had been covered by a
landslide, which preserved
some lovely mosaics with
geometric motifs such as the
Good Shepherd and *Psyche
and Cupids*. Finds from the
villa are in the Antiquarium.

🏠 **Duomo**
Piazza Duomo. 📞 *030-914 18 49.*
🕐 *8–11:30am, 4–6:30pm daily.*
🏛 **Museo Civico
Archeologico**
Via Santa Maria. 📞 *030-914 45 29
or 030-999 42 75.* 🕐 *3–7pm Tue,
Fri–Sun, hols.* ⬤ *Mon, Wed, Thu.*
🏛 **Villa Romana**
📞 *030-914 35 47.*
🕐 *Mar–14 Oct: 8:30am–7:30pm
Tue–Sun; 15 Oct–Feb: 9am–4:30pm
Tue–Sun.*
⬤ *Mon (Tue if Mon is hol).* 📷

The Valtènesi
and San Felice
del Benaco ❸

Brescia. 🏠 *2,500.*
ℹ️ Via Portovecchio 34, Desenzano
del Garda *(030-914 15 10).*

THE AREA BETWEEN Desenzano
and Salò, called Valtènesi, is
rich in medieval churches and
castles. At Padenghe, the Rocca
(9th–10th century) is reached
by a drawbridge. Nearby is
12th-century Sant'Emiliano.
The houses in Moniga del
Garda are protected by a 10th-
century wall with turrets. Here
stands Santa Maria della Neve,
built in the 14th century. The
Rocca di Manerba del Garda
(8th century) lies on a headland over the lake where a

The Rocca Scaligera at Sirmione, with its tower and battlements

Cappella del Santissimo Sacramento, Salò Duomo (18th century)

castle once stood. The ruins have become part of a regional park. At Solarolo, the 15th-century Santissima Trinità has a fresco cycle with the *Last Judgment*, while prehistoric finds from this area are in the **Museo Archeologico della Valtènesi** at Montinelle. The bay between the Punta Belvedere and Punta San Fermo headlands is dominated by San Felice del Benaco. To the south is the Madonna del Carmine sanctuary (1452). In the town centre the parish church has a *Madonna and Saints* by Romanino. Opposite Punta San Fermo is Isola di Garda. Tradition has it that the Franciscans in the 13th-century monastery introduced citrus fruit cultivation to Lake Garda.

🏛 Museo Archeologico della Valtènesi
Piazzale Simonati, Montinelle.
📞 0365-55 10 07. ◻ summer: 7:30–9pm Tue–Sat, 10am–noon Sun; winter: 2–4pm Sat; 10am–noon Sun. ● Mon.

Salò ❹

Brescia. 🏔 10,200. 🚌 Lungolago Zanardelli, Palazzo Municipale (0365-214 23).

A FORMER ROMAN town, in 1337 Salò became the seat of the Consiglio della Magnifica Patria, the governing body of 42 towns which met in the palazzo built by Sansovino in 1524 (now the Museo Archeologico). The late Gothic cathedral has a *Madonna and Saints* by Romanino (1529) and an altarpiece from 1476. Palazzo Fantoni is home to the Biblioteca dell'Ateneo di Salò and **Museo del Nastro Azzurro**, a military museum with items from 1796 to 1945. Palazzo Terzi-Martinengo at Barbarano was the seat of Mussolini's Salò puppet government.

🏛 Museo del Nastro Azzurro
Via Fantoni 49. 📞 0365-208 04. ◻ 5–7pm Mon–Fri, 5–8pm Sat; Jun–Aug & hols: 10am–1pm, 3–5pm; Sun in winter: 10am–noon, 3–5pm.

Gardone Riviera ❺

Brescia. 🏔 2,500. 🚌 Corso Repubblica 39 (0365-203 47).

B OASTING THE HIGHEST winter temperatures in Northern Italy, Gardone Riviera became a fashionable tourist resort in the late 19th century because of its mild dry climate, which is beneficial for those suffering from lung ailments. Two celebrated villas are Villa Alba and Villa Fiordaliso.

Gardone is also famous for the **Vittoriale degli Italiani**, Gabriele D'Annunzio's residence, where the poet collected over 10,000 objects including works of art, books and mementos, which he later donated to the state. In the garden are the Prioria, his residence, the Schifamondo with mementos, the Auditorium and the Mausoleum. On display are objects related to his exploits during and after World War I, such as his motor boat and aeroplane.

Another attraction is the **Giardino Botanico Hruska**, a fine botanic garden with over 2,000 Alpine, Mediterranean and subtropical species of plants.

D'Annunzio, who lived out his days at the Vittoriale degli Italiani

🏛 Vittoriale degli Italiani
Gardone. 📞 0365-29 65 11. ◻ Apr–Sep: 8:30am–8pm daily; Oct–Mar: 9am–5pm Mon–Fri, 9am–5:30pm Sat & Sun. ◙ **House** ◻ Apr–Sep: 9:30am–7pm Tue–Sun; Oct–Mar: 9am–1pm, 2–5pm Tue–Sun. ● Mon. ◙ ◙ ◙

🌿 Giardino Botanico Hruska
Via Motta 2. 📞 0365-203 47 (APT Gardone). ◻ 15 Mar–15 Oct: 9am–6pm daily. ◙

VINES, CHURCHES AND CASTLES

The Valtènesi area is known for its vineyards, where the rosé wine Chiaretto della Riviera del Garda is produced. A visit to the wineries here offers a chance to visit the inland region of this side of Lake Garda and also see the medieval fortresses of Soiano del Lago, Puegnago sul Garda and Polpenazze del Garda. In the cemetery of this last-mentioned village is the Romanesque church of San Pietro in Lucone, with its 15th-century frescoes depicting the lives of St Peter and the Apostles.

The medieval church of San Pietro in Lucone

Canvas by Celesti in the Santi Pietro e Paolo parish church, Toscolano

Toscolano Maderno **6**

Brescia. 🏔 *6,700.* 🚌 Lungolago Zanardelli 18, Maderno *(0365-641 330).*

THIS TOWN IS MADE UP OF THE two villages of Toscolano and Maderno. Sights of interest at Maderno are the Romanesque church of Sant'Andrea, with a panel by Paolo Veneziano, and the parish church of Sant'Ercolano, with paintings by Veronese and Andrea Celesti. Here the Gonzaga family built the Palazzina del Serraglio (17th century) for Vincenzo I's amorous assignations. Toscolano, ancient Benacum, was the largest town on Lake Garda in Roman times. At Santa Maria del Benaco, with 16th-century frescoes, archaeologists found Roman and Etruscan objects and the ruins of a mosaic-decorated villa (1st century AD). The parish church of Santi Pietro e Paolo has 22 canvases by Andrea Celesti. Gargnano boasts San Giacomo di Calino (11th–12th century) and San Francesco (1289), whose cloister has Venetian arches. Other sights are Villa Feltrinelli, Mussolini's residence during the Republic of Salò, and Villa Bettoni.

Limone sul Garda **7**

Brescia. 🏔 *990.* 🚌 Lungolago Zanardelli 18, Maderno *(0365-641 330).*

KNOWN FOR ITS mild climate, Limone may have been named after the lemon tree terraces (no longer used) typical of this area. Or the name may derive from *Limen* (border), since the Austrian frontier was here until 1918. In the town centre are the 15th-century church of San Rocco and a parish church (1685), with canvases by Celesti. Near Tignale is the **Montecastello Sanctuary** (13th–14th century) with a *Coronation of the Virgin* (14th century) and medallions by the school of Palma il Giovane. Towards Tremosine is the Brasa river gorge, in a panoramic setting.

🏛 **Montecastello Sanctuary**
Via Chiesa, Tignale. ◯ *9am–6pm daily mid-Mar–Oct.* 📞 *0365-730 20.*

Riva del Garda **8**

Trento. 🏔 *13,500.* 🚌 Giardini di Porta Orientale 8 *(0464-55 44 44).*

SITUATED AT a strategic point on the northern tip of the lake, in the Trentino region, Riva was under Austrian rule until 1918. The Rocca and Torre Apponale (13th century) were built to defend the town; an angel, the town symbol, stands on top of the tower. In the square opposite are Palazzo Pretorio (1370) and Palazzo del Provveditore (1482). The 12th-century Rocca is the home of the **Museo Civico**, with 14th–20th-century paintings. Santa Maria Assunta has two canvases by Piazzetta, while the octagonal, richly

frescoed Inviolata (1603) has works by Palma il Giovane. The impressive waterfalls of the Varone river, above Riva, are 80 m (262 ft) high.
Nearby Torbole was described by Goethe in *Italian Journey* and is a popular spot for sailing.

🏛 **Museo Civico**
Piazza Battisti 3. 📞 *0464-57 38 69.* ◯ *Mar–Oct: 9:30am–5:30pm Tue–Sun (10pm Jul & Aug).* ● *Nov–Feb.*

Malcesine **9**

Verona. 🏔 *3,500.* 🚌 Via del Capitanato 6/8 *(045-740 00 44).*

ONE OF THE MOST fascinating towns along the lake shore, Malcesine stands on a stretch of impervious rock, hence the name *mala silex*, inaccessible rock. The 12th-century **Castello** was rebuilt by the Scaligeri of Verona in 1277. It houses the Museo di Storia Naturale del Garda e del Monte Baldo, the lake's natural history museum, which among other things shows how the Venetians transported ships to Torbole (1438–40). The parish church contains a 16th-century *Deposition*. Towering above Malcesine is Monte Baldo (2,218 m, 7,275 ft), accessible by cable car, with nature trails and stunning views.

Deposition (15th century), Malcesine parish church

The Legend of Maria (c.1614–20) by Martino Teofilo Polacco, in the Inviolata at Riva del Garda

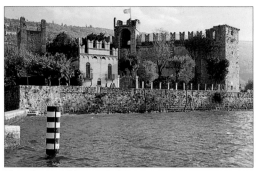

The castle at Torri del Benaco, built in 1393

Castello Scaligero
Via Castello. ☎ 045-657 03 33.
🕐 Apr–Oct: 9:30am–6:30pm daily;
Dec–Mar: 10am–4pm Sat & Sun.
● 3, 4 Jan; Nov; 25, 28, 29 Dec.

Torri del Benaco ⓾

Verona. 👥 2,500.
🛈 Lungolago Regina Adelaide,
Garda (045-627 03 84).

R OMAN CASTRUM TURRIUM was
a major stop between Riva
and Garda and has preserved
the typical grid plan. Due to
its strategic position, Torri was
fortified and a castle was built;
it is now a **museum**, with old
farm tools and prehistoric
finds. Santissima Trinità has
some 15th-century frescoes.

🏛 Museo del Castello
Via Fratelli Lavanda. ☎ 045-629 61 11.
🕐 Apr–May & Oct: 9:30am–12:30pm
daily; Jun–Sep: 9am–1pm, 2:30–
7:30pm daily; Dec: 2:30–5:30pm Sun.

Garda ⓫

Verona. 👥 3,500. 🛈 Lungolago
Regina Adelaide (045-627 03 84).

B UILT AROUND A SMALL BAY,
Garda was one of the
major towns along the lake,
controlling the southern
basin. Its name, then given to
the lake as well, comes from
the German *Warten* (fortress),
referring to the wall around
the historic centre with its
small port, accessible through
the Torre dell'Orologio tower
and gate. Among the historic
buildings are the 15th-century
Palazzo del Capitano, the
Iosa, the dock of Palazzo Car-

lotti designed by Sanmicheli,
and **Santa Maria Maggiore**
(18th century) with a painting
by Palma il Giovane and a
15th-century cloister. At the
new port is Villa Albertini,
with an English-style park,
while at Punta San Vigilio is
Villa Guarienti (1542), designed by Sanmicheli, where the
WWF offers a tour of the
Bronze Age rock engravings.

🏠 Santa Maria Maggiore
Piazzale Roma. ☎ 045-725 68 25.

Bardolino
and Lazise ⓬

Verona. 👥 5,900. 🛈 Piazzale Aldo
Moro (045-721 00 78).
🏺 antiques, 3rd Sun of month.

T HE CORNICELLO AND Mira-
bello headlands enclosing
Bardolino made it a natural
harbour. Originally it was a
prehistoric settlement and
then became a Roman camp.
The historic centre
has two early
medieval churches,
San Zeno and San
Severo. The first
still has its 9th-
century Carolingian
cruciform structure.
Romanesque San
Severo was founded
in the 9th century
but rebuilt in the
12th. It has 12th–
13th-century
frescoes with
battle scenes and
episodes from the
Bible, and a 10th-
century crypt.
Among the civic

buildings is the Loggia
Rambaldi, in the Rambaldi
family palazzo. Bardolino is
also famous for its wine.
Lazise also boasted a
prehistoric civilization. A
castle was built in the 11th
century and the lords of
Verona erected the walls in
the 1300s. The 16th-century
Venetian Customs House is all
that remains of the old harbour. Next to it is San Nicolò
(12th century), with Giotto
school frescoes. Near Colà
a Spa was recently opened.

Terme di Villa Cedri
Piazza di Sopra 4, Località Colà di
Lazise. ☎ 045-759 09 88.

Peschiera
del Garda ⓭

Verona. 👥 8,700. 🛈 Piazzale
Betteloni 15 (045-755 03 81).

P ESCHIERA HAS retained its
military image more than
any other town on Lake
Garda. The old town lies on
an island surrounded by a
star-shaped wall – "a fortress
beautiful and strong", says
Dante. The walls were reinforced by the Scaligeri of
Verona, rebuilt for the new
Venetian rulers by Sanmicheli
in 1556, and completed with
two forts by the Austrians two
centuries later. Besides the
frescoed 18th-century San
Martino, there is the 16th-
century Madonna del Frassino
sanctuary, with a beautiful
frescoed cloister.

San Zeno in Bardolino, crowned by a tower,
containing traces of its original frescoes

Gardaland ⑭

THIS THEME PARK was opened in 1975 and is one of the largest in Italy (500,000 sq m, 600,000 sq yds). The 38 attractions range from the rollercoaster to reconstructions of the pyramids and a jungle, the PalaBlù dolphin pool and the Village of the Elves, all ideal for families with children. The fun park facilities are good, including a wide range of refreshments, theme shops and souvenir photos. At busy times queues are kept informed about the length of the wait.

The canoe safari, one of the many attractions

PalaBlù
Italy's largest dolphin pool: four dolphins perform acrobatic tricks in front of the crowd.

Space Vertigo
There's a bacteriological alarm in the space station – everyone must escape! The only hope is to jump into space at top speed from a 40-m (131-ft) high tower. Thrills galore for everyone.

Arab Souk

Top Spin

Dinosaur Island
On a remote island – and without human interference – dinosaurs have continued to exist. You can join an expedition to study and help save them.

Monorail station

The floating tree trunks of the Colorado Boat confront the canyon rapids.

Magic Mountain
This super-fast rollercoaster is one of the most famous rides of all, with two hairpin bends and two death-defying spins. Only for the most intrepid of visitors.

The Valley of the Kings
Lovers of ancient Egypt can go into the temple of Abu Simbel, and discover the pharaohs' secrets among hieroglyphs, archaeologists and a mysterious green ray.

VISITORS' CHECKLIST

Peschiera del Garda. **☎** 045-644
97 77. **◯** 23 Mar–21 Jun & 11
Sep–30 Sep: 9:30am–6:30pm
daily; 22 Jun–10 Sep 9am–
midnight daily; Oct: 9:30am–
6:30pm Sat–Sun. **●** Nov–Mar.
▨ (free for **♿** and children
under 1m tall). Cameras for hire.
Weather report: **☎** 045-644 97
77, 045-644 95 55. **▮▮ ▮▮ ▮▮**
W www.gardaland.it

★ **Blue Tornado**
*Even more exciting than the
rollercoaster, this attraction
offers you the chance to
experience first-hand
the thrills of piloting
an American
fighter plane.*

Jungle Rapids
*Here you climb aboard
a rubber dinghy and
are taken over the rapids
of a canyon, past a
volcano, into the heart
of mysterious and
magical Southeast Asia
with its temples.*

★ **Fantasy Kingdom**
*Children will love this! The
talking trees, singing animals
and puppet show will keep
them entertained for hours.*

Prezzemolo
*Gardaland's mascot, Prezzemolo
(Parsley) the dragon, is always
at the park entrance to welcome
all new visitors.*

0 metres		100

0 yards		100

STAR FEATURES

★ **Blue Tornado**

★ **Fantasy Kingdom**

The stepped Motta ascent, the setting for the Ortafiori festivities in April and May

Lago d'Orta

🛈 APTL, Via Panoramica, Orta–San Giulio *(0322-90 56 14)*. 🚉 FS Novara-Domodossola line (848-88 80 88). 🚢 Nav. Lago d'Orta (0322-84 48 62).

LAKE ORTA, or Cusio, is the westernmost lake in the lower Alps region, characterized by soft hills and scenery. Villages are dotted around the lake, along the shore or perched among green terracing. The Mottarone, a ski resort, and the other mountains surrounding the lake offer attractive hiking trails.

As far back as the 1700s, Orta was a tourist attraction and many villas were built in large parks. The chief town is Orta San Giulio, on a promontory in the middle of the lake. The village alleyways wind around Piazza Motta, on which lies the Palazzetto della Comunità (1582) and where the stepped Motta ascent begins. Opposite the square is the island of San Giulio, converted to Christianity by the Greek deacon Julius, who built the 4th-century **basilica**. The church was restored in the 11th–12th centuries and has a 12th-century Romanesque marble pulpit and

15th-century frescoes. Next door is the Palazzo del Vescovo (16th–18th century). Another sight is the **Sacro Monte**, a sanctuary built in 1591 on the rise above Orta. Dedicated to St Francis, it consists of 20 chapels with 17th–18th-century terracotta statues and frescoes. Opposite, perched over a steep quarry, is the Madonna del Sasso sanctuary (1748).

On the northern tip of the lake is Omegna, whose medieval quarter boasts the late Romanesque collegiate church of Sant'Ambrogio.

At Quarna there is the **Museo Etnografico e dello Strumento a Fiato**, with displays of wind instruments, made in this village for centuries. Other interesting villages are Vacciago di Ameno, with the Calderara Collection of contemporary art, featuring 327 international avant-garde works of the 1950s and 1960s; Gozzano, with the church of San Giuliano (18th century), Palazzo Vescovile and the seminary; and, lastly, Torre di Buccione. San Maurizio d'Opaglio has a curious attraction: a museum devoted to the production of taps.

Figure on the pulpit, San Giulio

🔒 **Basilica di San Giulio**
Isola di San Giulio.
APTL, ring road, Orta San Giulio *(0322-90 56 14)*. 🕐 9:30am–12:15pm, 2–6:45pm Tue–Sat; 9:30–10:45am, 2–6:45pm (5:45pm solar time) Sun, hols; 11am–12:15pm Mon.

🔒 **Sacro Monte**
Via Sacro Monte. 📞 0322-91 19 60. **Chapels** 🕐 summer: 9:30am–6pm daily; winter: 9:30am–4pm daily (5pm hols).

🏛 **Museo Etnografico e dello Strumento Musicale a Fiato**
Quarna Sotto. 📞 0323-82 60 01. 🕐 Jul–mid-Sep: 10:30am–noon, 3–7pm Tue–Sun. ⬤ Mon.

Lago di Varese

🛈 IAT, Via Carrobbio 2, Varese *(0332-28 36 04)*. 🚉 Ferrovie Nord Milano, Milan-Laveno line to Gavirate (02-202 22). 🚌 Autolinee Zani (0332-73 11 10).

THIS LAKE BASIN was created by glacial movement during the Quaternary era. It offers pleasant scenery, with rolling hills and the Campo dei Fiori massif. In prehistoric times it was inhabited by a prehistoric civilization, the important remains of which were found on the island of Isolino Virginia (which can be reached from Biandronno), where they are on display at the **Museo Preistorico**.

Part of the lake shore is now protected as the Brabbia marsh nature reserve. Not far away, at Cazzago Brabbia, are ice-houses used to conserve fish in the 18th century. On the northern tip of the lake,

Fishing boats along the shores of the Lago di Varese

at Voltorre di Gavirate, the church of **San Michele** is worth a visit. It was part of a 12th-century Cluniac monastery and is now used for exhibitions. On the slopes of Campo dei Fiori you can see the lake of the **Sacro Monte** di Varese, a sanctuary made up of 14 17th-century chapels with frescoes and life-size statues narrating the Mysteries of the Rosary.

🏛 **Museo Preistorico**
Isolino Virginia.
📞 *0332-28 15 90 (Musei Civici di Varese).* ⏰ *Apr–Nov: 2–6pm Sat & Sun (Oct: 2–6pm Sun).* 🎫
⛪ **San Michele**
Voltorre di Gavirate. 📞 *0332-74 36 13.* ⏰ *during exhibitions.*
⛪ **Sacro Monte**
Varese. 📞 *0332-83 03 73.*
⏰ *daily.*

Lago d'Iseo

ℹ IAT, Lungolago Marconi 26, Iseo *(030-98 02 09).* 🚉 *FS to Brescia, then Ferrovie Nord Milano (02-84 47 75 00).* 🚌 *SAB (035-28 9 0 11).* ⛴ *Navigazione Lago d'Iseo (035-97 14 83).*

LAKE ISEO, ALSO KNOWN AS Sebino, extends between the provinces of Bergamo and Brescia. It is the seventh largest lake in Italy and the fourth in Lombardy, created by a glacier descending from the Val Camonica. The chief towns here are Iseo, Sarnico, Lovere and Pisogne. The historic centre of Iseo has retained its medieval character, with the church of

Sant'Andrea (1150), the Neo-Classical interior of which contains a painting by Hayez. Next to this is the tomb of the feudal landowner Giacomo Oldofredi and, on a hill at the entrance to the town, the Castello degli Oldofredi (both built in the 14th century), which in 1585 became a Capuchin monastery. At Provaglio d'Iseo there is the San Pietro in Lamosa Cluniac monastery, founded in 1030. Its 11th–12th-century Roman-esque church has frescoes by the school of Romanino. Sarnico, at the southern end of the lake, was an important commercial and industrial town. Among the Art Nou-veau houses built here by Giuseppe Sommaruga is Villa Faccanoni (1912), one of the best examples of this style.

The road that follows the western side of the lake rounds the Corno headland, which has a fine views of Monte Isola, the largest lake island in Europe, with its typical villages, dominated by the Madonna della Ceriola sanctuary and the 15th-century Rocca Oldofredi. At the northern end of the lake is Lovere, which has medieval tower-houses.

On the lakeside is the **Galleria dell'Accademia Tadini**, featuring fine works of art ranging from the 14th to the 20th century, including Jacopo Bellini, Strozzi, Tie-polo, Hayez and Canova. The church of Santa Maria in Valvendra (1483) has paint-ings by Floriano Ferramola

The Piramidi di Zone pinnacles, some reaching 30 m (98 ft)

and Moretto and a 16th-century wooden altarpiece on the high altar. At Pisogne is Santa Maria della Neve (15th century), with scenes of the Passion frescoed by Roma-nino (1534). From here you can go to the Val Camonica rock engravings park. The lake is also famous for its lovely scenery, including the Piramidi di Zone, pinnacles protected from erosion by the rock massif above them, and the Torbiere d'Iseo, a marshy area with peat bogs which is now a nature reserve.

🏛 **Galleria dell'Accademia Tadini**
Via Tadini, Lovere. 📞 *035-96 27 80.*
⏰ *mid-Apr–mid-Oct: 3–6pm Tue–Sat; 10am–noon, 3–6pm Sun & hols.*
⬤ *Mon.* 🎫

Lago d'Idro

ℹ Pro Loco, Via Trento 15, Idro *(0365-832 24).* 🚌 *SIA (02-86 46 23 50).*

THE HIGHEST LARGE LAKE in Lombardy (368 m, 1,207 ft above sea level) was turned into an artificial basin in 1932 to provide irrigation and hydroelectricity. It is domi-nated by the Rocca di Anfo, a fortress with a splendid panoramic view that was built over older fortifications by the Venetians in 1450, and then rebuilt many times. From here you can reach Bagolino, with its charming stone houses and San Rocco (1478), which contains a fresco cycle by Giovan Pietro da Cemmo.

Rocca Oldofredi, Monte Isola, the Martinengo residence since the 1500s

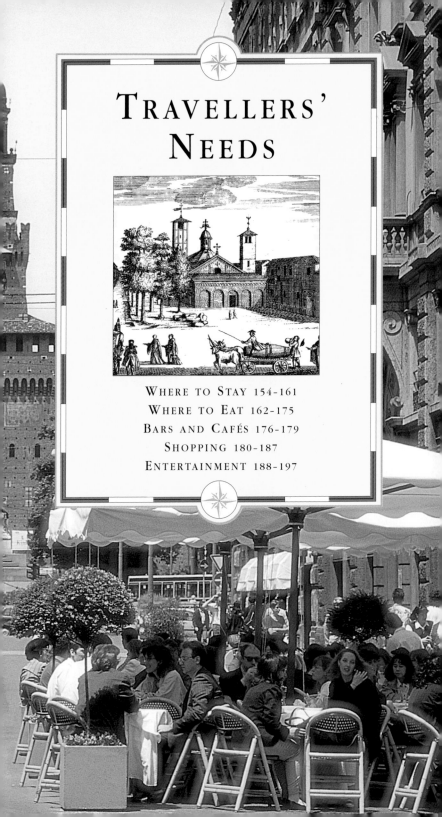

TRAVELLERS' NEEDS

WHERE TO STAY 154–161
WHERE TO EAT 162–175
BARS AND CAFÉS 176–179
SHOPPING 180–187
ENTERTAINMENT 188–197

WHERE TO STAY

I T IS NOT EASY TO FIND atmospheric hotels or charming guesthouses in Milan because the city caters mostly to businessmen and women and the majority of hotels are therefore geared to their needs, with working facilities in the rooms and public areas. This type of accommodation comes in the medium–high price range and usually offers either private parking or nearby garage facilities. The four-star hotels not only have prestigious restaurants that are among the best in the city, but may also have lovely inner gardens not seen from the street. It is best to book

**Porter, Hotel Palace,
Milan (see p159)**

accommodation well in advance, especially during the international fashion shows (held in March and October) and the many top trade fairs. At the lakes, on the other hand, the choice ranges from guesthouses to fascinating historic hotels, which have drawn visitors and celebrities from all over the world since the 19th century. The most luxurious are in charming 17th- and 18th-century villas, with flower-filled terraces, health clubs and heated pools. For more detailed information regarding accommodation in Milan and at the lakes, see pages 156–161.

CHOOSING A HOTEL

T HE ITALIAN FOR HOTEL is *albergo*. A *pensione* or *locanda* theoretically indicates a more modest guest-house, but in practice the distinctions are quite blurred.

Most of the hotels in Milan are concentrated in the Buenos Aires-Stazione Centrale area, near the Fiera and in the Città Studi district. The first group is situated for the most part in Piazza della Repubblica and near the main railway station, which is practical for visitors on a short stay. Some of the more interesting hotels are the **Buenos Aires** *(see p158)*, the **Palace** *(see p159)* and the **Duca di**

The elegant Four Seàsons Hotel in Milan (see p159)

Milano *(see p159)* – both 5-star – and the **Principe di Savoia** *(see p159)*, in 1930s style. Around the Fiera, large hotels cater for business visitors. The **Regency** *(see p157)* is smaller, with a warm atmosphere. At Città Studi you can find clean, inexpensive 2-star hotels: two examples are the **Aspromonte** *(see p158)* and the **San Francisco** *(see p158)*.

In the historic centre a few charming, small hotels remain. The **Antica Locanda Solferino** *(see p158)* has a family atmosphere. The **Grand Hotel et de Milan** *(see p159)* and the **Four Seasons** *(see p159)* are both elegant, historic hotels.

At the lakes hotels are more geared to holidaymakers and families. Some of Italy's most famous luxury hotels are sited

Entrance to the Hotel Regency *(see p157)* in Milan

around the lake shores. The **Des Iles Borromées** *(see p160)* at Lake Maggiore was once a royal residence. Lake Como boasts famous luxury hotels such as the **Grand Hotel Villa d'Este** *(see p160)* at Cernobbio, and the **Grand Hotel Villa Serbelloni** *(see p160)* at Bellagio.

BOOKING

A CCOMMODATION can be booked by phoning or sending a fax. The hotel will probably ask for a credit card number in advance. Almost all Milanese hotels have e-mail facilities and some, usually the luxury ones, have websites where you can book directly online. Milan is a busy commercial city so it is best to book well in advance.

The Grand Hotel Villa Serbelloni *(see p160)* at Lake Como

GRADING

A LONG WITH the rest of Italy, hotels in Milan and at the lakes are classified by a star system, from one (the lowest) to five stars. It is best to avoid one-star hotels in Milan (unlike the rest of Italy) however.

Two-star hotels usually offer bed and breakfast, and rooms may not have private bathrooms. Three-star hotels offer en-suite bathrooms, TV and sometimes a mini-bar; room service is usually available.

Four-star hotels, besides the above facilities, usually provide a laundry service, services for business travellers and (in Milan) a shuttle service to and from the airports. Five-star hotels are luxurious and offer exclusive restaurants and facilities for conferences.

At the lakes, accommodation ranges from luxury hotels to family-run guesthouses. There are also inexpensive youth hostels and campsites with tents and caravans (RVs). Some have self-catering (efficiency) apartments.

PRICES

A CCOMMODATION in Milan is generally expensive. Because Milan is primarily a business destination, there is little seasonal variation in pricing, and tariffs may even increase when the fashion shows are held and when there are major events like the Furniture Fair at the Fiera. Some of the larger hotels may also require you to take half-board (MAP) during your stay.

At the lakes, prices vary according to the season: in spring and summer, the peak tourist seasons, prices are higher. August, the Italian holiday month, is the busiest time. Many hotels expect you to take full board, especially in the summer months. Some hotels close for part of the year, usually in winter.

By law, prices have to be displayed in every hotel bedroom. Beware of extras: mini-bar drinks will be expensive. A view and air conditioning will add to costs, and hotel phone charges are higher than standard rates. By law, the hotel must issue you with a receipt when you pay, and the receipt should be kept until you leave Italy.

Sign of the Garda & Suisse hotel *(see p161)*

CHILDREN

I N GENERAL, CHILDREN are welcomed everywhere in Italy, but hotels may not go out of their way to provide special facilities. Some of the cheaper hotels may not be able to provide cots. However, virtually all hotels, from the simplest to the most grand, will put a small bed or two into a double room for families travelling together. The price is usually an additional 30–40 per cent of the double room rate per bed. Hotels around the lakes tend to be better equipped for children than the business hotels of Milan. Babysitting services are offered by some large hotels at the lakes.

PETS

F OR THOSE TRAVELLING with their dog or other pet, some hotels actively welcome animals and provide special facilities for them, especially at the lakes. In Milan it is more difficult to find hotels and guesthouses that accept pets, but some of the larger hotels have rooms specially furnished for clients and can even offer dog-sitting services. However, if you mean to travel with pets it is always a good idea to check these details when booking.

Four-poster bed in a room at the Villa Crespi *(see p161)*, Lake Orta

Choosing a Hotel

Hotels in Milan are notoriously expensive, but they all – from two to five stars – offer good services and facilities for business travellers. Hotels around the lakes are more geared to holidays and some are set in their own park with a pool. All the hotels listed below offer rooms with private bath and telephone.

	CREDIT CARDS	TERRACE OR GARDEN	PARKING	BAR	RESTAURANT

MILAN

CITY CENTRE: *Gran Duca di York* €€
Via Moneta 1. **Map** 7 B1. **(** 02-87 48 63. **FAX** 02-869 03 44.
A charming hotel in a historic building next to the Pinacoteca Ambrosiana.
Some rooms have a terrace. ● *Aug, Christmas.* **TV** ▤ **&** ▨ **Rooms:** 33

	■	●		●	

CITY CENTRE: *Sir Edward* €€€€
Via Mazzini 4. **Map** 7 C1. **(** 02-87 78 77. **FAX** 02-87 78 44.
W www.infosquare.it/siredward **@** siredw@infosquare.it
Almost in Piazza del Duomo, comfortable and inviting. **TV** ▤ **&** **Rooms:** 39

	■			●	

CITY CENTRE: *Spadari al Duomo* €€€€
Via Spadari 11. **Map** 7 C1. **(** 02-72 00 23 71. **FAX** 02-86 11 84.
W www.spadarihotel.com **@** reservations@spadarihotel.com
Situated opposite the Duomo, this hotel has designer furniture and works by
famous artists. Spacious rooms, some with a jacuzzi. **TV** ▤ **Rooms:** 39

	■			●	■

CITY CENTRE: *De La Ville* €€€€€
Via Hoepli 6. **Map** 4 D5. **(** 02-86 76 51. **FAX** 02-86 66 09.
W www.sinahotels.com **@** reservationdlv@sinahotels.it
Between Piazza del Duomo and La Scala, with bright, well furnished rooms.
Pleasant bar with wood panelling. **TV** ▤ **&** ▨ **Rooms:** 109

	■			●	■

CITY CENTRE: *Grand Hotel Duomó* €€€€€
Via San Raffaele 1. **Map** 7 C1. **(** 02-88 33. **FAX** 02-86 46 20 27.
@ info@grandhotelduomo.com
Recently remodelled. Many rooms have a view of the Duomo spires.
Mini-suites on two levels. Panoramic roof garden. **TV** ▤ **&** **Rooms:** 159

	■	●	■	●	■

NORTHWEST MILAN: *Antica Locanda dei Mercanti* €€€
Via San Tomaso 6. **Map** 3 B5. **(** 02-805 40 80. **FAX** 02-805 40 90.
W www.locanda.it **@** locanda@locanda.it
Near Castello Sforzesco and the Duomo, this tiny hotel offers a welcoming atmos-
phere: books at the guests' disposal and wake-up service with a bell. **Rooms:** 14

	■				

NORTHWEST MILAN: *Europeo* €€€
Via Canonica 38. **Map** 3 A3. **(** 02-331 47 51. **FAX** 02-33 10 54 10.
@ milpeo.booking@tiscalinet.it
An elegant hotel with extremely comfortable rooms. ● *Aug.* **TV** ▤ ▨ **Rooms:** 45

	■	●	■	●	

NORTHWEST MILAN: *Johnny* €€€
Via Prati 6. **Map** 2 D3. **(** 02-34 18 12. **FAX** 02-33 61 05 21. **@** johnny.hotel@tiscalinet.it
This small and comfortable family-run hotel offers good rates for long stays.
● *Aug, Christmas.* **TV** ▤ ▨ **Rooms:** 31

	■		■	●	

NORTHWEST MILAN: *Lancaster* €€
Via Sangiorgio 16. **Map** 2 E3. **(** 02-34 47 05. **FAX** 02-34 46 49. **@** h.lancaster@tin.it
In a late 19th-century palazzo near the RAI and the Fiera, with comfortable
rooms. Efficient, courteous staff. ● *Aug, Christmas.* **TV** ▤ ▨ **Rooms:** 30

	■			●	

NORTHWEST MILAN: *London* €€
Via Rovello 3. **Map** 3 B5. **(** 02-72 02 01 66. **FAX** 02-805 70 37. **@** hotel.london@traveleurope.it
A small hotel favoured by young American and British guests for its location
and reasonable rates. Spartan rooms. ● *Aug, Christmas.* **TV** ▤ **Rooms:** 29

	■			●	

NORTHWEST MILAN: *Metro* €€
Corso Vercelli 61. **Map** 2 D5. **(** 02-498 78 97. **FAX** 02-48 01 02 95. **@** hotelmetro@tin.it
In a recently remodelled building. Comfortable rooms. **TV** ▤ **&** ▨ **Rooms:** 37

	■		■	●	

NORTHWEST MILAN: *Montebianco* €€
Via Monterosa 90. **Map** 1 B3. **(** 02-48 01 21 30. **FAX** 02-48 00 06 58.
W www.hotelmontebianco.com Close to the Fiera, this charming building has spacious
rooms. Book well in advance when there are trade shows. **TV** ▤ ▨ **Rooms:** 46

	■	●	■	●	

Price categories for a standard double room per night, with tax, breakfast and service included:				
€ under €80				
€€ €80–130				
€€€ €130–180				
€€€€ €180–230				
€€€€€ over €230				

CREDIT CARDS
The hotel accepts all major credit cards.
TERRACE OR GARDEN
Garden or terrace reserved for guests.
PARKING
Private parking on premises.
Hotels usually charge for parking facilities.
BAR
The hotel has a bar that is also open to non-residents.
RESTAURANT
The hotel has a good restaurant that is also open to non-residents.

	CREDIT CARDS	TERRACE OR GARDEN	PARKING	BAR	RESTAURANT
NORTHWEST MILAN: *Ariosto* €€€ Via Ariosto 22. **Map** 2 E5. 02-481 78 44. **FAX** 02-498 05 16. www.brerahotels.com In an elegant quarter of Milan, this early 20th-century building has a grand staircase. Modern rooms. ● *Aug.* TV ▤ **Rooms:** 48	■	●	■	●	
NORTHWEST MILAN: *Domenichino* €€€ Via Domenichino 41–43. **Map** 1 B4. 02-48 00 96 92. **FAX** 02-48 00 39 53. www.hoteldomenichino.it @ hd@hoteldomenichino.it On a quiet street near the Fiera, with comfortable, spacious rooms and some suites. ● *2 wk Aug, Christmas.* TV ▤ �d **Rooms:** 77	■		■	●	
NORTHWEST MILAN: *King* €€€ Corso Magenta 19. **Map** 3 A5. 02-87 44 32. **FAX** 02-89 01 07 98. www.hotelking.com In a lovely palazzo on Corso Magenta, conveniently located between the city centre and the Fiera. Comfortable rooms, courteous staff. TV ▤ ⅰ ⅆ **Rooms:** 48	■		■		
NORTHWEST MILAN: *Palazzo delle Stelline* €€€ Corso Magenta 61. **Map** 6 F1. 02-481 84 31. **FAX** 02-48 19 42 81. www.palazzostelline.it Located in a palazzo which is a congress centre. Modern and well-equipped rooms. Close to the church with the *Last Supper.* ● *Aug.* TV ▤ ⅆ **Rooms:** 105	■	●	■	●	■
NORTHWEST MILAN: *Marriott Grand* €€€€€ Via Washington 66. **Map** 3 C2. 02-485 21. **FAX** 02-481 89 25. www.marriott.com Part of the hotel chain, offering luxurious, soundproofed rooms and one level for non-smokers. Large American breakfast. TV ▤ ⅆ **Rooms:** 323	■		■	●	●
NORTHWEST MILAN: *Regency* €€€€ Via Arimondi 12. **Map** 1 D1. 02-39 21 60 21. **FAX** 02-39 21 77 34. www.regencyhotel/milano.com @ regency@regency/milano.com This late 19th-century patrician residence is now a charming hotel. Romantic attic rooms. ● *3 wk Aug, Christmas.* TV ▤ **Rooms:** 59	■	●			
SOUTHWEST MILAN: *Ca' Bianca* €€€ Via Lodovico il Moro 117. **Map** 5 A5. 02-89 12 81 11. **FAX** 02-89 12 80 42. @ master@hotelcabianca.it A charming hotel in a characterful old house on the Naviglio. Comfortable, with balcony and terracotta floors. ● *Aug.* TV ▤ ⅰ ⅆ **Rooms:** 51	■	●	■	●	
SOUTHWEST MILAN: *Liberty* €€€ Viale Bligny 56. **Map** 8 D4. 02-58 31 85 62. **FAX** 02-58 31 90 61. Art Nouveau decor, in keeping with the style of this building. Modern furniture in the rooms and marble bathrooms. ● *Aug.* TV ▤ **Rooms:** 52	■	●	■	●	
SOUTHWEST MILAN: *Regina* €€€€ Via Cesare Correnti 13. **Map** 7 B2. 02-58 10 69 13. **FAX** 02-58 10 70 33. www.hotelregina.it @ info@hotelregina.it In a converted 18th-century Milanese residence, with cosy, attractively furnished rooms. Near the Navigli canals. ● *Aug, Christmas.* TV ▤ ⅆ ⅰ **Rooms:** 45	■	●		●	
SOUTHWEST MILAN: *Zurigo* €€€ Corso Italia 11/A. **Map** 7 C2. 02-72 02 22 60. **FAX** 02-72 00 00 13. @ zurigo@brerahotels.it www.brerahotels.com An ecological hotel, serving organic breakfast. Bicycles for guests. Simple but comfortable rooms. ● *Christmas.* TV ▤ ⅆ ⅰ **Rooms:** 41	■		■	●	
SOUTHWEST MILAN: *Carrobbio* €€€€ Via Medici 3. **Map** 7 B2. 02-89 01 07 40. **FAX** 02-805 33 34. www.traveleurope.it/hotelcarrobbio.htn @ hotelcarrobbio@traveleurope.it A small luxury hotel in old Milan. Cosy, attractively furnished rooms. ● *Christmas.* TV ▤ **Rooms:** 43	■	●	■	●	
SOUTHWEST MILAN: *Pierre* €€€€ Via Edmondo De Amicis 32. **Map** 7 A2. 02-72 00 05 81. **FAX** 02-805 21 57. All the rooms are different: luxuriously furnished and with marble bathrooms. A hearty buffet breakfast is served. ● *Aug, Christmas.* TV ▤ ⅆ **Rooms:** 51	■		■	●	●

For key to symbols see back flap

<table>
<tr><td colspan="2">

Price categories for a standard double room per night, with tax, breakfast and service included:

€ under €80
€€ €80–130
€€€ €130–180
€€€€ €180–230
€€€€€ over €230

</td><td colspan="5">

CREDIT CARDS
The hotel accepts all major credit cards.
TERRACE OR GARDEN
Terrace or garden reserved for guests.
PARKING
Private parking on premises.
Hotels usually charge for parking facilities.
BAR
The hotel has a bar that is also open to non-residents.
RESTAURANT
The hotel has a good restaurant that is also open to non-residents.

</td></tr>
</table>

	CREDIT CARDS	TERRACE OR GARDEN	PARKING	BAR	RESTAURANT
SOUTHEAST MILAN: *Piacenza* €€€ Via Piacenza 4. **Map** 8 F4. 📞 02-545 50 41. **FAX** 02-546 52 69. 🌐 www.hotelpiacenza.com One of the few hotels in this area, Piacenza offers cosy, plainly furnished rooms and good amenities. Courteous staff. ● *Christmas.* 📺 🍽 🛏 **Rooms:** 24	■		■	●	
NORTHEAST MILAN: *Aspromonte* €€ Piazza Aspromonte 12/14. Just off **Map** 4 F4. 📞 02-236 11 19. **FAX** 02-236 76 21. 🌐 www.venere.it/milano/aspromonte 📧 hotelasp@tin.it A small hotel offering quality at a reasonable price. The well-furnished rooms have every comfort. 📺 🍽 🛏 **Rooms:** 19	■	●	■	●	
NORTHEAST MILAN: *Antica Locanda Solferino* €€ Via Castelfidardo 2. **Map** 3 C3. 📞 02-657 01 29. **FAX** 02-657 13 61. 📧 info@anticalocandasolferino.it A uniquely fascinating inn, frequented by artists and regulars. Book well in advance. ● *Aug.* 📺 **Rooms:** 11	■	●			
NORTHEAST MILAN: *Baviera* €€€ Via P Castaldi 7. **Map** 4 E3. 📞 02-659 05 51. **FAX** 02-29 00 32 81. 🌐 www.hotelbaviera.com 📧 info@hotelbaviera.com An impeccably run 3-star hotel near the main railway station. Well furnished rooms. Good value for money. 📺 🍽 🛏 **Rooms:** 50	■		■	●	
NORTHEAST MILAN: *San Francisco* €€ Viale Lombardia 55. **Map** 4 F3. 📞 02-236 03 02. **FAX** 02-26 68 03 77. 🌐 www.hotel-sanfrancisco.it 📧 sf@hotel-sanfrancisco.it A reasonably priced family-run hotel with simple rooms. Small garden with a pergola. Located in the Città Studi. 📺 🍽 🛏 **Rooms:** 31	■	●			
NORTHEAST MILAN: *Auriga* €€€€ Via Pirelli 7. **Map** 4 E1. 📞 02-66 98 58 51. **FAX** 02-66 98 06 98. 🌐 www.virtualia.it/auriga 📧 hotelauriga@virtualia.it Luxury rooms with amenities for businessmen. ● *Aug, Christmas.* 📺 🍽 **Rooms:** 52	■			●	
NORTHEAST MILAN: *Buenos Aires* €€€ Corso Buenos Aires 26. **Map** 4 F3. 📞 02-29 40 01 69. **FAX** 02-29 40 24 94. 📧 info@hotelbuenosaires/milan.com A small hotel in the heart of the Porta Venezia shopping district. Pleasant, soundproofed rooms with well-equipped bathrooms. 📺 🍽 ♿ 🛏 **Rooms:** 25	■			●	
NORTHEAST MILAN: *Lombardia* €€€ Viale Lombardia 74–76. **Map** 4 F3. 📞 02-289 25 15. **FAX** 02-289 34 30. 📧 hotelomb@tin.it Recently renovated. Some rooms look over a small courtyard garden. Well cared for. Buffet breakfast. ● *Aug.* 📺 🍽 ♿ 🛏 **Rooms:** 79	■	●	■	●	■
NORTHEAST MILAN: *Cavour* €€€ Via Fatebenefratelli 21. **Map** 3 C4. 📞 02-657 20 51. **FAX** 02-659 22 63. 🌐 www.hotelcavour.it Close to the Brera and the fashion quarter, this hotel has large, elegant rooms. Efficient, friendly service. 📺 🍽 ♿ **Rooms:** 113	■			●	■
NORTHEAST MILAN: *Manzoni* €€€€ Via S Spirito 20. **Map** 4 D4. 📞 02-76 00 57 00. **FAX** 02-78 42 12. 🌐 hotelmanzoni.com 📧 hotel.manzoni@tin.it An old-fashioned atmosphere, excellent and friendly service, in the heart of the fashion district. ● *Aug, Christmas, New Year.* 📺 🍽 **Rooms:** 52	■		■	●	■
NORTHEAST MILAN: *Ritter* €€€ Corso Garibaldi 68. **Map** 3 B3. 📞 02-29 00 68 60. **FAX** 02-657 15 12. 📧 comfort@tiscalinet.it High-level 3-star hotel tucked away in the Brera quarter. Terrace-solarium and small garden. Lavish buffet breakfast. 📺 🍽 ♿ 🛏 **Rooms:** 88	■	●		●	
NORTHWEST MILAN: *Hermitage* €€€€€ Via Messina 10. **Map** 3 A1. 📞 02-33 10 77 00. **FAX** 02-33 10 73 99. 🌐 www.monrifhotels.it 📧 hermitage.res@monrif.it A classic hotel close to the RAI, with a garden and the well-known restaurant "Il Sambuco" (*see p171*). Bright, spacious rooms. ● *3 wk Aug.* 📺 🍽 ♿ 🛏 **Rooms:** 131	■	●		●	

NORTHEAST MILAN: *Sanpi* €€€€€
Via Lazzaro Palazzi 18/20. **Map** 4 E3. █ 02-29 51 33 41. **FAX** 02-29 40 24 51.
w www.hotelsanpimilano.it   The rooms vary in size and have satellite and
pay TV as well as a safe. Garden and babysitting service.
● *3 wk Aug, Christmas and New Year.* **TV** 目 **Ġ Rooms:** *71*

NORTHEAST MILAN: *Sheraton Diana Majestic* €€€€€
Viale Piave 42. **Map** 4 F4. █ 02-205 81. **FAX** 02-20 58 20 58. w www.sheraton.com
Art Nouveau-style hotel built in 1905 overlooking a large garden. Handsome
period furniture in the lounge, foyer and rooms. ● *Aug.* **TV** 目 **ᗏ Ġ Rooms:** *107*

NORTHEAST MILAN: *Four Seasons* €€€€€
Via Gesù 8. **Map** 4 D5. █ 02-79 69 76. **FAX** 02-77 08 50 00.
w www.fourseasons.com @ milano@fourseasons.com
Milan's most exclusive hotel. Situated in the fashion district in a converted
monastery. Two good restaurants. **TV** 目 **Ġ ᗏ Rooms:** *118*

NORTHEAST MILAN: *Grand Hotel et de Milan* €€€€€
Via Manzoni 29. **Map** 4 D4. █ 02-72 31 41. **FAX** 02-86 46 08 61.
w www.grandhoteletdemilan.it @ infos@grandhoteletdemilan.it
Giuseppe Verdi died in this historic hotel boasting fine 19th-century furniture.
The bar with Art Nouveau skylights is impressive. **TV** 目 **Ġ ᗏ Rooms:** *95*

NORTHEAST MILAN: *Excelsior Hotel Gallia* €€€€€
Piazza Duca d'Aosta 9. **Map** 4 E1. █ 02-678 51. **FAX** 02-66 71 32 39.
w www.lemeridien-excelsiorhotelgallia.it @ guest@excelsiorhotelgallia.it
For years the Gallia and the Principe di Savoia have been *the* hotels in Milan.
The foyer and public areas are still luxurious, with lovely large mirrors and
chandeliers. The royal suite is a real "museum". **TV** 目 **Rooms:** *237*

NORTHEAST MILAN: *Palace* €€€€€
Piazza della Repubblica 20. **Map** 4 E3. █ 02 633 61. **FAX** 02-65 44 85.
w www.westen.com @ res049palacemilan@starwoodhotels.com
A splendid foyer-lounge for special occasions. Spacious, luxuriously furnished
rooms with every comfort, some with Turkish bath. ● *Aug.* **TV** 目 **Ġ Rooms:** *244*

NORTHEAST MILAN: *Principe di Savoia* €€€€€
Piazza della Repubblica 17. **Map** 4 D2. █ 02-623 01. **FAX** 02-659 58 38.
w www.luxurycollection.com @ hotelprincipedisavoia@luxurycollection.com
A favourite with royalty and VIPs. A 1930s atmosphere. The white façade
is sumptuous. A myriad of services for guests. **TV** 目 **Ġ ᗏ Rooms:** *404*

THE LAKES

LAKE MAGGIORE: *Villa Carlotta* €€€
Belgirate. Via Sempione 121–125. █ 0322-764 61. **FAX** 0322-767 05.
w www.bestwestern.it @ villacarlotta.no@bestwestern.it
In the middle of a large botanic garden. Large, well equipped rooms. The
restaurant is part of the "Buon Ricordo" chain. **TV** 目 **Ġ 🏊 ᗏ Rooms:** *129*

LAKE MAGGIORE: *Pironi* €€
Cannobio. Via Marconi 35. █ 0323-706 24. **FAX** 0323-721 84. w www.pironihotel.it
@ info@pironihotel.it   Tastefullly furnished rooms in a converted 15th-century
palazzo in the quiet streets of Cannobio's historic centre. ● *Nov–Mar.* **TV Rooms:** *12*

LAKE MAGGIORE: *Villa Belvedere* €€
Cannobio. Via Casali Cuserina 2. █ 0323-701 59. **FAX** 0323-719 91.
@ hotel.villabelvedere@cannobio.net   A beautiful villa surrounded by a large park
in a quiet position. Fine views. ● *mid-Oct–Mar.* **TV** ᗏ 🏊 **Rooms:** *18*

LAKE MAGGIORE: *Castello di Frino* €€
Ghiffa. Via C Colombo 8. █ 0323-591 81. **FAX** 0323-597 83.
This small 16th-century castle in a panoramic position stands in a lovely park.
Frescoed rooms with period furniture. ● *mid-Oct–Feb.* **Ġ ᗏ 🏊 Rooms:** *14*

LAKE MAGGIORE: *Park Hotel Paradiso* €€
Ghiffa. Via Marconi 20. █ 0323-595 48. **FAX** 0323-595 48.
A delightful early 20th-century villa with a pool. Public areas with Art Nouveau
decor. Rooms overlook the lake. ● *Nov–mid-Mar.* ᗏ 🏊 **Rooms:** *15*

LAKE MAGGIORE: *Verbano* €€€
Isola dei Pescatori. V Ugo Ara 2. █ 0323-304 08. **FAX** 0323-331 29. w www.hotelverbano.it
@ hotelverbano@tin.it   This pretty red house is on the Isola dei Pescatori. The rooms
have views of Isola Bella and Palazzo Borromeo. ● *Jan, Feb.* **Ġ ᗏ Rooms:** *12*

Price categories for a standard double room per night, with tax, breakfast and service included:

€ under €80
€€ €80–130
€€€ €130–180
€€€€ €180–230
€€€€€ over €230

CREDIT CARDS
The hotel accepts all major credit cards.
TERRACE OR GARDEN
Garden or terrace reserved for guests.
PARKING
Private parking on premises.
Hotels usually charge for parking facilities.
BAR
The hotel has a bar that is also open to non-residents.
RESTAURANT
The hotel has a good restaurant that is also open to non-residents.

	CREDIT CARDS	TERRACE OR GARDEN	PARKING	BAR	RESTAURANT
LAKE MAGGIORE: Villaminta €€€	■	●	■		
LAKE MAGGIORE: Des Iles Borromées €€€€€	■	●	■	●	■
LAKE COMO: Florence €€€	■	●		●	■
LAKE COMO: Grand Hotel Villa Serbelloni €€€€€	■	●	■	●	■
LAKE COMO: Grand Hotel Villa D'Este €€€€€	■	●	■	●	■
LAKE COMO: Le Due Corti €€€	■	●		●	■
LAKE COMO: Terminus €€€€	■	●	■	●	■
LAKE COMO: San Giorgio €€	■	●	■		
LAKE COMO: Villa Flora €	■	●	■		
LAKE COMO: Du Lac €€€	■	●	■	●	
LAKE COMO: Royal Victoria €€	■	●	■	●	■
LAKE GARDA: Grand Hotel Fasano €€€€		●	■	●	■

LAKE MAGGIORE: Villaminta €€€
Stresa. Via Sempione Nord 123. (0323-93 38 18. FAX 0323-93 39 55.
W www.stresa.net/hotel/villaminta @ h.villaminta@stresa.net
North of Stresa is this beautiful villa in a park overflowing with flowers. The rooms have a superb view of the islands. ● Nov–Mar. TV 🏠 ≈ Rooms: 62

LAKE MAGGIORE: Des Iles Borromées €€€€€
Stresa. Lungolago Umberto I 67. (0323-93 89 38. FAX 0323-324 05.
W www.borromees.it @ borromees@borromees.it
A historic hotel on the Piedmontese side, once a favourite with royalty and now VIPs. Luxurious suites and public areas. ● Christmas TV 🍽 & 🏠 ≈ Rooms: 173

LAKE COMO: Florence €€€
Bellagio. Piazza Mazzini 46. (031-95 03 42. FAX 031-95 17 22.
W www.bellagio.co.nz @ hotflore@tin.it
A small lakefront hotel in two 19th-century houses. ● Nov–Mar. TV Rooms: 32

LAKE COMO: Grand Hotel Villa Serbelloni €€€€€
Bellagio. Via Roma 1. (031-95 02 16. FAX 031-95 15 29.
W www.villaserbelloni.it @ inforequest@villaserbelloni.it
A stupendous hotel for over a century. The monumental entrance stairway is crowned by a Murano glass chandelier. ● Nov–Mar. TV 🍽 & 🏠 ≈ Rooms: 83

LAKE COMO: Grand Hotel Villa D'Este €€€€€
Cernobbio. Via Regina 40. (031-34 81. FAX 031-34 88 44.
W www.villadeste.it @ info@villadeste.it
This luxury hotel is world-famous. Set in a huge park, with magnificent rooms and an excellent restaurant. ● Jan–Feb. TV 🍽 & 🏠 ≈ Rooms: 166

LAKE COMO: Le Due Corti €€€
Como. Piazza Vittoria 12/13. (031-32 81 11. FAX 031-32 88 00. @ hotelduecorti@virgilio.it
Once a 17th-century monastery, this hotel has rooms that overlook the two courtyards. Restaurant in the former stable. TV 🍽 & 🏠 ≈ Rooms: 64

LAKE COMO: Terminus €€€€
Como. Lungo Lario Trieste 14. (031-32 91 11. FAX 031-30 25 50.
W www.terminus.com @ info@albergoterminus.com
This hotel has preserved its Art Nouveau-style atmosphere. TV 🍽 🏠 & Rooms: 38

LAKE COMO: San Giorgio €€
Lenno. Via Regina 81. (0344-404 15. FAX 0344-415 91.
An early 20th-century building in a pleasant garden leading to the lake. Lovely views from rooms with a balcony. ● Mid-Oct–Mar. TV 🍽 Rooms: 26

LAKE COMO: Villa Flora €
Torno. Lungolago Castelli 7/11. (031-41 92 22. FAX 031-41 83 18.
Turn-of-the-century villa in a lovely garden. The public areas have period furniture. Large rooms, some with a terrace. ● Nov–mid-Mar. TV ≈ Rooms: 20

LAKE COMO: Du Lac €€€
Varenna. Via del Pristino 4. (0341-83 02 38. FAX 0341-83 10 81. W www.albergodulac.com
In a truly romantic position, a lovely 19th-century house on the lakefront. Some rooms have a breathtaking view. ● Mid-Nov–Feb. TV 🍽 & 🏠 Rooms: 17

LAKE COMO: Royal Victoria €€
Varenna. Piazza San Giorgio 5. (0341-81 51 11. FAX 0341-83 07 22.
W www.royalvictoria.com @ hotelroyalvictoria@promo.it
A fine palazzo in the main square. The restaurant is excellent. TV 🏠 Rooms: 43

LAKE GARDA: Grand Hotel Fasano €€€€
Fasano. Corso Zanardelli 190. (0365-29 02 20. FAX 0365-29 02 21.
W www.grand-hotel-fasano.it @ info@grand-hotel-fasano.it
This 19th-century building was the hunting lodge of the Austrian imperial family. Luxuriously furnished. ● Nov–Mar. TV 🍽 & 🏠 ≈ Rooms: 87

LAKE GARDA: *Villa del Sogno* €€€€
Fasano. Via Zanardelli 107. (*0365-29 01 81.* FAX *0365-29 02 30.*
W *www.gardalake.it/villadelsogno* @ *villadelsogno@gardalake.it*
A *fin de siècle* villa with one of the best views of the area. The rooms, some with terraces, have Art Nouveau touches. ● *Nov–Mar.* TV ▤ ▦ **Rooms:** *30*

LAKE GARDA: *Villa Capri* €€€
Gardone. Corso Zanardelli 172. (*0365-215 37.* FAX *0365-227 20.*
W *www.hotelvillacapri.it*
This 3-star family-run hotel is in a superb location. The "Villa Capri" annexe has eight rooms with a view of the lake. ● *Nov–Mar.* TV ▤ ▦ ▦ **Rooms:** *55*

LAKE GARDA: *Grand Hotel* €€€€
Gardone. Corso Zanardelli 84. (*0365-202 61.* FAX *0365-226 95.*
W *www.grandgardone.it*
Impressive late 19th-century building dominating the Gardone lakeside. Winston Churchill and D'Annunzio stayed here. ● *Nov–Mar.* TV ▤ ▦ ▦ **Rooms:** *180*

LAKE GARDA: *Villa Fiordaliso* €€€€
Gardone. Corso Zanardelli 150. (*0365-201 58.* FAX *0365-29 00 11.*
W *www.villafiordaliso.it* @ *info@villafiordaliso.it*
A fascinating lakeside villa where D'Annunzio once lived. Magnificent frescoed ceilings and Carrara marble in the lounges and in the suite dedicated to Claretta Petacci. Gourmet restaurant. ● *Christmas.* TV ▤ **Rooms:** *7*

LAKE GARDA: *Villa Giulia* €€€
Gargnano. Viale Rimembranza 20. (*0365-710 22.* FAX *0365-727 74.*
W *www.gardalake.it/hotel-villagiulia* @ *hvgiulia@gardanet.it*
This splendid villa with a Neo-Gothic façade offering luxury and privacy. Rooms overlook the lake or the park. ● *Mid-Oct–Mar.* TV ▦ ▦ **Rooms:** *25*

LAKE GARDA: *Du Lac et Du Parc* €€€€
Riva del Garda. Viale Rovereto 44. (*0464-55 15 00.* FAX *0464-55 52 00.*
W *www.garda.com/dulac* @ *hoteldulac@anthese.it*
A large hotel in a spectacular, spacious park. The rooms are comfortable, a good size and well equipped. ● *Nov–Mar.* TV ▤ ▦ ▦ ▦ **Rooms:** *170*

LAKE GARDA: *Laurin* €€€€
Salò. Viale Landi 9. (*0365-220 22.* FAX *0365-223 82.*
W *www.laurinsalo.com* @ *laurinbs@tin.it*
Friezes, frescoes and cornices fill the walls and ceilings of this 1910 villa. Art Nouveau in the public areas and rooms. ● *Dec–Feb.* TV ▤ ▦ ▦ **Rooms:** *38*

LAKE GARDA: *Palace Hotel Villa Cortine* €€€€€
Sirmione. Via Grotte 6. (*030-990 58 90.* FAX *030-91 63 90.*
W *www.hotelvillacortine.com* @ *info@hotelvillacortine.com*
A luxurious Neo-Classical villa. Enormous rooms with period furniture, elegant public areas and a park. Impeccable service.
● *Nov–Mar.* TV ▤ ▦ ▦ **Rooms:** *54*

LAGO D'ISEO: *L'Albereta* €€€€
Erbusco. Via V Emanuele 11. (*030-776 05 50.* FAX *030-776 05 73.*
W *www.albereta.it* @ *info@albereta.it*
A masterpiece of the "maestro" Gualtiero Marchesi, who has created this *relais* out of an old country mansion *(see also p175).* TV ▤ ▦ **Rooms:** *56*

LAGO D'ISEO: *I Due Roccoli* €€
Iseo. Invino, Via Bonomelli. (*030-982 29 77.* FAX *030-982 29 80.*
W *www.idueroccoli.com* @ *relais@idueroccoli.com*
This lovely rustic complex includes the residence, with elegant rooms, and a farmhouse converted into a good restaurant. ● *Nov–mid-Mar.* TV ▦ ▦ **Rooms:** *13*

LAGO D'ORTA: *Hotel San Rocco* €€€€
Orta San Giulio. Via Gippini 11. (*0322-91 19 77.* FAX *0322-91 19 64.*
W *www.hotelsanrocco.it* @ *info@hotelsanrocco.it*
A 17th-century convent, now a sophisticated hotel. The simply furnished rooms overlook either a lake or a garden. Private boat for guests. TV ▦ **Rooms:** *74*

LAGO D'ORTA: *Villa Crespi* €€€€
Orta San Giulio. Via Fava 8. (*0322-91 19 02.* FAX *0322-91 19 19.*
W *www.lagodortahotels.com* @ *villacrespi@tin.it*
An incredible villa in Islamic style built in 1880. Rooms have precious textiles and four-poster beds. The restaurant is excellent.
● *Jan–Feb.* TV ▤ ▦ **Rooms:** *14*

For key to symbols see back flap

WHERE TO EAT

ILAN IS A COSMOPOLITAN CITY and offers a wide range of restaurants in all price categories. As well as Milanese and Tuscan cooking (the latter has become a real speciality of the city), ethnic cuisine has recently come to the fore – from North African to Oriental and even South American, reflecting the city's multicultural character. The fish restaurants are excellent, offering skilfully prepared fish and seafood.

The Barchetta chef,
Bellagio *(see p173)*

Restaurants are at their most crowded at the weekend, and it is often best to book in advance. Sunday brunch has become part and parcel of the Milanese life style, and a number of cafés offer this late morning meal. At the lakes there are restaurants with terraces overlooking the water, and cafés with tables outside. Menus are dominated by fish dishes and local specialities. For more detailed information, see the chart on pages 166–75, with a selection of 122 restaurants.

CHOOSING A RESTAURANT

IN MILAN the Brera and Navigli districts are filled with restaurants. Around the Brera the fashion crowd love **La Briciola** *(see p170)*, while vegetarians head for **Joia** *(see p171)*. Near the Navigli is **Pizzeria Tradizionale** *(see p167)* where fans queue for a table. Near Porta Genova is **Osteria dei Binari** *(see p168)*, serving Lombard and Piedmontese dishes. The **Centro Ittico** *(see p171)* and **Malavoglia** *(see p171)*, near the fish market, have excellent fresh fish.

Classic restaurants in the centre include **Boeucc** *(see p166)* and **Al Girarrosto da Cesarina** *(see p171)*. Also popular are **Aimo e Nadia**

The Pizzeria Tradizionale sign, Milan *(see p167)*

(see p168), in the Bande Nere district, **Il Pesce d'Oro** *(see p171)*, near the Città Studi, and **Alfredo Gran San Bernardo** *(see p167)*, near the Certosa.

Some of Italy's best restaurants are in beautiful locations near the lakes. At Lake Maggiore, **Il Sole di Ranco** *(see p172)* is one of Italy's finest. At Lake Como good places include **Il Griso** hotel restaurant *(see p173)* at Malgrate (Lecco), the **Barchetta** *(see p173)* at Bellagio and **Raimondi del Villa Flori**, a hotel restaurant near Como *(see p173)*. Lake Garda boasts excellent restaurants, such as **Villa Fiordaliso** *(see p174)*, at Gardone. At Erbusco (Lake Iseo), is **Gualtiero Marchesi** *(see p175)*, the restaurant of Italy's most famous chef.

The counter at La Briciola, in the Brera quarter of Milan *(see p170)*

To prevent disappointment, book a table ahead if there is a restaurant you are particularly keen on trying.

EATING HOURS

LUNCH is generally served between 1 and 2:30pm. Dinner is usually at about 8pm and goes on until about 11pm (or later in summer).

ETIQUETTE

THE MILANESE are very dress-conscious and smart dress will also ensure better service. Smoking is still popular in Italy and non-smoking areas in restaurants are rare.

TYPES OF RESTAURANTS

MILAN OFFERS an unusually wide range of types of cuisine for an Italian city. Alongside traditional Italian cooking you can also find Asian, North African and Mexican food of all kinds. Classic Milanese cooking survives in the traditional rest-

L'Ami Berton restaurant in the Città Studi area of Milan *(see p171)*

aurants of the centre. International cuisine is found in places frequented by business people. Italian regional cooking, from Tuscan to Piedmontese, Neapolitan and Sicilian, is increasingly popular in Milan.

There are several different types of restaurant. Traditionally, a *ristorante* is smarter and more expensive than an *osteria* or a *trattoria*, but the divisions are increasingly blurred. A pizzeria is usually an inexpensive place to eat and many serve pasta, meat and fish dishes as well as pizza. Those with wood-fired ovens *(forno a legna)* are the most highly rated. Milan's pizzerias tend to be more expensive than in the rest of Italy but the quality is excellent thanks to the many Neapolitan pizza chefs in the city. An *enoteca* or *vineria* is a place to taste wine and sample snacks.

Genuine small trattorias still abound as well as the increasingly rare *latterie* (dairies), which are small, crowded kitchens.

The Milan fish market is one of the best in Italy, and the city's excellent seafood restaurants guarantee superfresh fish.

At the lakes, much use is made of local fish such as carp, tench and shad, and you will also find regional specialities – in particular, Piedmontese, Valtellinese and Veneto cooking.

Gualtiero Marchesi's restaurant at Erbusco, Lake Iseo *(see p175)*

Raimondi del Villa Flori, Lake Como *(see p173)*

The wine cellar in the famous Il Sole di Ranco restaurant, Lake Maggiore *(see p172)*

READING THE MENU

A CLASSIC ITALIAN dinner begins with an *antipasto* or starter. The first course *(il primo)* is likely to be pasta or risotto but may be a hearty soup. The main course *(il secondo)* consists of meat or fish served with a side dish of vegetables *(contorno)*. Dessert *(il dessert)* follows and may consist of ice cream, fruit or pastries. Coffee *(il caffè)* comes next, and perhaps a digestif. A classic Milanese dinner might consist of *nervetti*, or *gnervitt (see p164)*, followed by *risotto alla milanese (see p164)*, and then a veal cutlet *(costoletta; see p165)*. Other typical dishes are *ossobuco (see p165)*, and *casoeûla (see p165)*.

Vegetarians will find that many pasta dishes are meat-free and that spring is a good time to try new young vegetables. Autumn is also good for non-meat eaters, as pumpkins, wild mushrooms and chestnuts start to appear on the menu. Cheeses are also a good option.

PAYING

M ENUS ARE USUALLY posted outside restaurants, with prices. An unavoidable extra is the cover charge *(coperto)*, which is charged per person. In general Milanese restaurants accept major credit cards, except for some of the smaller, family-run trattorias, where you will need cash. Commonly accepted cards include Visa and MasterCard. Even restaurants in the smaller villages around the lakes now increasingly accept credit cards. When paying for a meal (the Italian for the bill is *il conto*), it is normal to leave a small tip.

WHEELCHAIR ACCESS

U NFORTUNATELY, NOT ALL Milanese restaurants have facilities for the disabled. Wheelchair access may be even more of a problem at the lakes, with restaurants often sited at the top of long slopes or paths with steps. It is therefore advisable to telephone the restaurant beforehand for advice.

CHILDREN'S FACILITIES

L ESS EXPENSIVE PLACES such as trattorias and pizzerias are ideal for children. They may be less welcome in Milan's sophisticated restaurants. Restaurant owners at the lakes are more accustomed to families with children, and can often provide smaller portions if required.

What to Eat in Milan and at the Lakes

Classic Milanese cuisine boasts a long tradition, and dishes such as *costoletta* (breaded veal cutlet), *ossobuco* (veal shin with marrow) and risotto with saffron are well known in Italy and abroad. At the lakes, locally caught lake fish is widely used, especially whitefish, trout, pike and perch. At Lake Garda they produce good quality, light olive oil, and good wines such as Bardolino and Valpolicella (red) and Lugana, Bianco di Custoza and Soave (white).

Lake Garda olive oil

Gnervitt con Cipolle *is a Milanese antipasto consisting of calf cartilage with onions, oil and vinegar.*

Bread with olive oil

Rice

Vegetable stock

Fresh chopped basil

MINESTRONE

As well as vegetables, the Milanese version of minestrone soup includes just-cooked rice. It is often served with toasted bread.

Agnolotti con Pesce Persico *consists of stuffed pasta parcels filled with perch, broccoli and parsley. It is a typical dish from Lake Maggiore and Lake Orta.*

Risotto alla Milanese *is a traditional Milanese first course. The risotto is made yellow by the addition of saffron when the rice is almost done.*

Risotto Trota e Zucca *is a Lake Garda typical first course – risotto with pumpkin and trout, flavoured with chives and served with butter.*

Bigoli con le Aole *is a pasta dish. Thick spaghetti is served with aole or small freshwater fish. It is a traditional recipe from Lake Garda.*

Farfalle ai Funghi Porcini *is made with pasta butterflies and a sauce of fresh porcini mushrooms, parmesan and butter.*

Tinca Ripiena *is tench, stuffed with a mixture of breadcrumbs, parmesan cheese, bay leaf and parsley, and then baked.*

Rognone di Vitello Trifolato *is a Milanese dish of sliced veal kidneys, oil and garlic. It is served with hot polenta.*

Luganega
sausage

CASOEÛLA

This very rich Milanese
dish is based on pork
and cabbage and is
often served with
polenta made with
maize flour.

Pork chop

**Savoy
cabbage**

Pork skin

**Polenta made
with yellow flour**

Costoletta alla Milanese *is
an authentic Milanese veal
cutlet of tender veal loin.
The meat is covered with
breadcrumbs and then lightly
fried in butter.*

Ossobuco alla Milanese *is a
cut of veal including the bone
and its marrow. The meat is
braised and served with risotto.*

Luccio alla Gardesana, *a
Lake Garda speciality, is
freshly caught pike served with
vegetables, capers and olive oil.*

Coregone in Crosta *is a lake
fish flavoured with aniseed, basil
and lemon and cooked in a crusty
casing of coarse salt.*

Pesce Persico Fritto, *a
speciality from Lake Como, is
prepared by flouring pieces of
fresh perch and then lightly
frying them in oil.*

Semifreddo al Limone *is
a Garda dessert: ice cream
parfait made of lemon, cream
and eggs. It is delicious with
strawberry sauce.*

Panettone *is the classic
Milanese Christmas cake. This
dome-shaped sponge cake is
made with flour, eggs, sugar,
candied fruit and raisins.*

FRANCIACORTA WINES

Franciacorta is the area bordered by Lake Iseo, the
outskirts of the town of Brescia, the beginning of the
Po River valley and the Oglio River and is well known
for its good wines. The red Terre di Franciacorta, aged
for one or two years, is good with first courses and
roast meat. The white Terre di Franciacorta has a mini-
mum alcohol level of 11 per cent and goes well with
fish dishes. Sparkling Franciacorta wine *(spumante)*
makes a good aperitif and celebration wine.

Bottles of Franciacorta wines

Choosing a Restaurant

L IKE ANY OTHER large city, Milan offers a wide range of restaurants and types of cuisine. Traditional Milanese cooking is slowly giving way to other Italian regional fare, ethnic cooking and the *nouvelle cuisine* of creative chefs. Around the Northern Italian lakes the local gastronomic tradition is much more deep-rooted.

	Credit Cards	Attended Parking	Fixed-Price Menu	Seafood Restaurant	Traditional Cuisine
MILAN					
CITY CENTRE: *Serendib* €€ Via Pontida 2. **Map** 3 B2. 02-659 21 39. Undoubtedly the best-run Sri Lankan restaurant in Milan. Excellent vegetables with curry or spicy coconut. ● *midday; Aug.*	▩				
CITY CENTRE: *Bistrot Duomo* €€€ Via San Raffaele 2, La Rinascente. **Map** 7 C1. 02-87 71 20. The menu centres around meat dishes, including fine Milanese veal cutlets, but there is also excellent fish. Try the desserts. View of the spires on the Duomo. ● *Sun, Mon midday; Aug.*	▩	●	▩		▩
CITY CENTRE: *Boeucc* €€€ Piazza Belgioioso 2. **Map** 4 D5. 02-76 02 02 24. Located in an old palazzo, a classic Belle Epoque restaurant: spacious rooms with crystal chandeliers and precious mirrors. Typical Milanese cuisine, with risotto and *ossobuco.* ● *Sat, Sun midday; Aug, Easter, Christmas.* 🍷 🍴	▩	●			▩
CITY CENTRE: *Hostaria Borromei* €€€ Via Borromei 4. **Map** 7 B1. 02-86 45 37 60. In the courtyard of a lovely palazzo in the old centre, a dozen tables with yellow linen tablecloths and soft candlelight. Lombard cuisine in a romantic setting. ● *Sat midday, Sun; Aug, Christmas.* 🏠	▩				▩
CITY CENTRE: *Trattoria Milanese* €€€ Via Santa Marta 11. **Map** 7 B1. 02-86 45 19 91. One of the few surviving trattorias in the heart of town, this place has been serving typical Milanese food since 1919. ● *Tue; Aug.*	▩				▩
CITY CENTRE: *Marino alla Scala* €€€€ Piazza della Scala 5. **Map** 3 C5. 02-80 68 82 01. In the Trussardi building with a great view of the Scala opera house. Well-prepared Lombard cooking. The novelty of this bright restaurant is that you can eat at any time of day. ● *Sun; 10–20 Aug, public holidays.*	▩				▩
CITY CENTRE: *Biffi Scala & Toulà* €€€€€ Piazza della Scala 2. **Map** 3 C5. 02-86 66 51. The proximity to the Scala and splendid dining room make for a truly special atmosphere. Milanese cooking featuring, among other things, fried rice and veal cutlets. ● *Sat midday, Sun; Aug; 1–7 Jan.* 🍴	▩				▩
CITY CENTRE: *Peck* €€€€€ Via V Hugo 4. **Map** 7 C1. 02-87 67 74. One of the best restaurants in Milan, rich in gastronomic tradition. Only super-fresh, top-quality ingredients. ● *Sat midday, Sun; Aug, Christmas.* 🍷	▩		▩	●	▩
CITY CENTRE: *Savini* €€€€€ Galleria Vittorio Emanuele II. **Map** 8 D1. 02-72 00 34 33. One of Milan's historic restaurants, in business since 1867. Elegance and impeccable service. Classic Milanese cuisine. ● *Sun; 1–6 Jan, Aug.* 🍷 🍴	▩		▩		▩
NORTHWEST MILAN: *Tagiura* €€ Via Tagiura 5. **Map** 5 C2. 02-48 95 06 13. At first it looks like a bar, until you see three rooms behind the counter. Piacenza cuisine, with salami, cured meats and home-made pasta. Tables in the evening by reservation only. ● *Sun, Mon–Wed, Sat eve; Aug.* 🍷	▩				▩
NORTHWEST MILAN: *Leo* €€€ Via Trivulzio 26. **Map** 1 B5. 02-40 07 14 45. Fresh fish cooked the old-fashioned way. An informal atmosphere and cordial service. The shellfish sauté is excellent; try the *pennette* with prawns, mixed fried fish and delicious grilled razor clams. Good value for money. ● *Sun, Mon; Aug, 24 Dec–6 Jan.*				●	

Price categories for a three-course meal for one, including drinks (except for wine), cover charge, service and taxes. € under €20 €€ €20–40 €€€ €40–50 €€€€ €50–60 €€€€€ over €60	**CREDIT CARDS** Restaurant that accepts the major credit cards. **ATTENDED PARKING** Parking under restaurant supervision. **FIXED-PRICE MENU** Restaurant with a choice of two or three fixed-price menus, usually cheaper than eating *à la carte*. **SEAFOOD RESTAURANT** Specializing in fish and seafood dishes. **TRADITIONAL CUISINE** The cooking is based on typical regional fare.	CREDIT CARDS	ATTENDED PARKING	FIXED-PRICE MENU	SEAFOOD RESTAURANT	TRADITIONAL CUISINE

NORTHWEST MILAN: *Osteria della Cagnola* €€€
Via D Cirillo 14. **Map** 2 F3. 02-331 94 28.
Near RAI and the Fiera, this small, characteristic tavern offers some of the best examples of Milanese cooking. Besides the classic *gnervitt*, risotto and *ossobuco*, there is *baccalà* (salt cod). ● Sun; Aug, Christmas, New Year.
— Credit Cards ■; Traditional Cuisine ■

NORTHWEST MILAN: *Quattro Mori* €€€
Largo M Callas 1. **Map** 3 B5. 02-87 84 83.
Facing Castello Sforzesco, this restaurant features excellent cooking, including fish dishes. Impeccable service. ● Sat midday, Sun; Aug, Christmas, New Year.
— Credit Cards ■; Attended Parking ●; Seafood Restaurant ●; Traditional Cuisine ■

NORTHWEST MILAN: *Taverna della Trisa* €€€
Via Ferruccio 1. **Map** 2 E2. 02-34 13 04.
A Trentino restaurant with dark wood decor. The specialities are *speck* (smoked ham), *canederli* (dumplings) in broth and *finferli* mushrooms. Excellent Teroldego wine. ● Sun (fortnightly) Mon; Aug, Christmas, New Year.
— Credit Cards ■; Seafood Restaurant ■; Traditional Cuisine ●

NORTHWEST MILAN: *Alfredo Gran San Bernardo* €€€€
Via Borghese 14. **Map** 2 D1. 02-331 90 00.
For years, a kind of temple of traditional Milanese cuisine. Among the best specialities are meatballs served as an antipasto, assorted risottos and a first-rate *casoeûla*. ● Sun (also Sat Jun & Jul); Aug, Dec–Jan.
— Credit Cards ■; Traditional Cuisine ■

NORTHWEST MILAN: *Primo Novecento* €€€€
Via Ruggero di Lauria 17. **Map** 2 D1. 02-33 61 16 43.
Early 1900s decor and atmosphere. Good fried vegetables and fish, and octopus stewed in tomatoes. ● Sat midday, Sun; 3 wk Aug, 26 Dec–7 Jan.
— Credit Cards ■; Seafood Restaurant ●

NORTHWEST MILAN: *Trattoria Franca* €€€€
Viale Certosa 235. **Map** 2 D1. 02-38 00 62 38.
A trattoria where great attention is paid to every detail. Many home-made products from the family farm. An example of how an unforgettable dinner can be achieved with home cooking. ● Sat, Sun; Aug, Christmas and New Year.
— Credit Cards ■; Traditional Cuisine ■

SOUTHWEST MILAN: *Al Pont de Ferr'* €€
Ripa di Porta Ticinese 55. **Map** 6 D4. 02-89 40 62 77.
A tavern with varied wines, excellent cured meats, cheeses, flans and vegetable pies, soups and good first courses. ● Sun; Aug, Christmas and New Year.
— Credit Cards ■

SOUTHWEST MILAN: *L'Oca Giuliva* €€
Viale Bligny 29. **Map** 7 C4. 02-58 31 28 71.
A lively place decorated with models of geese (*oca giuliva* means happy goose). Mediterranean food with Puglian touches. ● Mon; Aug, Christmas, New Year.
— Credit Cards ■

SOUTHWEST MILAN: *Marghera 37* €€
Via Marghera 37. **Map** 1 C5. 02-481 43 86.
This restaurant has three dining rooms and an indoor garden. Try the *risotto mari e monti* (with porcini mushrooms and prawns). Fish specialitites. ● Wed.
— Credit Cards ■; Seafood Restaurant ●

SOUTHWEST MILAN: *Osteria Grand Hotel* €€
Via Ascanio Sforza 75. **Map** 7 A4. 02-89 51 15 86.
A trattoria featuring fresh ingredients and traditional dishes. The gnocchi with smoked ricotta cheese are delicious. ● midday, Mon, Aug, New Year.
— Credit Cards ■

SOUTHWEST MILAN: *Pace* €€
Via G Washington 74. **Map** 5 C1. 02-46 85 67.
This Tuscan trattoria offers good value for money. Try the antipasti, the fillet or sizeable *fiorentina* steak. ● Wed, Sat midday; Easter, Aug, Christmas.
— Credit Cards ■

SOUTHWEST MILAN: *Pizzeria Tradizionale con cucina di pesce* €€
Ripa di Porta Ticinese 7. **Map** 6 D4. 02-839 51 33.
Besides the excellent pizza, prepared with quality ingredients, try the breaded fish and linguine with lobster. In the summer you can sit outside, near the Naviglio. Booking ahead is advisable. ● Wed midday, Christmas, New Year.
— Credit Cards ■; Seafood Restaurant ●

Price categories for a three-course meal for one, including drinks (except for wine), cover charge, service and taxes.

€ under €20
€€ €20–40
€€€ €40–50
€€€€ €50–60
€€€€€ over €60

CREDIT CARDS
Restaurant that accepts the major credit cards.
ATTENDED PARKING
Parking under restaurant supervision.
FIXED-PRICE MENU
Restaurant with a choice of two or three fixed-price menus, usually cheaper than eating *à la carte*.
SEAFOOD RESTAURANT
Specializing in fish dishes.
TRADITIONAL CUISINE
The cooking is based on typical regional fare.

	Price	Credit Cards	Attended Parking	Fixed-price Menu	Seafood Restaurant	Traditional Cuisine
SOUTHWEST MILAN: *Shri Ganesh* Via Lombardini 8. **Map** 6 E4. 02-511 09 33. A pleasant setting in which to try the specialities of Indian cuisine. The chicken tandoori and lamb tikka are good, judiciously spiced. ● *midday; Tue, Aug.*	€€	■		■		
SOUTHWEST MILAN: *Aurora* Via Savona 23. **Map** 5 B3. 02-89 40 49 78. Antique furniture and classic Piedmontese cooking in this good trattoria. House specialities are boiled meat and dessert. ● *Mon midday.*	€€€	■		■		
SOUTHWEST MILAN: *Osteria dei Binari* Via Tortona 1. **Map** 6 D3. 02-89 40 94 28. Enjoy Lombard-Piedmontese dishes in a traditional house. Tempting antipasti, *ossobuco*, desserts galore. Piano bar in winter. ● *midday; Sun.*	€€€	■		■		■
SOUTHWEST MILAN: *Rifugio Pugliese* Via Boni 16. **Map** 6 D2. 02-48 00 09 17. The menu in the shape of a mussel offers a range of Puglian specialities. The *burrata* (mozzarella) served with cherry tomatoes is excellent, as are the home-made *orecchiette* pasta with different sauces. ● *Sun; Aug.*	€€€	■		■		
SOUTHWEST MILAN: *Al Porto* Piazzale Generale Cantore. **Map** 6 F3. 02-89 40 74 25. A fish restaurant in a converted customs house, a favourite with celebrities. Well-prepared cuisine based on classic and traditional dishes. Good antipasti and a decent mixed grill. ● *Sun, Mon midday; Aug, 23 Dec–6 Jan.*	€€€€	■	●		●	
SOUTHWEST MILAN: *L'Assassino* Via Amedei 8. **Map** 7 C2. 02-80 561 44. A traditional Tuscan trattoria. The spaghettini sautéed with fresh tomatoes and basil and the Chianina steak are very good. ● *Mon, 23 Dec–3 Jan.*	€€€€	■				
SOUTHWEST MILAN: *L'Ulmet* Via Olmetto 21, corner of Via Disciplini. **Map** 7 B2. 02-86 45 27 18. Antique furniture and a fireplace, a warm family atmosphere. Elegant Italian cuisine with some traditional regional dishes as well. The pastries and grappas are very good. ● *Sun, Mon midday; Aug, Christmas–6 Jan.*	€€€€	■				
SOUTHWEST MILAN: *Osteria di Porta Cicca* Ripa di Porta Ticinese 51. **Map** 6 D4. 02-837 27 63. In the heart of the Navigli district is this pleasant, bright tavern. Imaginative, well-prepared cuisine. Fish and meat dishes. ● *Sat midday, Sun; Easter, Aug, Christmas.*	€€€€				●	
SOUTHWEST MILAN: *Aimo e Nadia* Via Montecuccoli 6. **Map** 5 A1. 02-41 68 86. For years, one of the best restaurants in Milan. The Moroni family has kept up top standards with the utmost consistency. The dishes are the quintessence of simplicity and perfection. ● *Sat midday, Sun; Aug, New Year–6 Jan.*	€€€€€	■		■		
SOUTHWEST MILAN: *La Scaletta* Piazzale Stazione Porta Genova 3. **Map** 6 F3. 02-58 10 02 90. An elegant restaurant featuring creative cooking based on seasonal products. One of the best-known (and best) in town. ● *Sun, Mon midday; Aug.*	€€€€€	■				
SOUTHWEST MILAN: *Sadler* Via Conchetta, corner of Via Troilo 14. **Map** 7 A5. 02-58 10 44 51. One of the best places in town, with high-level creative cooking. The chef, who once worked at the famous Porta Cicca, is known for his extraordinary fish dishes and delectable desserts. ● *Sun midday; 9–31 Aug.*	€€€€€	■		■	●	
SOUTHEAST MILAN: *Pizzeria napoletana La Taverna* Via Anzani 3. **Map** 8 F. 02-59 90 07 93. Typical Neapolitan pizzeria-friggitoria (with fried food). Melting, thin pizza cooked to perfection. Good Neapolitan dishes. ● *Mon; Easter, Aug, Christmas.*	€	■				

SOUTHEAST MILAN: *Al Merluzzo Felice* €€
Via Lazzaro Papi 6. **Map** 8 F4. 02-545 47 11.
Sicilian food including fish antipasti and numerous first courses. The
cannoli (pastry rolls) with ricotta are delicious. *Sun; 12 Aug–1 Sep.*

SOUTHEAST MILAN: *Cueva Maja* €€
Viale Monte Nero 19. **Map** 8 E2. 02-55 18 57 40.
One of the best Mexican restaurants in town. Wide choice of cocktails.
Meat dishes with spicy sauces and melted cheese. *Mon; Easter, Aug, Christmas.*

SOUTHEAST MILAN: *Dongiò* €€
Via Corio 3. **Map** 8 F4. 02-551 13 72.
Home-made Calabrian-Piacentine dishes are featured in this trattoria. Try the
salami (especially the *coppa* – cured pork neck), the fresh pasta with hot chilli
and grilled caciocavallo cheese. *Sat midday, Sun; Aug, Christmas and New Year*

SOUTHEAST MILAN: *Taverna degli Amici* €€
Via Spartaco 4. **Map** 8 F2. 02-55 19 40 05.
A small restaurant with wooden tables. Wide selection of Italian wines. Popular
for its meat dishes and mixed grills. *Sat midday, Sun; Aug; Christmas, New Year.*

SOUTHEAST MILAN: *Trattoria dei Decemviri* €€
Via dei Decemviri 14. **Map** 8 F1. 02-70 10 24 42.
Exceptionally fresh fish in a simple, informal setting. An excellent
Neapolitan *pastiera* tart. *Mon; Aug, Christmas–6 Jan.*

SOUTHEAST MILAN: *La Piola di Mariagrazia e Diego* €€€
Via Perugino 18. **Map** 8 F2. 02-55 19 59 45.
A fish-only trattoria run by a family from Foggia. Excellent raw fish
antipasti, unforgettable home-made pasta.The house desserts are good.
Sat midday, Sun; Aug, Christmas–6 Jan.

SOUTHEAST MILAN: *Masuelli San Marco* €€€
Viale Umbria 80. **Map** 8 F3. 02-55 18 41 38.
A traditional Milanese trattoria with authentic home cooking. The dishes
vary according to the day. Excellent Piedmontese specialities, too.
Sun, Mon midday; 18 Aug–16 Sep, Christmas–6 Jan.

SOUTHEAST MILAN: *Porcao Churrascaria* €€€
Via Abbadesse 30. **Map** 4 D. 02-688 38 83.
An authentic *churrascaria* (grill-room) in Milan. Brazilian dishes and
Brazilian waiters. Grilled meat of all kinds. *Sun; Aug.*

SOUTHEAST MILAN: *Trattoria del Pescatore* €€€
Via Vannucci 5. **Map** 8 E4. 02-58 32 04 52.
The scent of delicious cooking comes from the inviting open kitchen.
Spaghetti with mullet roe and squid, lobster Catalan, excellent myrtle liqueur.
Book well in advance. *Sun; Aug, Christmas and New Year.*

SOUTHEAST MILAN: *Da Giacomo* €€€€
Via Sottocorno 5. **Map** 4 F5. 02-76 02 33 13. www.todine.net-dagiacomo
In an area with a large number of trattorias, Giacomo's stands out for
its fish dishes and delicious desserts. *Mon, Tue midday; Aug, Christmas–6 Jan.*

SOUTHEAST MILAN: *Mauro* €€€€
Via Colonnetta 5. **Map** 8 E1. 02-546 13 80.
An elegant restaurant offering a range of fish specialities. Try the pappardelle
with prawns (shrimp) and curry and excellent baked turbot with potatoes.
Efficient, friendly service. *Sat midday, Mon; 2 wk mid-Aug, Christmas and New Year.*

SOUTHEAST MILAN: *Yar* €€€€
Via Mercalli 22. **Map** 7 C3. 02-58 30 52 34.
This combination restaurant-bistro offers top-quality Russian food in an elegant
setting. Various types of caviar, salmon and sturgeon. *Sun; Aug.*

SOUTHEAST MILAN: *Giannino* €€€€€
Via Sciesa 8. **Map** 8 F1. 02-55 19 55 82.
This historic restaurant has a splendid copper hood in the open kitchen and a
lovely winter garden. Chef Davide Oldani adds a dash of creativity
to classic dishes. *Sun, Mon midday; 1–7 Jan, 2 wk mid-Aug.*

NORTHEAST MILAN: *Massawa* €
Via Sirtori 6. **Map** 4 F4. 02-29 40 69 10.
Eritrean cuisine. The main course is *zighini*: sourdough bread
with meat and spicy vegetables and, on Friday, with fish. *Mon.*

Price categories for a three-course meal for one, including drinks (except for wine), cover charge, service and taxes. € under €20 €€ €20-40 €€€ €40-50 €€€€ €50-60 €€€€€ over €60	CREDIT CARDS Restaurant that accepts the major credit cards. ATTENDED PARKING Parking under restaurant supervision. FIXED-PRICE MENU Restaurant with a choice of two or three fixed-price menus, usually cheaper than eating à la carte. SEAFOOD RESTAURANT Specializing in fish dishes. TRADITIONAL CUISINE The cooking is based on typical regional fare.	CREDIT CARDS	ATTENDED PARKING	FIXED-PRICE MENU	SEAFOOD RESTAURANT	TRADITIONAL CUISINE

Restaurant		CC	AP	FP	SR	TC
NORTHEAST MILAN: *La Bitta* — Via del Carmine 3. **Map** 3 B4. 02-72 00 31 85. An acclaimed trattoria offering mostly fish: from lightly fried crayfish with courgettes *(zucchini)* to a delicious fillet alla Voronov (with mustard, cream and brandy). Excellent value for money. Sun, Sat midday; Aug.	€€	■		■	●	
NORTHEAST MILAN: *Il Doge di Amalfi* — Via Sangallo 41. **Map** 4 F5. 02-73 02 86. This popular restaurant-pizzeria is next to the Ciak theatre. The pizza is excellent, as are the fish dishes. Mon; Aug, Christmas–6 Jan.	€€	■		■	●	
NORTHEAST MILAN: *Il Ristorante il Coriando* — Via dell'Orso 1. **Map** 3 C5. 02-869 32 73. A pleasant restaurant offering fish dishes and typical Milanese cuisine. Easter, Christmas.	€€	■		■	●	
NORTHEAST MILAN: *Mandi Osteria Friulana* — Via E De Marchi 5, corner of Via di Giustizia. **Map** 4 D4. 02-670 42 95. A typical Friuli trattoria at the Naviglio della Martesana. Among the tempting antipasti are Suaris ham and salami. Try the ravioli, and then the classic *frico* (fried cheese pancake) with polenta. midday, Sun; 1–25 Aug, Christmas, New Year.	€€	■				
NORTHEAST MILAN: *Piero e Pia* — Piazza Aspari 2. **Map** 4 F3. 02-71 85 41. A pleasant setting for Piacenza specialities: *coppa* (cured pork neck), *pisarei e fasò* (peas and beans) and pork shank. Sun; 2 wk Aug, Christmas, New Year.	€€	■				
NORTHEAST MILAN: *Vecchia Napoli* — Via Chavez 4. **Map** 4 F1. 02-261 90 56. This authentic pizzeria has received prizes for the best pizza in Europe. Always very crowded but well worth your while. Sun midday, Mon; Aug.	€€	■				
NORTHEAST MILAN: *Gianni e Dorina – Il Pontremolese* — Via G Pepe 38. **Map** 3 B1. 02-60 63 40. The fascinating Isola quarter boasts this elegant (but relaxed) restaurant, where Dorina offers Tuscan fare from Lunigiana, using only the freshest top-quality ingredients. Sat midday, Sun; Aug, Christmas.	€€€	■				
NORTHEAST MILAN: *La Briciola* — Via Marsala, at the corner of Via Solferino. **Map** 3 C3. 02-65 36 99. Parisian bistro atmosphere in the heart of Brera with many plants and mirrors. Very popular with fashion and theatre people. Fried rice and browned *carpaccio* (thinly sliced veal with oil). Sun, Mon midday; Aug, Christmas–6 Jan.	€€€	■				
NORTHEAST MILAN: *Malavoglia* — Via Lecco 4. **Map** 4 E3. 02-29 53 13 87. Sicilian fish specialities. Hot and cold seafood appetizers, pasta with sardines, spaghetti with fish sauce as well as pasta alla Norma (with aubergines/eggplant, tomatoes and ricotta). midday, Mon; Aug, Christmas–6 Jan.	€€€	■			●	
NORTHEAST MILAN: *Matarel* — Corso Garibaldi 75. **Map** 3 B3. 02-65 42 04. At the beginning of the Brera quarter is this classic Milanese restaurant: *gnervitt*, risotto and the *rostin negàa* (veal cutlet). Tue, Wed midday; June–July.	€€€	■				■
NORTHEAST MILAN: *Mykonos* — Via Tofane 5. **Map** 4 F1. 02-261 02 09. In a traditional house at the end of the Naviglio della Martesana is this classic Greek tavern. Book ahead. midday; 10 days Aug.	€€€	■				■
NORTHEAST MILAN: *Osteria Corte Regina* — Via Rottole 60. **Map** 4 F1. 02-259 33 77. Sophisticated cooking and elegant decor in a farmstead on the north-eastern outskirts of Milan. Tasty fish. Sat midday, Sun; 2 wk mid-Aug, Christmas, New Year.	€€€	■	●		●	■

NORTHEAST MILAN: *Ran*   €€€
Via Bordoni 8. **Map** 4 D1. **(** *02-669 69 97.* **W** www.ristoranteran.com
The Japanese restaurant in Milan. The decor is simple and the chefs
are *sushi* masters. Try the "barchetta" mix: raw seabass, salmon and
octopus with rice and radish. The *tempura*, a delicate mixture of
deep-fried crayfish and vegetables, is superb. ● *Midday, Sun; 2 wk Aug.*

NORTHEAST MILAN: *Taiwan*   €€€
Via Adda 10. **Map** 4 E2. **(** *02-670 24 88.*
Delicious Taiwanese cuisine. Specialities include steamed bread stuffed
with crispy pork, giant crab with meat sauce, turbot stewed with mushrooms
and bamboo. Book ahead for Chinese New Year. ● *Tue; 2 wk mid-Aug.*

NORTHEAST MILAN: *Valtellina*   €€€
Via Taverna 34. **Map** 8 F. **(** *02-756 11 39.*
This restaurant bases its menu on salame, meat and mushrooms. Excellent
antipasti and home-made appetizers in oil. ● *Mon; Aug, Christmas–6 Jan.*

NORTHEAST MILAN: *Al Girarrosto da Cesarina*   €€€€
Corso Venezia 31. **Map** 5 E4. **(** *02-76 00 04 81.*
This very centrally located restaurant is ideal for business lunches.
Fish and meat with a Tuscan touch. ● *Sat, Sun midday; Aug, Christmas–6 Jan.*

NORTHEAST MILAN: *Centro Ittico*   €€€€
Via F Aporti 35. **Map** 4 F1. **(** *02-26 14 37 74.*
Near the fish market, with the freshest fish in town, cooked simply and with
skill. The raw shellfish is excellent. ● *Sun, Mon midday; Aug, Christmas–6 Jan.*

NORTHEAST MILAN: *Ilia*   €€€€
Via Lecco 1. **Map** 4 E3. **(** *02-29 52 18 95.*
This Tuscan trattoria is becoming one of the best in Milan. Delicious
deep-fried appetizers are served while you're waiting for the first course.
Traditional tripe and Florentine steaks. ● *Fri, Sat midday; Aug, Christmas–10 Jan.*

NORTHEAST MILAN: *Joia*   €€€€
Via P Castaldi 18. **Map** 4 E3. **(** *02-29 52 21 24.*
First-class vegetarian food in an elegant setting. Creative dishes based on pasta,
vegetables and pulses (legumes). ● *Sat midday, Sun; Easter, Aug, Christmas–6 Jan.*

NORTHEAST MILAN: *La Terrazza di Via Palestro*   €€€€
Via Palestro 2. **Map** 4 E4. **(** *02-76 00 22 77.* **W** www.acena/laterrazza.it
A fish restaurant famous for its "Mediterranean sushi". Creative Ligurian
cuisine, exemplified by the minestrone with pesto and scorpion-fish. View of
the Porta Venezia gardens. ● *Sun, Sat eve; 2 wk mid-Aug, Christmas–mid-Jan.*

NORTHEAST MILAN: *Il Pesce d'Oro*   €€€€€
Via Nullo 14, corner of Via Goldoni. **Map** 4 E5. **(** *02-70 12 34 76.*
An elegant restaurant with a good selection of fish and a wonderful wine
list. Their speciality is fillets of fish baked in a crusty pastry.
● *Sat midday, Sun; Aug.*

NORTHEAST MILAN: *Il Sambuco*   €€€€€
Via Messina 10. **Map** 3 A2. **(** *02-33 61 03 33.*
The Hermitage hotel restaurant, which specializes in fish. The octopus and squid
stew and the potato, prawn and leek flan are very good. Mondays are dedicated
to steak eaters. ● *Sat midday, Sun; 1–25 Aug, Christmas–New Year.*

NORTHEAST MILAN: *Il Teatro dell'Hotel Four Seasons*   €€€€€
Via del Gesù 8. **Map** 4 D5. **(** *02-77 08 14 35.*
This restaurant reflects the aspirations of the best hotel in Milan, both in decor
and in the preparation and presentation of its dishes. Marvellous shellfish antipasti and risottos, splendid choice of desserts. ● *Midday, Sun; Aug, Dec.*

THE LAKES

LAKE MAGGIORE: *La Vecchia Arona*   €€
Arona. Lungolago Marconi 17. **(** *0322-24 24 69.*
This small, sophisticated restaurant offers great value for your money
with its tasting menu. A wide selection of French cheeses
and a matching wine cellar. ● *Fri; Jun, Nov.*

LAKE MAGGIORE: *Del Barcaiolo*   €€€€
Arona. Piazza del Popolo 23. **(** *0322-24 33 88.*
Located in the 14th-century Palazzo del Podestà, with a lovely open kitchen.
Chargrilled meat and fish, and rustic antipasti. ● *Wed; 15 days Feb & Aug.*

	CREDIT CARDS	ATTENDED PARKING	FIXED-PRICE MENU	SEAFOOD RESTAURANT	TRADITIONAL CUISINE
LAKE MAGGIORE: *Taverna del Pittore* €€€€€ **Arona.** Piazza del Popolo 39. (0322-24 33 66. A fine terrace overlooking the lake, elegant decor and beautifully cooked dishes. The fish – both from the lake and the sea – is good and painstakingly prepared. ● *Mon; 15 Dec–20 Jan.*	■			●	
LAKE MAGGIORE: *Del Lago* €€€€€ **Cannobio.** Carmine Inferiore, Via Nazionale 2. (0323-705 95. Probably one of the best restaurants in the area. The elegant cuisine is based on super-fresh fish from the sea. Well-stocked wine cellar, splendid view of the lake. ● *Tue, Wed midday; Nov–Feb.*	■	●	■	■	
LAKE MAGGIORE: *Piccolo Lago* €€€€ **Fondotoce.** Via Turati 87. (0323-58 67 92. A small inn overlooking the Mergozzo lake. Traditional local dishes, with some influence from the sea, which you can enjoy in summer along with the stunning views from the terrace. ● *Mon, Jan.*	■	●	■		■
LAKE MAGGIORE: *Il Porticciolo* €€€€ **Laveno.** Via Fortino 40. (0332-66 72 57. A beautiful lakeside villa. The elegant restaurant offers creative cuisine characterized by the fresh home-made produce, such as the pasta, the bread and the desserts. ● *Tue, Jan–Feb.*	■	●	■		■
LAKE MAGGIORE: *L'Antico Maniero* €€€€ **Lesa.** Via alla Campagna 1. (0322-74 11. This splendid restaurant is a converted 18th-century castle in the middle of an ancient park. Period consoles, mirrors and chandeliers make for an even more old-world atmosphere. Well-prepared dishes, with delicate combinations of fish and vegetables. ● *Mon; Sun eve; 1–15 Jan, 1–15 Nov.*	■	●	■		■
LAKE MAGGIORE: *Il Torchio* €€ **Pallanza.** Via Manzoni 20. (0323-50 33 52. Rustic but elegant, with a wooden beamed ceiling and attractively presented tables. The home-made ravioli and grilled fish are wonderful. ● *Tue.*	■			●	
LAKE MAGGIORE: *Milano* €€€€ **Pallanza.** Corso Zanitello 2. (0323-55 68 16. A restaurant with a splendid veranda over the lake. The specialities are fish from the lake and exquisite desserts. ● *Tue; mid-Jan–mid-Feb, 1 wk Jun.*	■	●		●	
LAKE MAGGIORE: *Il Sole di Ranco* €€€€€ **Ranco.** Piazza Venezia 5. (0331-97 65 07. w www.soleranco.relaischateaux.fr @ ivanett@tin.it One of the Relais & Châteaux chain, with a stupendous view. The Brovelli family has run this restaurant for five generations, making it one of the best in Italy. ● *Mon (except summer), Tue; Jan.*	■	●	■		■
LAKE MAGGIORE: *Da Mosé* €€€€ **Sesto Calende.** Lisanza, Via Ponzello 14. (0331-97 72 10. A small villa in the middle of a pleasant garden on the road to Angera. Inviting, elegant decor and attentive staff. The selection of fish is good, the cheeses exceptional. ● *Mon–Tue, midday Wed–Fri; Jan, Aug, Christmas.*	■	●	■	●	
LAKE MAGGIORE: *Piemontese* €€€€ **Stresa.** Via Mazzini 25. (0323-302 35. A restaurant with a long tradition in the heart of Stresa. Ingredients are chosen with care. The spaghetti with onions and chilli and pâté de foie gras with fondue are excellent. ● *Mon, Sun eve (Oct–May); Dec–Jan.*	■		■		■
LAKE COMO: *Silvio* €€ **Bellagio.** Via Carcano 12. (031-95 03 22. This small hotel-restaurant is famous for its local cuisine at reasonable prices. *Lavarello* (a lake fish) is offered in a variety of ways. ● *6 Jan, Feb.*		●		●	■

Lake Como: *Barchetta* €€€
Bellagio. Salita Mella 13. 031-95 13 89.
This restaurant, with its romantic pergola with geraniums, is in one of the most interesting parts of Bellagio. The chef prepares local recipes with the utmost care, choosing exceptionally fresh ingredients. A wide range of lake fish and a highly tempting choice of cakes. Tue (except summer); Nov–Feb.

Lake Como: *Crotto dei Platani* €€€
Brienno. Via Regina 73. 031-81 40 38. www.crottodeiplatani.it
Situated in a natural cave *(crotto)*, this restaurant features good local fare. Try the lake shad, prepared in different ways. Tue, Wed–Fri midday (Nov), hols.

Lake Como: *Gatto Nero* €€€
Cernobbio. Rovenna, Via Monte Santo 69. 031-51 20 42.
Just above Cernobbio, on the road to Monte Bisbino, is this pleasant place with a marvellous view of the lake. It features Lombard cuisine. The chopped kidneys cooked in brandy are especially good. Mon, Tue midday.

Lake Como: *Musichiere* €€€
Cernobbio. Via Cinque Giornate 32. 031-34 22 95.
www.vademecumitalia.com/musichiere The menu is based on healthy, hearty food with fresh ingredients. Try the gnocchi *alla Alessandro Volta* with tomatoes, onions, bacon and taleggio cheese, or the classic trout *alla Musichiere*, stuffed and oven-baked. Sun; 1 wk Jan, 2 wk Aug.

Lake Como: *Trattoria del Vapore* €€€
Cernobbio. Via Garibaldi 17. 031-51 03 08. In the heart of town. A very pleasant trattoria with flavourful, well prepared local food. The risotto with perch and lake carp are very good. Tue; Christmas– 25 Jan.

Lake Como: *Locanda dell'Oca Bianca* €€€
Como. Trecallo, Via Canturina 251. 031-52 56 05. www.ocabianca.it
In a carefully renovated farmhouse near Como, creative recipes are mixed with local dishes such as home-made pasta with vegetables and mountain pasture cheeses. Mon; Jan, 1 wk mid-Aug.

Lake Como: *Raimondi del Villa Flori* €€€€
Como. Via Cernobbio 12. 031-338 20.
A charming room with fine views of the lake and the park. Good, well-prepared international cuisine. Mon, Sat midday; Dec, Jan.

Lake Como: *Navedano* €€€€€
Como. Via Pannilani. 031-30 80 80.
An elegant, well-kept restaurant featuring many fish dishes, such as the exquisite roast seabass with sautéed potatoes. Tue; 2 wk Aug, 2 wk Jan.

Lake Como: *Locanda dell'Isola Comacina* €€€€
Isola Comacina. 0344-567 55.
What makes this place special is its location on an uninhabited island. A boat takes you to the restaurant pier from Sala Comacina. Only typical local dishes. Tue (in spring); Nov–Mar.

Lake Como: *Nicolin* €€€
Lecco. Via Ponchielli 54. 0341-42 21 22.
A historic restaurant belonging to the Cattaneo family, run by father and son. The cooking ranges from classic Lombard dishes to the elegant creations of the son Giovanni. Try the soused (pickled) fish rolls. Tue; Aug, 1st wk Jan.

Lake Como: *Al Porticciolo 84* €€€€
Lecco. Via Valsecchi 5. 0341-49 81 03.
Top-quality seafood. The hot and cold antipasti and home-made pasta dishes with shellfish sauce are delicious. midday (except hols), Mon, Tue; Aug.

Lake Como: *Il Griso* €€€€€
Malgrate. Via Provinciale 51. 0341-20 20 40.
Classic, elegant, famous: these adjectives perfectly describe a pillar of Lecco's gastronomic tradition. The best in international cuisine, with dishes including both meat and fish. The pâté de foie gras is delectable, and the prawns (shrimp) are extra-fresh. 15 days Dec–Jan.

Lake Como: *Il Ricciolo* €€€
Mandello Olcio. Via Provinciale 165. 0341-73 25 46.
This intimate restaurant celebrates Lake Como cuisine. The speciality is *brodetto lariano* (fish soup), but tagliatelle with river crayfish and perch with lemon are also good. Sun eve, Mon, Tue–Sat midday; 2 wk Sep, Christmas–15 Jan.

For key to symbols see back flap

Price categories for a three-course meal for one, including drinks (except for wine), cover charge, service and taxes. € under €20 €€ €20-40 €€€ €40-50 €€€€ €50-60 €€€€€ over €60	**CREDIT CARDS** Restaurant that accepts the major credit cards. **ATTENDED PARKING** Parking under restaurant supervision. **FIXED-PRICE MENU** Restaurant with a choice of two or three fixed-price menus, usually cheaper than eating *à la carte*. **SEAFOOD RESTAURANT** Specializing in fish dishes. **TRADITIONAL CUISINE** The cooking is based on typical regional fare.			

	CREDIT CARDS	ATTENDED PARKING	FIXED-PRICE MENU	SEAFOOD RESTAURANT	TRADITIONAL CUISINE
LAKE COMO: *Imperialino* €€€€ **Moltrasio.** Via Antica Regina 26. ☎ 031-34 66 00. One of the Imperiale Hotel restaurants, in a nice position over the lake. Local cuisine, with strong flavours. ● *Mon (except summer); Jan–mid-Feb.* ▦	▦	●		●	
LAKE COMO: *La Tirlindana* €€€ **Sala Comacina.** Piazza Matteotti 5. ☎ 0344-566 37. Sit at tables in the lakeside square. Known for its delicious ravioli stuffed with lemon-flavoured cheese. ● *Mon, Tues–Fri (Nov–Feb); 31 Oct–18 Nov.* ▦	▦	●		●	
LAKE COMO: *Vecchia Varenna* €€ **Varenna.** Contrada Scoscesa 10. ☎ 0341-83 07 93. In summer you eat on the splendid terrace facing the lake; in the winter in two cosy rooms. Typical valley and lake cuisine. Try the risotto finished with *scimudin* cheese. ● *Mon; Jan.* ▦	▦			●	▦
LAKE GARDA: *Bagatta alla Lepre* €€€€ **Desenzano.** Via Bagatta 33. ☎ 030-914 23 13. Desenzano is generally a good place to eat out, and this relatively recent restaurant is especially recommended for its excellent fish, fine wine list and friendly staff. ● *Tue, Wed midday.* ▯	▦			●	
LAKE GARDA: *Cavallino* €€€€ **Desenzano.** Via Gherla 30, corner of Via Murachette. ☎ 030-912 02 17. A pleasant courtyard restaurant. Cavallino features fish, from the lake and the sea. The scallops and lobster are excellent, as is the pastry with Sauternes-flavoured zabaglione. ● *Mon, Tue midday; Nov, 2nd wk Jan.* ▯ ▮ ▦	▦	●	▦	●	
LAKE GARDA: *Esplanade* €€€€ **Desenzano.** Via Lario 3. ☎ 030-914 33 61. A superb terrace over the lake and elegant decor. Fabulous cooking, with a range of combinations of lake, sea and land. Try the seafood terrine and pasta and risotto with spicy seafood sauce. ● *Wed.* ▯ ▮ ▦	▦	●		●	
LAKE GARDA: *Locanda agli Angeli* €€€ **Gardone.** Piazza Garibaldi 2, road to Vittoriale. ☎ 0365-208 32. In the pedestrian-only alleys of upper Gardone, opposite the Vittoriale, is this small inn with good cooking. Try the delicious risotto with trout and pumpkin and the fragrant home-made breadsticks. ● *Mon; Nov–Feb.* ▯	▦			●	▦
LAKE GARDA: *Villa Fiordaliso* €€€€€ **Gardone.** Corso Zanardelli 150. ☎ 0365-201 58. Ⓦ www.villafiordaliso.it One of the elegant Relais & Châteaux chain, in a splendid converted villa overlooking the lake. This is one of the best restaurants in Italy, featuring creative, skilfully prepared and presented dishes. The *spaghetti chioggiotti* with shellfish are delectable. ● *Mon; Tue midday; Nov–Feb.* ▯ ▮ ▦	▦	●	▦	●	
LAKE GARDA: *Tortuga* €€€€€ **Gargnano.** Via XXIV Maggio 5. ☎ 0365-712 51. This small, elegant restaurant is a firm fixture on the Lake Garda gastronomic scene. The food is based on fresh local products such as exquisite lake fish with oil and Garda capers. ● *Mon eve (except summer), Tue; mid-Jan–Feb.* ▯ ▮	▦		▦	●	
LAKE GARDA: *Capriccio* €€€€ **Manerba.** Montinelle, Piazza San Bernardo 6. ☎ 0365-55 11 24. On a hill, with the terrace offering a breathtaking view. Seafood is the main-stay here, especially molluscs and crustaceans. The raw vegetable and seafood salad with Garda olive oil is superb. ● *Tue; Jan, Feb.* ▯ ▮ ▦	▦	●	▦	●	▦
LAKE GARDA: *Trattoria al Combattente* €€ **Peschiera del Garda.** San Benedetto, Via Sabino 29. ☎ 045-755 32 27. This pleasant trattoria between Peschiera and Sirmione serves only dishes based on fish caught in Lake Garda. Its forte is the mixed hot and cold antipasti. ● *Mon.* ▦	▦			●	▦

LAKE GARDA: *Restel de Fer* €€
Riva del Garda. Via Restel de Fer 10. (0464-55 34 81.
W www.restel-de-fer.de @ resteldef@tin.it
A simple place where you can enjoy the specialities of upper Lake Garda. The
dishes include medieval recipes. Excellent olive oil. ● *midday, Tue, Nov–Jan.*

LAKE GARDA: *Locanda San Vigilio* €€€€€
San Vigilio. Punta San Vigilio. (045-725 66 88.
This small, enchanting inn in a fascinating part of Lake Garda has
seven rooms for those who want to linger in this paradise. Ask for a table
in the loggia facing the lake, where you can enjoy the view and a fine
risotto with radicchio, after sampling the fine buffet. ● *Tue; Nov–Feb.*

LAKE GARDA: *La Rucola* €€€€
Sirmione. Via Strentelle 3. (030-91 63 26.
An elegant restaurant in the historic centre, with brick walls and soft lighting.
The risotto with leeks and salame and the pike fillet with pancetta and
cabbage are good. Two tasting menus. ● *Thu, Fri midday; Jan–mid-Feb.*

LAKE GARDA: *Vecchia Lugana* €€€€
Sirmione. Lugana, Piazzale Vecchia Lugana 1. (030-91 90 12.
This restaurant is near the Sirmione peninsula, and has offered top-level
cuisine for years. The mixed fish grill is famous for the abundance
and quality of the fish. ● *Mon, Tue; Jan–mid-Feb.*

LAKE GARDA: *Osteria dell'Orologio* €€
Salò. Via Butturini 26. (0365-29 01 58.
A pleasant two-storey place in the historic centre of Salò, like an old-fashioned
wine bar with a kitchen, serving local wines and a few excellent dishes,
including home-made pappardelle with partridge. ● *Wed; mid-Jun–mid-July.*

LAKE GARDA: *Antica Trattoria Alle Rose* €€€
Salò. Via Gasparo da Salò 33. (0365-432 20.
Recently restored, Gianni Briarava's restaurant, a milestone in lower Lake
Garda gastronomy, is now open. ● *Wed; Nov–Dec.*

LAKE GARDA: *Aurora* €€
Soiano del Lago. Via Ciucani 1. (0365-67 41 01.
Simple, savoury cooking at this friendly country restaurant. The ravioli
with *bagos* cheese and stewed whitefish are very good. ● *Wed.*

LAGO D'ISEO: *Mongolfiera dei Sodi* €€€
Erbusco. Via Olina 18. (030 726 83 03.
The three rooms have antique furniture and a fireplace. The quality cuisine
is Tuscan-Lombard. Try the house Florentine steak. ● *Tues.*

LAGO D'ISEO: *Gualtiero Marchesi* €€€€€
Erbusco. Via Vittorio Emanuele 11. (030-776 05 62.
Italy's most famous chef, Gualtiero Marchesi, presides over this restaurant in a
splendid Relais, on a winery estate in Franciacorta. Unique class and atmosphere. The risotto with saffron is exceptional. ● *10 Jan–20 Feb.*

LAGO D'ISEO: *Osteria Il Volto* €€
Iseo. Via Mirolte 33. (030-98 14 62.
This restaurant offers good value for money. The marinated fish
is good and the fillet of perch with herbs is delicious.
Franciacorta wines. ● *Wed; Thu midday; Jan, Jul.*

LAGO D'ISEO: *Al Desco* €€€
Sarnico. Piazza XX Settembre 19. (035-91 07 40.
Signora Nadia's fish courses go beyond all expectations: the freshest of
ingredients, careful preparation and magnificent flavour. The meticulously
shelled fried prawns are exceptional. ● *Mon; Tue midday; Jan.*

LAGO D'ORTA: *Taverna Antico Agnello* €€€
Orta San Giulio. Via Olina 18. (0322-902 59.
A rustic atmosphere in a 17th-century house. Among the specials: breast of
duck Tartar and *lasagnette* with goat's milk cheese. ● *Tue; mid-Dec–mid-Feb.*

LAGO D'ORTA: *Al Sorriso* €€€€€
Soriso. Via Roma 18. (0322-98 32 28.
One of Italy's top restaurants. The delights of Luisa Valazza's cooking attract
clients from all over the world. Every ingredient, from the oil to the lamb, is
guaranteed genuine and home-produced. The cheese trolley and wine list
alone deserve an award. ● *Mon, Tue midday; Aug; Jan.*

For key to symbols see back flap

BARS AND CAFÉS

Logo of Bar Jamaica (see p179)

IN GENERAL, MILANESE bars and cafés are places to go for lunch or an aperitif. Breakfast for most Milanese office workers tends to consist of a cappuccino with a croissant, usually consumed at the bar counter. In the Brera quarter, cafés are lively and full of atmosphere. In the early evening they are popular places to relax in with colleagues and friends. Fashions come and go and a café that is "in" one month may be suddenly empty a few months later. To counteract such swings, many Milanese bars have initiated a "happy hour",

when drinks are cheaper. Cafés are usually more crowded during the lunch break, when office workers stop for a quick salad or quiche. As well as cafés, Milan also has excellent cake shops or *pasticcerie*, where you can sample pastries and cakes. For a more formal afternoon tea there are tea rooms (*sala da thè*), which are also packed at lunchtime. Many are historic places with period furniture. At the lakes, some of the more enterprising bars and cafés offer entertainment in the evening, either with a piano bar area or a small band.

WHERE TO LOOK

IN MILAN, THERE ARE plenty of places to choose from, whether you are going out for an aperitif or to eat snacks, and the choice will vary from area to area. In the atmospheric Brera quarter the bars usually have tables outside in summer. These places are popular with the fashion set and art students. **Jamaica** *(see p179)* is one established institution, an ideal place for a cocktail before dinner as well as for a chicken salad for lunch or an after-dinner drink. **Sans Égal** *(see p179)* is equally popular; on Sunday afternoons they show football (soccer) live on television, and in the evening the place is filled with young rock music buffs.

Around the Navigli, which is a pedestrian precinct from

8pm on, all the bars and cafés have tables set out outside in summer, and it is possible to forget that Milan is a bustling commercial city altogether.

The Conca del Naviglio area is always busy. There are numerous places to try such as the **Caffè della Pusterla** *(see p179)*, located in the renovated medieval walls of the city, the **Tribeca Lounge** *(see p178)*, which is a good place to try for Sunday brunch, and the **Colonial Fashion Café** *(see p178)*, deservedly famous for its aperitifs.

In the Ticinese quarter **Coquetel** *(see p178)* is a popular place, especially during happy hour, when the young Milanese get together for an early evening drink.

For those with a sweet tooth who like croissants and

Sans Égal business card (see p179)

pastries for breakfast, the place to go is **Angela** *(see p178)*, near the Fiera, or **Sissi** *(see p178)*, where you can enjoy cream pastries. If you like brunch, a habit that is increasingly popular in Milan, you can choose from among **Café l'Atlantique** *(see p178)*, a favourite with VIPs, **Speak Easy** *(see p178)*, which also serves good salads, and the **Orient Express** *(see p178)*, with its appealingly old-fashioned look.

HISTORIC CAFÉS AND BARS

SOME OF MILAN'S most frequented cafés and pastry shops have a long tradition, and are housed in old palazzi with fine interiors. One interesting historic pasticceria is **Sant'Ambroeus** *(see p179)*, famous for its traditional panettone. Another ornate setting for breakfast and an aperitif is **Taveggia** *(see p179)*, which has been a favourite with the Milanese since 1910. Don't miss **Zucca**

Watching life go by at a café in Piazza del Duomo

in **Galleria** *(see p179)*, (formerly Camparino), a historic, old-fashioned bar and the place where the world-famous Campari drink was invented. Another must is **Cova** *(see p179)*, a café-pastry shop in Via Montenapoleone in business since 1817. In the heart of the fashion district, it is perfect for a cup of mid-afternoon hot chocolate or an evening aperitif. Lastly, the **Bar Magenta** *(see p178)* has been popular year in and year out and is now an evening haunt for the young Milanese crowd.

The historic Cova pastry shop in Via Montenapoleone *(see p179)*

WHAT TO ORDER

A VAST SELECTION of beers, wines, aperitifs, excellent cocktails and non-alcoholic drinks is served in Milanese bars. A wide range of international beers is available as well as the Italian brands Peroni and Moretti. The current fashion is for Latin-American cocktails, which are gradually replacing classics like the Alexander and Bloody Mary. Almost every bar produces its own house aperitif.

**A tray of savouries
served with aperitifs**

Italy is a wine-producing country and the regions of Piedmont, Lombardy and the Veneto all have extensive areas under vine. Piedmont is best known for its red wines, Barolo and Barbaresco, and the more affordable Barbera and Dolcetto. Good reds are also made in Franciacorta in Lombardy *(see p165)*, in the Valtellina and near Verona where Bardolino and Valpolicella are made. These regions' white wines include Gavi, Soave, Bianco di Custoza and Lugana, and there are some very good sparkling wines.

Most bars provide snacks to go with early evening drinks. These may be simple, such as peanuts, or more elaborate. For generous snacks, try **Honky Tonks** *(see p178)*, where they serve Ascoli olives and pasta salad, as well as the classic *pinzimoni* dips with raw vegetables and canapés, during happy hour.

USEFUL HINTS

I T IS BEST TO GET AROUND by public transport as parking is notoriously difficult in Milan and popular bars are likely to be surrounded by scooters, motorbikes and cars. Most bars and cafés operate two price tariffs, with higher prices charged for sitting down at a table. Ordering and consuming at the bar counter is the most economical option, but you may prefer to linger and "people-watch".

Many bars operate a "happy hour" from 6:30 to 9:30pm, when drinks such as cocktails are sold at half-price. As a result these places become extremely crowded. At bars attracting younger people the music can be very loud, so if peace and quiet are needed, "happy hour" may not suit.

BARS IN HOTELS

U NLIKE THE OTHER BARS in town, those in the large hotels are mostly used as venues for business rendez-vous. They are ideal for this purpose, splendidly furnished, and usually quiet. The discretion and privacy creates ideal conditions for discussing business matters.

Among the most distinguished are the bar in the **Hotel Palace** *(see p159)*, with a fountain in the middle, and the Foyer, the bar in the **Hotel Four Seasons** *(see p159)*. The latter is decorated with theatre set designs. Extra charm is added by an antique fireplace, recreating the plush atmosphere of old Milanese palazzi.

The Foyer in the Hotel Four Seasons

HAPPY HOUR

Colonial Fashion Café

Via De Amicis 12. **Map** 7 A2.
█ 02-89 42 04 01.
◯ 8am–2am.

Fitted out with furniture and objects from all over the world, many reminiscent of the colonial style, this café is very popular for its aperitifs and also offers a wide range of delicious snacks.

Coquetel

Via Vetere 14. **Map** 7 B3.
█ 02-836 06 88.
◯ 8am–2am.

For years this establishment has been popular with young Milanese. It is especially busy in the summer, when people stroll around the grassy stretches of the adjacent Piazza della Vetra, and drop in for a beer and a chat. The cocktails are very good. Happy hour is from 6:30 to 8:30pm.

Honky Tonks

Via Fratelli Induno, corner of Via Lomazzo. **Map** 2 F1.
█ 02-345 25 62.
◯ 6pm–2am Mon–Sat. ● Sun.

This establishment in a converted garage is famous for the variety and sheer quantity of the snacks offered during happy hour. The counter is laden with heaps of Ascoli olives, croquettes, stuffed *focaccia* (flat bread) and cured meats of every kind. A good choice of traditional and Caribbean cocktails.

Magenta

Via Carducci 13. **Map** 3 A5 & 7 A1.
█ 02-805 38 08.
◯ 8am–3am Tue–Sun. ● Mon.

This historic café is ideal for a light lunch snack or a beer in the evening. Try an aperitif at the counter with delicious savouries and *bruschetta*. The good atmosphere attracts smart young Milanese, as well as students from the Università Cattolica and the San Carlo secondary school, both of which are nearby.

Makia

Corso Sempione 28. **Map** 2 E2.
█ 02-33 60 40 12. ◯ 10am–2am.
● Aug.

This chic cocktail bar-restaurant offers tasty Italian/European dishes at lunch, dinner and Sunday brunch as well as a great selection of snacks served on the original American 1930s bar at cocktail hour.

BRUNCH

Café L'Atlantique

Viale Umbria 42. **Map** 8 F4.
█ 02-55 19 39 06.
@ atlantique@iol.it
w www.paginegialle.it/atlantique
◯ 9pm–3am Tue–Sun
(from noon Sun).

This establishment boasts original, extravagant decor, including a famously huge chandelier. The Sunday brunch attracts many young locals. Atlantique is also a disco and a restaurant.

Orient Express

Via Fiori Chiari 8. **Map** 3 C4.
█ 02-805 62 27.
◯ 8am–2am daily.

The decor, atmosphere and service are all reminiscent of the good old days, when the famous Orient Express was in its heyday. Bar, restaurant and Sunday brunch.

Speak Easy

Via Castelfidardo 7. **Map** 3 C2.
█ 02-65 36 45. ◯ noon–3pm, 7pm–3am daily (noon–5pm Sun).

"Eat as much as you like" is the motto in this place in the Brera quarter, which offers a tantalizing, varied buffet and fresh salads.

Tribeca Lounge

Via Conca del Naviglio 22.
Map 7 A2. █ 02-89 42 03 96.
◯ 7pm–2am Thu–Tue. ● Wed.

The owners, including TV host Simona Ventura and star goalkeeper Gianluca Pagliuca, were inspired by the style of the famous New York district, after which their establishment was named. The buffet, with hot and cold dishes, is exceptional. Also on offer, quality *à la carte*.

BREAKFAST

Angela

Via Ruggero di Lauria 15. **Map** 2 D1.
█ 02-34 28 59. ◯ 8am–7:30pm Tue–Sun (8.30–1.30pm, 3–7pm Sat & Sun). ● Mon.

This small pastry shop near the Fiera has a counter where you can pause and enjoy breakfast. Go for the pastries with custard or whipped cream, the warm puff pastry with ricotta cheese and the fresh croissants with hot custard.

De Cherubini

Via Trincea delle Frasche 2.
Map 7 B3 & B4. █ 02-54 10 74 86.
◯ 6:45am–11pm daily.

On the south side of Piazza XXIV Maggio, under a colonnade, lies this lovely café cum pastry shop. Good dishes at lunchtime, snacks with pre-dinner drinks and excellent croissants. Grab an outside table in good weather.

Leonarduzzi

Via Aurelio Saffi 7. **Map** 2 F5.
█ 02-439 03 02. ◯ 7:15am–10pm Tue–Sun. ● Mon.

This ice cream parlour and pastry shop is famous for its crème patissière. The pastry rolls and cream puffs are delicious. Try the home-made yogurt or vanilla ice cream.

Marchesi

Via Santa Maria alla Porta 11a.
Map 7 B1. █ 02-87 67 30.
◯ 7:30am–8pm Tue–Sun
(8:30am–1pm Sun). ● Mon.

This historic pastry shop, in the centre between Via Meravigli and Piazza Cordusio, offers croissants, savouries, salads, a vast assortment of cakes and delicious tartlets.

San Carlo

Via Bandello 21, corner of Corso Magenta. **Map** 6 E1. █ 02-49 82 030. ◯ 6:30am–10:30pm Tue–Sun.

A stone's throw from Santa Maria delle Grazie, this pastry shop features delicious chocolate-based delicacies and irresistible cream-filled pastries.

Sissi

Piazza Risorgimento 20. **Map** 4 F5 & 8 F1. █ 02-76 01 46 64.
◯ 7am–8pm Tue–Sun. ● Mon.

A small pastry shop featuring a host of tempting morsels, including custard-filled croissants or raw ham savouries. The pretty courtyard with its pergola is ideal for Sunday afternoon tea.

SNACKS

Coin – The Globe

Piazza Cinque Giornate 1a.
Coin department store, 8th floor.
█ 02-55 18 19 69.
◯ noon–2am Mon–Sat. ● Sun.

This restaurant, bar and food market, on the top floor of the Coin department store, is similar to those in Harrod's or Macy's. The restaurant offers light lunches and traditional dinners, both high quality. The bar offers fine aperitifs, and you will find delectable delicatessen specialities in the food market.

De Santis

Corso Magenta 9. **Map** 3 A5 & 6 F1.
▮ 02-87 59 68. ◻ noon–3pm,
8pm–1am Mon–Sat. ● Sun, Aug,
Christmas.

This compact place specializes in
filled rolls. On the walls are banknotes from all over the world and
signed photographs of celebrities
who have enjoyed choosing from
150 types of sandwich, made with
fresh, tasty ingredients.

El Tombon
de San Marc

Via San Marco 20. **Map** 3 C3.
▮ 02-659 95 07. ◻ 12:30–2pm,
5pm–2am Mon–Sat. ● Sun, Aug.

A historic establishment that has
resisted passing fashions since the
1930s. A warm, intimate atmosphere. Sandwiches and salads
as well as excellent soups and
various hot and cold dishes.

Latteria di Via Unione

Via dell'Unione 6. **Map** 7 C1.
▮ 02-87 44 01.
◻ 11:30am–4pm Mon–Sat. ● Sun.

This dairy in the heart of town
offers good vegetarian dishes.
Get there early, because it is small
and usually quite crowded.

Luini

Via Santa Radegonda 16. **Map** 7 C1.
▮ 02-86 46 19 17. ◻ 8am–2pm,
4–8pm Mon–Sat. ● Sun, Mon pm.

For over 30 years this baker's
has featured Puglian panzerotti
(ravioli) filled with tomatoes
and mozzarella.

Salumeria Armandola

Via della Spiga 50. **Map** 4 D4.
▮ 02-76 02 16 57.
◻ 8am–7pm Mon–Sat. ● Sun.

People drop in here for a quick
bite at the counter. The chef's
specialities include baked pasta,
roasted meat and a range of
vegetable and side dishes.

BARS AND CAFÉS

Biffi

Corso Magenta 87. **Map** 3 A5 & 6 F1.
▮ 02-48 00 67 02.
◻ 7:30am–8pm Tue–Sun. ● Mon.

This historic bar-pastry shop dates
from the end of the 19th century.
Biffi is famous for its milk rolls
with cured ham or butter and
anchovies. The home-made
panettone, made every year, is
one of the best in Milan.

Caffè della Pusterla

Via De Amicis 24. **Map** 7 A2.
▮ 02-89 40 21 46.
◻ 7am–1:30am Mon–Sat. ● Sun.

This charming café is located in
the former Pusterla, or minor gate,
in Milan's medieval walls. A wide
range of cocktails and a fine wine
list too. The savouries served with
the aperitifs are also very good.

Cova

Via Montenapoleone 8. **Map** 4 D5.
▮ 02-76 00 05 78.
◻ 8am–8:30pm Mon–Sat. ● Sun.

Founded in 1817, this elegant
pastry shop is right in the heart of
the fashion district and is an ideal
place for a pause during your
shopping spree. Cova is well-
known for its chocolates and
stuffed panettone.

Jamaica

Via Brera 32. **Map** 3 C4.
▮ 02-87 67 23.
◻ 9am–2am. ● Aug.

This historic Milanese café is
the haunt of artists and intellectuals, who flock to this
fascinating corner of the Brera
quarter. Busy at all hours. Drinks
as well as good huge salads.

Sant'Ambroeus

Corso Matteotti 7. **Map** 4 D5.
▮ 02-76 00 05 40.
◻ 7:45am–8:15pm. ● Aug.

The atmosphere in what is probably Milan's most elegant pastry
shop is plush, with sumptuous
window displays and slick service.
The tarts, pralines and cakes are
famous. There is a lovely tearoom
inside and tables outside under the
arcade opposite.

Sans Égal

Vicolo Fiori 2. **Map** 3 4B.
▮ 02-869 30 96.
◻ 10am–2am Tue–Sun. ● Mon.

In an alley in the Brera quarter,
this multi-faceted establishment
is a sports pub on Sunday, a small
lunch-time restaurant during the
week, a drinks bar in the evening
and a music pub at night.

Taveggia

Via Visconti di Modrone 2. **Map** 8 E1.
▮ 02-76 02 12 57. ◻ 7:30am–
8:30pm Tue–Sun. ● Mon.

Another historic Milanese pastry
shop, inaugurated in 1910. Great
rice pudding, many different
types of croissants and various
delicacies. Taveggia is also
popular for its aperitifs.

Victoria Café

Via Clerici 1. **Map** 3 C5.
▮ 02-805 35 98.
◻ 5pm–3am.

Behind Piazza della Scala is this
Parisian-style fin de siècle café with
red lamps on the tables, lace cur-
tains and red leather seats. Popular
for aperitifs and after dinner.

Zucca in Galleria

Piazza del Duomo 21. **Map** 7 C1.
▮ 02-86 46 44 35. ◻ 7:30am–
8:30pm Tue–Sun. ● Mon.

This famous bar (formerly Camparino) in the Galleria has period
decor and tables outside. The
world-famous Campari drink was
created here in the late 1800s.

LAKE BARS & CAFÉS

Matella (Lake
Maggiore)

Via Ruga 1, Pallanza. ▮ 0323-50 19
88. ◻ 7:30am–midnight Wed–Mon.
● Tue; mid-Oct–mid-Nov.

Bar-pasticceria shop in the
19th-century arcades of Palazzo
Municipale featuring amaretti
(macaroons). Nice tables for a
drink outside.

Mimosa (Lake Garda)

Via RV Cornicello 1, Bardolino.
▮ 045-621 24 72. ◻ 8am–2am.
● Nov–Feb.

The barman at Mimosa is a true
cocktail "magician". There is also a
garden where you can listen to the
music from the piano bar while
sipping your drink or enjoying
good home-made ice cream.

Monti (Lake Como)

Piazza Cavour 21, Como.
▮ 031-30 11 65. ◻ 7am–1am
Wed–Mon. ● Tue.

Bar-pastry shop in lovely Piazza
Cavour, with tables outside and
a view of the lake. Perfect for
sipping tea and tasting pastries
in tranquil surroundings.

Vassalli (Lake Garda)

Via San Carlo 84, Salò.
▮ 0365-207 52.
◻ 8am–10pm Wed–Mon. ● Tue.

This historic bar-pastry shop in
Salò has been popular for over a
century. The aperitifs and cocktails
are good, but Vassalli is most well-
known for its desserts, such as the
exquisite bacetti di Salò chocolates
and the lemon mousse.

For key to symbols see p291

Shops and Markets

W HETHER BUYING OR just looking, shopping is a real pleasure in Milan. As well as the window displays of the leading national and international fashion designers – whose outlets are all within the area between Via Manzoni, Via Montenapoleone, Via della Spiga and Via Sant'Andrea, the so-called "quadrilateral" – you can find small shops and stores throughout the city. Shops are generally smart and stylish, especially in the city centre, as good design is highly regarded in Italy, and Milan is one of the most affluent cities. For those who are interested in interior design there is plenty of choice among the specialist shops, while lovers of antiques will love the Brera and Navigli quarters, where regular outdoor antique markets are held. Milan also has some excellent *pasticcerie*, where you can purchase authentic delicacies and traditional Milanese confectionery. At the lakes the choice is widest in the bigger towns, and includes clothes shops, craft shops and wine shops selling local produce.

Shopping in Milan

OPENING HOURS

S HOPS IN MILAN are usually open from 9:30am to 1pm and then from 3:30 to 7:30pm. However, many shops in the city centre and the department stores stay open all day, without a break, and major bookshops stay open until 11pm.

Shops are closed on Sunday and Monday mornings, except over Christmas, when they are usually open every day of the week. Food shops, on the other hand, close on Monday afternoon, with the exception of supermarkets.

During the summer holiday period, shops generally close for most of August, apart from the department stores which maintain their normal opening hours, even during this rather inactive month.

Window shopping in fashionable Via Montenapoleone

The Coin department store in Piazza Cinque Giornate

DEPARTMENT STORES

I N COMMON WITH other Italian towns, there are not many department stores in Milan. One of the most central is **La Rinascente**, which is open seven days a week and stays open until 10pm. Opposite the Duomo, it is perhaps the most prestigious department store in the city. Over eight floors everything from clothing, perfumes, toys and stationery to food is sold. The restaurant has a view of the Duomo and an exhibition space for art shows.

In Piazza Cinque Giornate there is the **Coin**, with quality products at medium-range prices, including clothes and household goods. **Upim**, in Piazza San Babila, is more downmarket and sells clothes and other articles at really low prices. Lastly, there is the **Centro Bonola**, a huge shopping centre that includes a huge Coop supermarket and an Upim department store, as well as 60 shops and numerous bars and cafés.

MARKETS

I TALY'S OUTDOOR MARKETS are always fun and Milan has some good specialist markets. The Mercatone dell'Antiquariato, held on the last Sunday of the month at the Alzaia Naviglio Grande, is an extensive antiques market with more than four hundred exhibitors offering antique objects and bric-a-brac. Every Saturday at the Darsena on Viale d'Annunzio there is the Fiera di Senigaglia, where you can find almost anything, from clothing to records and ethnic handicrafts.

The Mercato dell'Antiquariato in the Brera area, between Via Fiori Chiari and Via Madonnina, is also worth a visit. Every third Saturday of

The Fiera di Senigallia along the Darsena

the month antiques, books, postcards and jewellery go on sale here. Lastly, don't miss the Mercato del Sabato on Viale Papiniano, which offers great designer-label bargains, clothes, shoes and bags.

FOOD SHOPS

GOURMETS WILL appreciate the well-stocked Milanese delicatessens and food shops. Perhaps the most famous is **Peck**, which since 1883 has been synonymous with fine food and delicacies. It is a large firm with 150 employees, and the shops are known for the high quality of the produce and the delicious recipes. Besides the main delicatessen in Via Spadari, selling hams, salami and cheeses of all kinds, there is also a popular Peck *rosticceria* in Via Cantù where you can buy the best ready-made dishes in Milan.

Another top-quality establishment is **Il Salumaio** on

Corso Vittorio Emanuele, a popular street for shopping

Via Montenapoleone, which is both a delicatessen and a restaurant offering international, impeccably prepared and presented dishes.

N'Ombra de Vin is one of Milan's most famous *enoteche*, where you'll find the best Italian wines. For those who love chocolate, **Neuhaus Maitre Chocolatier** is paradise. Its specialities are fresh praline and home-baked cakes – if you feel the need, Neuhaus will even deliver.

Garbagnati is the best-known baker in town, and is especially known for *panettone*. Garbagnati has been making this traditional Milanese cake with a natural leavening process since 1937.

Go to **Fabbrica di Marroni Giovanni Galli** for sweet things; this shop has made the best marrons glacés in Milan since 1898. Equally famous is **L'Angolo di Marco**, in the Brera quarter, a delightful *pasticceria* (pastry shop) offering delectable treats of all kinds. At **Ranieri** they make a *panettone* with pineapple, and sweets and pastries with fresh fruit. Last but not least, **Marchesi** is the best place to go for meltingly good chocolates, both milk and dark.

SALES

SHOPS IN MILAN hold sales *(saldi)* twice a year: in early July and then in January, immediately after Epiphany. Discounts may even be as much as 70 per cent, but be wary and check goods carefully before you buy, especially if the discount

looks overgenerous. Shop-owners may use the sales as an excuse to get rid of old stock or defective clothing. For all-year-round bargains, try the numerous outlet shops: Il Salvagente at Via Bronzetti 16 is the most famous shop to head for.

Clothing and Accessories

THE CLOTHES SHOPS OF MILAN are known all over the world because of their associations with famous Italian fashion designers. The city centre fashion district is stormed each year by Italians and foreigners alike in search of the latest top fashion items. However, Milan is not just about expensively priced goods, and the true secret of pleasurable shopping can lie in discovering the less well-known shops which offer good prices and still work to high standards of quality.

CLASSIC CLOTHING

WOMEN IN SEARCH of impeccable classic clothing for themselves and their children should seek out the **Pupi Solari** shop, which also makes wedding dresses to order. Lovers of colourful sports clothes, on the other hand, will be more than satisfied at **Urrà**. Elegant children's apparel and shoes can be found at **Gusella**, while **Host** features men's sports and informal clothes. Elegant, stylish clothes for men can also be found at **Bardelli** or **Gemelli**, and **Ravizza** is an ideal shop for those who prefer classic wear with a casual touch. **Ermenegildo Zegna** is the place to go for stylish men's classic clothing made of the best quality fabrics. **Boggi** offers both classic and sports clothes at reasonable prices. Lastly, the recently renovated **Neglia** has two floors filled with fashionable menswear, from clothing to accessories.

DESIGNER WEAR

ALMOST ALL THE SHOPS that feature the latest in top designer clothes are in or near the city centre (see pp106–7). **Hugo Boss** is a recently opened shop of some size, selling elegant clothes for men. **Giò Moretti**, an institution in Via della Spiga, features articles by the top names as well as pieces by up-and-coming fashion designers. **Marisa** is a shop specializing in Italian and foreign designers and there is always something new and interesting, while **Banner** has clothes for the young and

sophisticated. **Biffi** is famous for its wide-ranging selection of top designer clothes.

Among non-Italian fashion designers there is **Calvin Klein**, who is growing more and more popular, and **Jil Sander**. **Guess**, the well-known New York designer, offers the latest lines.

The diffusion lines of the most famous designers can be found in the fashion district, where the main names have their own branches, from **Miu Miu** to **Gieffeffe**, **D&G** and **Emporio Armani**. Armani's Via Manzoni store also houses an art gallery and a sushi bar. Lastly, **Antonio Fusco** attracts an enthusiastic clientele.

ACCESSORIES

FOR GOOD QUALITY sports shoes there is **Tod's**. Less well-known but equally good is the **Stivaleria Savoia**, which features classic styles that can also be made to measure. **Guido Pasquali** is proud of his stylish traditional and modern shoes.

Ferragamo, the Italian designer known all over the world for his top fashion styles, offers elegant classic shoes. More bizarre and unconventional articles can be found at **La Vetrina**, while **Camper** features original shoes known for their fine workmanship. **Garlando** offers a vast range of styles and colours that aim at the young people's market.

Crocodile, ostrich and leather handbags can be found at **Colombo**, while **Valextra** features high-quality

SIZE CHART

Children's clothing

Italian	2–3	4–5	6–7	8–9	10–11	12	14	14+ (age)
British	2–3	4–5	6–7	8–9	10–11	12	14	14+ (age)
American	2–3	4–5	6–6X	7–8	10	12	14	16 (size)

Children's shoes

Italian	24	25½	27	28	29	30	32	33	34
British	7½	8	9	10	11	12	13	1	2
American	7½	8½	9½	10½	11½	12½	13½	1½	2½

Women's dresses, coats and skirts

Italian	38	40	42	44	46	48	50	52
British	6	8	10	12	14	16	18	20
American	4	6	8	10	12	14	16	18

Women's blouses and sweaters

Italian	40	42	44	46	48	50	52
British	30	32	34	36	38	40	42
American	6	8	10	12	14	16	18

Women's shoes

Italian	36	37	38	39	40	41
British	3	4	5	6	7	8
American	5	6	7	8	9	10

Men's clothing

Italian	44	46	48	50	52	54	56	58
British	34	36	38	40	42	44	46	48
American	34	36	38	40	42	44	46	48

Men's shirts

Italian	36	38	39	41	42	43	44	45
British	14	15	15½	16	16½	17	17½	18
American	14	15	15½	16	16½	17	17½	18

Men's shoes

Italian	40	41	42	43	44	45	46
British	7	7½	8	9	10	11	12
American	7½	8	8½	9½	10½	11	11½

suitcases and briefcases. For something original head for the **Atelier Anne Backhaus**, where they make handbags and accessories using different materials.

The **Mandarina Duck** shops have stylish sports bags, luggage, casual handbags and knapsacks. **Borsalino** is the place to go for top-quality classic hats. **Giusy Bresciani** has more original designs, as well as gloves and other highly stylish accessories. **Cappelleria Melegari** deals in hats imported from all over the world and they

can do hat alterations in their workshop if a customer requires. A wide range of ties and knitwear can be found at **Fedeli** and at **Oxford**, where you can also find good ranges of men's shirts.

JEWELLERY

E LEGANT, CLASSIC JEWELLERY is featured at **Calderoni**, which has designed jewels for smart Milanese women since 1840, and **Cusi**, which has been in business since 1885. **Faraone** is known for high-class jewellery, while Mario

Buccellati has gold and silver pieces of elegant workmanship. Another historic shop is **Bulgari**, known for its beautiful jewellery and watches. **Merù** features original and modern hand-crafted jewels. Jewellery dating from the 19th century to 1950 is to be found at **Mirella Denti**. For modern costume jewellery, you will find a good collection at **Donatella Pellini**, and **Sharra Pagano** also has a good choice of the latest costume jewellery and jewellery styles, made of original materials.

DIRECTORY

CLASSIC CLOTHING

Bardelli
Corso Magenta 13. **Map 3** A5. 02-86 45 07 34.

Boggi
Via Durini 28. **Map 8** D1. 02-76 00 55 82.

Ermenegildo Zegna
Via Verri 3. **Map 4** D5. 02-76 00 64 37.

Gemelli
Corso Vercelli 16. **Map 2** D5. 02-48 00 00 57.

Gusella
Corso V Emanuele II 37b. **Map 8** D1. 02-79 65 33.

Host
Piazza Tommaseo 2. **Map 2** E5. 02-43 60 85.

Neglia
Corso Venezia 2. **Map 4** E4. 02-79 52 31.

Pupi Solari
Piazza Tommaseo 2. **Map 2** E5. 02-46 33 25

Ravizza
Via Hoepli 3. **Map 4** D5. 02-869 38 53.

Urrà
Via Solferino 3. **Map 3** C2. 02-86 43 85.

DESIGNER WEAR

Antonio Fusco
Via Sant'Andrea 11. **Map 4** D5. 02-76 00 29 57.

Banner
Via Sant'Andrea 8a. **Map 4** D5. 02-76 00 43 61.

Biffi
Corso Genova 6. **Map 7** A2. 02-831 16 01.

Calvin Klein
Via Durini 14. **Map 8** D1. 02-76 00 73 28.

D&G
Corso Venezia 7. **Map 4** E4. 02-76 00 40 91.

Emporio Armani
Via Durini 24. **Map 8** D1. 02-76 02 03 06.
Via Manzoni 31. **Map 3** C5. 02-62 69 07 29.
www.armani-viamanzoni31.com

Gieffeffe
Corso Venezia 2. **Map 4** E4. 02-76 00 40 72.

Giò Moretti
Via della Spiga 4. **Map 4** D4. 02-76 00 31 86.

Guess
Piazza San Babila 4b. **Map 4** D5. 02-76 39 20 70.

Hugo Boss
Corso Matteotti 11. **Map 4** D5. 02-76 39 46 67.

Jil Sander
Via P Verri 6. **Map 4** D5. 02-777 29 91.

Marisa
Via della Spiga 52. **Map 4** D4. 02-76 00 20 82.

Miu Miu
Corso Venezia 3. **Map 4** E4. 02-76 00 17 99.

ACCESSORIES

Atelier Anne Backhaus
Corso di Porta Vigentina 10. **Map 8** D3. 02-58 30 27 93.

Borsalino
Galleria V Emanuele II. **Map 7** C1. 02-86 45 72 42.

Camper
Via Torino 15. **Map 7** B1. 02-805 71 85.

Cappelleria Melegari
Via Paolo Sarpi 19. **Map 3** A2. 02-31 20 94.

Colombo
Via della Spiga 9. **Map 4** D4. 02-76 02 35 87.

Fedeli
Via Montenapoleone 8. **Map 4** D5. 02-76 02 33 92.

Ferragamo
Via Montenapoleone 3. **Map 4** D5. 02-76 00 00 54.

Garlando
Via Madonnina 2. **Map 3** B4. 02-87 46 65.

Giusy Bresciani
Via Morone 8. **Map 3** C5. 02-76 00 42 30.

Guido Pasquali
Via Sant'Andrea 1. **Map 4** D5. 02-78 35 08.

La Vetrina
Via Statuto 4. **Map 3** B3. 02-65 42 78.

Mandarina Duck
Corso Europa. **Map 8** D1. 02-78 22 10.

Oxford
Via Verri 2. **Map 4** D5. 02-76 02 34 04.

Stivaleria Savoia
Via Petrarca 7. **Map 2** E4. 02-46 34 24.

Tod's
Via della Spiga 22. **Map 4** D4. 02-76 00 24 23.

Valextra
Piazza San Babila 1. **Map 4** D5. 02-76 00 29 89.

JEWELLERY

Bulgari
Via della Spiga 6. **Map 4** D4. 02-77 70 01.

Calderoni
Via Montenapoleone 23. **Map 4** D5. 02-76 00 12 93.

Cusi
Via Montenapoleone 21/a. **Map 4** D5. 02-76 02 19 77.

Donatella Pellini
Via Santa Maria alla Porta 13. **Map 7** B1. 02-72 01 05 69.

Faraone Tiffany
Via della Spiga 19/a. **Map 4** D4. 02-76 01 36 56.

Mario Buccellati
Via Montenapoleone 4. **Map 4** D5. 02-76 00 21 53.

Merù
Via Solferino 3. **Map 3** C3. 02-86 46 07 00.

Mirella Denti
Via Montenapoleone 29. **Map 4** D5. 02-76 02 25 44.

Sharra Pagano
Corso Garibaldi 35. **Map 3** B3. 02-29 51 41 73.

Design and Antiques

$\mathbf{M}$ILAN IS THE ACKNOWLEDGED CAPITAL of modern design and a paradise for enthusiasts, who can spend their free time browsing in the numerous shops and showrooms throughout the city. Every spring the Salone del Mobile, the famous Milan furniture fair, attracts all the top designers and trade buyers. During the fair, many of Milan's interior design shops extend their opening hours and put on various events for trade experts and visitors.

INTERIOR AND INDUSTRIAL DESIGN

$\mathbf{A}$T **De Padova**, elegant, studiously avant-garde objects for the home, including furniture, are made of the finest materials. For stylish lighting there is **Artemide**, which is known for its superb modern designs, created by well-known names, and **Flos**, in Corso Monforte, which features sleek ultra-modern lighting of all kinds.

Fontana Arte is a kind of gallery and a leading light in the field of interior design. Founded in 1933, its displays include splendid lamps, mostly crystal.

Da Driade, located in the heart of the fashion district, features objects created in the last 30 years which have since become collectors' items. **Galleria Colombari**, on the other hand, offers modern antiques as well as a range of contemporary design objects.

Spazio Cappellini is a showroom for informal and elegant furniture, while **Zani & Zani** features interior design accessories, displayed in a chessboard pattern to show off the individual objects at their best.

Kartell stocks various articles for the home and the office, while **Arform** specializes in Scandinavian design. **Venini** is an institution in the production of blown Venetian glass vases, while **Barovier & Toso** offers extremely high-quality chandeliers and vases, and **Cassina** features products by leading designers.

Eclectica offers its customers individual and extravagant design articles from the 1930s and 1940s, as well as imported and ethnic products and various handicrafts.

Koivu, in Corso Europa, specializes in designer furniture and interior design pieces of Scandinavian inspiration, mostly made of wood. Those who love stylish period furniture should stop by **L'Utile e il Dilettevole**, where 19th-century taste prevails, and **Dimorae**, where the furniture is beautifully displayed in welcoming settings.

San Patrignano Casa d'Arte stocks furniture, wallpaper, and genuinely handcrafted fabrics and embroidery for the modern home.

MEGASTORES

$\mathbf{T}$HE MEGASTORE, where you can purchase almost anything under the sun, from the tiniest household article to a large piece of furniture, is now becoming the rage in Milan as well as in other Italian cities. These large establishments *(empori)* are usually open late in the evening and on Sunday and are frequently able to offer their customers various additional services.

High Tech was one of the first to offer this new mode of shopping. Come here for exotic furniture, fabrics and wallpaper for the home, kitchenware, perfume and accessories imported from all over the world.

B612 is a large centre dedicated entirely to travel and travellers, the only such centre in Italy. Clothing and equipment are found in two big areas – the warm countries area and the cold countries area. In addition, there is a bookshop, a library and a travel agency, as well as a cyberbar, where you can surf the net and have a coffee.

10 Corso Como is an unusual place featuring designer articles and objects from the Middle and Far East. It also has a gallery and an interesting café/bar.

The ultramodern and unconventional **Moroni Gomma** offers boots, raincoats, kitchenware and interior design and household articles, all made of plastic or rubber *(gomma)*.

FABRICS AND LINEN FOR THE HOME

$\mathbf{F}$OR ELEGANCE and high-class interior design, Milan cannot be beaten. There are many shops which specialize in fabrics and linen which can be made to order.

Etro, in Via Pontaccio, is famous for its fabrics and stylish accessories. In the same street is **KA International**, a sales outlet for a Spanish chain of fabric shops, offering excellent value for money. Among the many other articles, **Lisa Corti** features original Indian cotton and cheesecloth fabrics with floral and stripe decorative patterns. **Mimma Gini** has characteristic fabrics from India, Japan and Indonesia; **Castellini & C** is known mostly for its linen articles.

Original and exclusive fabrics can be found at **Fede Cheti**. Among the shops featuring household linen, **Pratesi**, in the heart of the fashion district, is known for its classic and elegant ranges, while **Jesurum** is famous for its embroidered materials and fine lace cloth. **Zucchi** is a very well-known name in Italy for beautifully made fabrics.

Bed linen and table linen in both modern and practical styles are featured at **Mirabello**. Since 1860 **Frette** has been a guarantee of high quality bed linen, table linen and articles for the bathroom such as towels and bathrobes. They also offer delivery throughout the world as well as advice and help from an interior designer.

ANTIQUES

MILAN HAS NUMEROUS antique shops and workshops. Subert, in Via della Spiga, specializes in 18th-century furniture and scientific instruments. In the same street is **Mauro Brucoli**, where they specialize in 19th-century furniture

and objects as well as splendid jewellery dating from the same period. At Franco Sabatelli, which is also a furniture restorers, you can find picture frames of all periods, some even dating to the 16th century.

Lovers of 18th- and 19th-century British furniture must head for Old English Furniture, which also has a fine stock of medical and scientific instruments. If you prefer the unusual and even bizarre object, try **L'Oro dei Farlocchi**, a historic antique gallery in the Brera area.

Blanchaert & Arosio is one of Milan's best-known shops for antique glass, with Murano chandeliers and Venini vases.

At **Antichità Caiati** you will find 17th- and 18th-century Italian paintings, and valuable canvases are also sold at **Antichità Gianetti**, as well as majolica, 18th-century Oriental screens and 16th–19th-century furniture. **Carlo Orsi** has exclusive antiques, including bronze sculpture, splendid paintings, fine furniture, ivory pieces and precious stones.

DIRECTORY

INTERIOR AND INDUSTRIAL DESIGN

Arform
Via della Moscova 22.
Map 3 B3.
02-655 46 91.

Artemide
Corso Monforte 19. Map
4 E5. 02-76 00 69 30.

Barovier & Toso
Via Manzoni 40. Map 4
D5. 02-76 00 09 06.

Cassina
Via Durini 16. Map 8 D1.
02-76 02 07 58.

Da Driade
Via Manzoni 30. Map 4
D5. 02-76 02 30 98.

De Padova
Corso Venezia 14. Map 4
E4. 02-77 72 01.
www.depadova.it

Dimorae
Corso Magenta 69. Map 3
A5. 02-48 01 18 03.

Eclectica
Corso Garibaldi 3. Map 3
B2. 02-87 61 94.

Flos
Corso Monforte 9. Map 4
E5. 02-76 00 36 39.

Fontana Arte
Via Santa Margherita 4.
Map 3 C5.
02-86 46 45 51.

Galleria Colombari
Via Solferino 37. Map 3
C2. 02-29 00 25 33.

Kartell
Via Turati, corner of Corso
Porta 1. Map 4 D3.
02-659 79 16.

Koivu
Corso Europa 12. Map 8
D1. 02-76 02 08 21.

L'Utile e il Dilettevole
Via della Spiga 46. Map 4
D4. 02-76 00 84 20.

San Patrignano Casa d'Arte
Via Bigli 3. Map 4 D5.
02-76 01 40 29.

Spazio Cappellini
Via Statuto 12. Map 3 B3.
02-29 01 33 53.

Venini
Via Montenapoleone 9.
Map 4 D5.
02-76 00 05 39.

Zani & Zani
Via San Damiano (corner
of Corso Venezia).
Map 4 E4.
02-79 80 96.

MEGASTORES

10 Corso Como
Corso Como 10.
Map 3 C2.
02-29 00 26 74.

B612
Via Ludovico Muratori
13/13A. Map 8 F4.
02-54 12 12 70.

High Tech
Piazza XXV Aprile 12.
02-624 11 01.

Moroni Gomma
Corso Matteotti 14.
Map 4 D5.
02-79 62 20.
Via Giusti 10. Map 3 A2.
02-33 10 65 65.

Mondadori Multicenter
Via Marghera 28. Map 1
C5. 02-48 04 71.

FABRICS AND LINEN FOR THE HOME

Etro
Via Montenapoleone 5.
Map 4 D5.
Via Bigli 2. Map 4 D5.
02-76 00 54 50.
posta@etro.it

Fede Cheti
Via Manzoni 23. Map 3
C5. 02-86 46 40 05.

Frette
Via Montenapoleone 21.
Map 4 D5.
02-76 00 37 91.
Via Manzoni 11. Map 3
C5. 02-86 45 06 46.
Corso Vercelli 23–25. Map
2 D5. 02-498 97 56.

Jesurum
Via Verri 4. Map 4 D5.
02-76 01 50 45.
www.jesurum.it

KA International
Via Pontaccio 3. Map 3
B4. 02-86 45 12 44.
Via Marghera 14. Map 1
C5. 02-48 00 63 53.

Lisa Corti
Via Conchetta 6. Map 7
A5. 02-58 10 00 31.

Mimma Gini
Via Santa Croce 21. Map
7 B3. 02-89 40 07 22.

Mirabello
Via Montebello, corner of
Via San Marco. Map 4 C3.
02-65 48 87.
www.mirabellomilano.it

Pratesi
Via Montenapoleone 27/e.
Map 4 D5.
02-76 01 27 55.

Zucchi
Via Ugo Foscolo 4.
02-89 01 14 14.

ANTIQUES

Antichità Caiati
Via Gesù 17. Map 4 D5.
02-79 48 66.

Antichità Gianetti
Via Gesù 7. Map 4 D5.
02-76 00 83 62.

Blanchaert & Arosio
Via Nirone 19. Map 7 A1.
02-86 45 17 00.

Carlo Orsi
Via Bagutta 14.
02-76 00 22 14.

Mauro Brucoli
Via della Spiga 17. Map 4
D4. 02-76 02 37 67.

L'Oro dei Farlocchi
Via Madonnina, opposite
No. 5. Map 3 B4.
02-86 05 89.

Books and Gifts

MILAN IS WELL SUPPLIED WITH good bookshops, many offering foreign-language publications as well as books in Italian. The larger bookstores in the centre are usually open late in the evening and also on Sunday. They have plenty of space where you can quietly browse through the books on display at your leisure. In addition there are plenty of small bookshops, many stocking rare or out-of-print books. Around the University there are many specialist bookshops. Music fans can head for the megastores and the many music shops in town, while the specialist gift article shops will help those interested in buying presents to take home.

BOOKSHOPS

THE **Mondadori Multicenter** is centrally located, open every day until 11pm and on Sunday as well. It spreads out over two floors. On the ground floor, next to the newspapers and periodicals (including international ones), are the new releases, both fiction and non-fiction for visitors who read Italian. The mezzanine contains books of all kinds.

Computer buffs should head for the recently opened **Mondadori Informatica**, which is a paradise for anyone interested in IT.

Another large, well-stocked and very popular bookstore is **Rizzoli** in the Galleria Vittorio Emanuele, which has a fine arts section.

Feltrinelli has four bookshops in Milan, which are open every day including Sunday. The brand-new main bookshop in Piazza del Duomo, almost 500 sq m (5,380 sq ft) in size, has over 60,000 books and offers various services, such as wedding lists, to its customers.

Five-floor **Hoepli** is a serious bookstore steeped in tradition. It specializes particularly in scientific publications and subscriptions to foreign periodicals. The **American Bookstore** and **English Bookshop** specialize in English-language literature and the **Libreria Francese Ile de France** has a good selection of publications in French. For second-hand books, go to **Il Libraccio**, which has a number of branches. Besides school textbooks, it has various books, comic books and even CDs.

A small shop where opera fans can find interesting publications is **Il Trovatore**. Out-of-print editions, scores and libretti are offered together with valuable rarities such as facsimiles of scores by Donizetti or Verdi with the composers' signatures. This music store also provides a catalogue of its publications.

Books Import specializes in art show catalogues and art history books, and books on architecture, design and photography, almost all of which are published abroad. Their section on hobbies is particularly good.

L'Archivolto, which specializes mostly in architecture and design, also has a section on antiques with books from the 1500s to the present. This shop also has modern design objects on display. The **Libreria della Triennale** also deals mainly in books on architecture and design, but has a well-stocked children's book section as well.

Art lovers will also enjoy the **Libreria Bocca**, in the Galleria Vittorio Emanuele. The **Libreria dei Ragazzi** is the only bookshop in town entirely given over to children's books, with games and educational books. The **Libreria del Mare**, as its name suggests, offers a wide range of prints and books on the sea (*il mare*), while the **Libreria Milanese** has books (including photographic ones), prints, posters and gadgets concerning Milan. **Milano Libri**, always up with the latest trends, has a section on high fashion and another on photography. **Luoghi e Libri** specializes in travel books, novels and non-fiction, and the **Libreria Magenta** offers a good range of foreign newspapers and periodicals. Comic-book fans should visit **La Borsa del Fumetto**, which also has rare and old editions.

Besides travel guides, the **Libreria dell'Automobile** has handbooks and illustrated books on cars and motorcycles. **Libreria dello Sport** features books and videos on all sports, and **Libreria dello Spettacolo** specializes in theatre and biographies of famous actors and actresses.

MUSIC, CDS & RECORDS

MUSIC LOVERS WILL revel in the **Virgin Megastore**, which stocks a huge quantity of compact discs, music cassettes and video cassettes, as well as books, periodicals and gadgets concerning music. This store also sells tickets to concerts.

Another good music shop is the **Ricordi Media Store**, which has parts and scores as well as books on composers and their works. It is open even on Sunday (until 8pm), offers discounts on items at least once a month and also has a ticket office for concerts. **Messaggerie Musicali**, on three floors, boasts a vast range of records, tapes and CDs as well as a well-stocked section with books on music in various foreign languages.

The **Bottega Discantica** is a paradise for lovers of opera and church and symphonic music. **Supporti Fonografici** is a shop with a British flavour: besides the latest trends in music, there are records that are almost impossible to find elsewhere and a wide range of Italian and foreign periodicals as well as rare music-themed T-shirts. **Buscemi Dischi** is one of the best-stocked and low-priced music shops and is especially recommended for jazz lovers.

Rasputin, in Piazza Cinque Giornate, specializes in rock music, particularly from American bands, and offers a good assortment of the latest chart releases at reasonable prices.

GIFTS

VISITORS IN SEARCH of gifts would do well to try **Fiorucci** to start with. This large and very centrally located store sells everything from clothing to costume jewellery, household goods, gadgets and fun items.

If circumstances call for a more sophisticated gift, head for **Albrizzi**, a famous bookbinder's dealing in quality notebooks, albums and other handcrafted articles. Another good alternative in this field is **La Piccola Legatoria**, where visitors will find excellent handcrafted stationery, including writing paper and cardboard articles.

Smokers will love **Lorenzi** which, besides a vast assortment of knives, scissors and toilet and gift articles, has high-quality pipes and accessories for smokers. Again for

the smoker, **Savinelli** is an institution in Milan. Since 1876 it has sold pipes of all kinds, at all prices, up to unique and extremely expensive ones.

For toys or games, try the **Città del Sole**, which stocks Milan's largest assortment of traditional wooden toys, educational games and board games for both children and adults. **Movo**, in business since 1932, is the domain of model-making enthusiasts, while **Pergioco** specializes in video games and DVDs, as well as computer games.

DIRECTORY

BOOKSHOPS

American Bookstore
Via Camperio 16. **Map** 3 B5. 02-87 89 20.

Books Import
Via Maiocchi 11. 02-29 40 04 78.

English Bookshop
Via Mascheroni 12. **Map** 2 E4. 02-469 44 68.
w www.yesplease.it

Feltrinelli
Via Manzoni 12. **Map** 3 C5. 02-76 00 03 86.
Via Foscolo 1–3. 02-86 99 69 03.
Corso Buenos Aires 20. **Map** 4 F3. 02-29 53 17 90.
Via P Sarpi 15. **Map** 3 A2. 02-349 02 41.

Hoepli
Via Hoepli 5. **Map** 4 D5. 02-86 48 71.

Il Libraccio
Via Arconati 16. 02-55 19 08 97.
Via Corsico 9. **Map** 6 F3. 02-837 23 98.
Via Santatecla 5. 02-87 83 99.
Viale Vittorio Veneto 22. **Map** 4 E3. 02-655 56 81.

Il Trovatore
Via Carlo Poerio 3. 02-76 00 16 56.

L'Archivolto
Via Marsala 2. **Map** 3 C3. 02-659 08 42.

La Borsa del Fumetto
Via Lecco 16. **Map** 4 E3. 02-29 51 38 83.

Libreria Bocca
Galleria Vittorio Emanuele II 12. **Map** 7 C1. 02-86 46 23 21.

Libreria dei Ragazzi
Via Unione 3. **Map** 7 C1. 02-72 00 41 66.
w www.libreriadeiragazzi.it

Libreria del Mare
Via Broletto 28. **Map** 3 B5. 02-89 01 02 28.
w www.libreriadelmare.it

Libreria dell'Automobile
Corso Venezia 43. **Map** 4 E4. 02-76 02 81 08.

Libreria della Triennale
Viale Alemagna 6. **Map** 2 F3. 02-87 78 12.

Libreria dello Spettacolo
Via Terraggio 11. **Map** 7 A1. 02-86 45 17 30.

Libreria dello Sport
Via Carducci 9. **Map** 3 A5. 02-805 53 55.
w www.libreriadellosport.it

Libreria Francese Ile de France
Via San Pietro all'Orto 10. **Map** 4 D5. 02-76 00 17 67.

Libreria Magenta
Corso Magenta 65. **Map** 3 A5. 02-481 61 50.

Libreria Milanese
Via Meravigli 18. **Map** 3 B5. 02-86 45 31 54.

Luoghi e Libri
Via M Melloni 32. **Map** 4 F5. 02-738 83 70.

Milano Libri
Via Verdi 2. **Map** 3 C5. 02-87 58 71.

Mondadori
Corso Vittorio Emanuele II 34. **Map** 8 D1. 02-76 00 58 33.

Mondadori Informatica
Via Berchet 2. 02-58 16 37 83.
Corso di Porta Vittoria. **Map** 8 F1. 02-55 19 22 10.
Via Marghera 28. **Map** 1 C5. 02-48 04 73 03.

Rizzoli
Piazza Cavour. **Map** 4 D4. 02-659 56 82.
Galleria Vittorio Emanuele II 79. **Map** 7 C1. 02-86 46 10 71.

MUSIC, CDs & RECORDS

Abottega Discantica
Via Nirone 5. **Map** 7 A1. 02-86 29 66.

Buscemi Dischi
Corso Magenta 31. **Map** 3 A5. 02-86 45 52 65.

Messaggerie Musicali
Galleria del Corso 2. 02-76 05 54 31.

Rasputin
Piazza Cinque Giornate 10. **Map** 8 F1. 02-55 01 64 28.

Ricordi Media Store
Galleria Vittorio Emanuele II. **Map** 7 C1.

02-86 46 02 72.
Corso Buenos Aires 33. **Map** 4 F3. 02-29 52 62 44.

Supporti Fonografici
Corso di Porta Ticinese 106. **Map** 7 B2. 02-89 40 04 20.

Virgin Megastore
Piazza del Duomo 8. **Map** 7 C1. 02-88 00 11.

GIFTS

Fiorucci
Galleria Passarella 1. 02-76 00 32 76.

BOOKBINDING

Albrizzi
Via Bagutta 8. 02-76 00 12 18.

La Piccola Legatoria
Via Palermo 11. **Map** 3 B3. 02-86 11 13.

ARTICLES FOR SMOKERS

Lorenzi
Via Montenapoleone 9. **Map** 4 D5. 02-76 02 28 48.

Savinelli
Via Orefici 2. **Map** 7 C1. 02-87 66 60.

TOYS AND GAMES

Città del Sole
Via Orefici 13. **Map** 7 C1. 02-86 46 16 83.

Movo
Piazzale Principessa Clotilde 8. **Map** 4 D2. 02-655 48 36.

Pergioco
Via San Prospero 1. 02-86 46 34 14.

ENTERTAINMENT IN MILAN

THE ENTERTAINMENT SCENE is lively in Milan and there is plenty of choice for those who love night life, given the hundreds of clubs that animate the Brera and Navigli quarters in particular. Pubs, discos and nightclubs with live music, as well as late-night bistros, are filled every evening with people who come from all corners of Italy. The theatres offer the public a rich and varied programme: La Scala represents the top in opera and ballet. Major music concerts are usually held in the Palavobis arena (formerly PalaTrussardi) or at the Filaforum at Assago. Milan is equally generous to sports lovers. Every Sunday from September to May the San Siro stadium plays host to the matches of local football teams Inter and Milan. It also stages national and international championship matches. Sometimes matches are also scheduled during the week. Horse racing takes place all year round at the Ippodromo racecourse. Milan's many sports and leisure clubs cater to those who like to play as well as watch sports.

Ronaldo, star player of the Inter club

INFORMATION

IN ORDER TO FIND OUT the latest information on the many evening events in Milan, check the listings in *Vivi-Milano*, a Wednesday supplement to the newspaper *Corriere della Sera*. Every Thursday the daily paper *La Repubblica* publishes *Tutto Milano*, which is also full of useful information.

The APT tourist offices in Piazza del Duomo and the Stazione Centrale (main railway station) provide free copies of the brochure *Milano Mese*, with all the information you need concerning art shows, light and classical music concerts, jazz and other cultural events in town. You can also use the Internet and log on to the *Inmilano* website: (www.rcs.it/quotidiani/inmilano/benven.htm) for information on Milanese nightlife, exhibitions, cultural events and other forms of entertainment.

BUYING TICKETS

TICKETS FOR THE THEATRE and various concerts can be purchased in specialist booking offices such as **Ricordi Box Office**, **La Prevendita**, at the Virgin Megastore, and at **Last Minute Tour** (inside the Fiorucci store) or **Ticket web** (telephone reservations and online www.ticketweb.it). **Prenoticket** accepts telephone reservations only, while for La Scala you have to go to the box office at the theatre or book through the theatre's website (www.teatroallascala.org).

Tickets for football (soccer) matches can be purchased directly from the stadium box offices. Alternatively tickets for Inter matches can be bought from the Banca Popolare di Milano, Banca Briantea, Banca Agricola Milanese and Milano Ticket. Tickets for AC Milan matches are sold by Cariplo bank, various businesses (40 bars and shops) and Milan Point, whose listings are shown at the Milan Club.

Tickets for the annual Formula 1 Grand Prix, held in September at the Autodromo Nazionale in Monza, are sold at the **Automobile Club Milano**, **Acitour Lombardia** and **AC Promotion**. The Monza race track is usually open to visitors at weekends when there are no other events going on. Cars and motorbikes can be driven on the track when it is free. For more information, enquire at the **Autodromo Nazionale**.

Alcatraz, one of the trendiest discos in Milan (*see p191*)

The Last Minute Tour ticket office at Fiorucci

The Filaforum at Assago is a sports arena which is also used for concerts *(see p191)*

CHILDREN

FAMILIES visiting Milan with children should be warned that the city does not have extensive specialist entertainment available for them. However, some of the museums and galleries are quite child-friendly. To stimulate the young imagination and provide lots of interesting educational material, there are the Planetarium *(see p120)* and the Science and Technology Museum *(see p88)*, as well as the Civic Aquarium *(see p68)*.

As far as shows and spectacles are concerned, the **Nuovo Arti** motion picture theatre shows children's films, and the **Teatro delle Marionette** is a children's puppet theatre.

If on the other hand you opt for pure entertainment, the amusement park at the **Idroscalo** is a good choice.

From June to September **Aquatica** is a popular place to take children: slides, pools and shows make this aquatic park a children's paradise that will entertain both the youngsters and adults alike.

Children over the age of 12 who are keen on video games can try out one of the numerous amusement arcades in the city.

A good place for entertaining smaller children only is the **Play Planet**. This is a recreation centre where the kids can let off some steam and use up a lot of energy or become involved in some of the creative workshops that are on offer. Play Planet is open all year round, and there are also two rooms in which birthday parties can be held.

In sunny weather there are always local public parks to take children to. The most suitable parks for children are the ones at Porta Venezia and Via Palestro, where theoretically no one is allowed to enter unless they are accompanied by a child. By contrast, Parco Sempione (between Piazza Castello and Piazza Sempione) is used mostly by adults, for sports activities or to walk their dogs.

Young tourists enjoying an ice cream

DIRECTORY

TICKET AGENCIES

AC Promotion
Piazza Eleonora Duse 1.
Map 4 F4.
📞 02-76 00 25 74.

Acitour Lombardia
Corso Venezia 43. **Map** 4 E4.
📞 02-76 00 63 50.

Autodromo Nazionale
Parco di Monza.
📞 039-248 21.

Automobile Club Milano
Corso Venezia 43. **Map** 4 E4.
📞 02-774 51.

La Prevendita
Virgin Megastore, Piazza Duomo 8.
Map 7 C1.
📞 02-88 00 11.

La Scala
📞 02-86 07 75.

Last Minute Tour
At **Fiorucci** *(see p187)* (no telephone reservations taken).

Ticket Web
Via Cappuccini 11. **Map** 7 A1.
📞 02-76 00 91 31.
🌐 www.ticketweb.it

Prenoticket
📞 02-542 71.

Ricordi Box Office
Galleria Vittorio Emanuele II.
Map 7 C1. 📞 02-869 06 83.

CHILDREN

Aquatica
Via G Airaghi 61.
📞 02-48 20 01 34.
🌐 www.parcoaquatica.com

Idroscalo (Fun Park)
Via Rivoltana 64.
📞 02-756 03 93.

Nuovo Arti
Via Mascagni 8. **Map** 4 E5.
📞 02-76 02 00 48.

Play Planet
Via Veglia 59.
📞 02-668 88 38.
🌐 www.play-planet.it

Teatro delle Marionette
Via degli Olivetani 3b.
Map 6 E1.
📞 02-469 44 40.

Nightlife

ONE OF THE CHARACTERISTICS that distinguishes Milan from other Italian cities is the way in which the city really comes alive at night. From Tuesday to Saturday the city's pubs, bars, cafés and discotheques are generally packed, though there are fewer Milanese and more people from outside the city on Saturdays. Monday and, to a certain extent, Sunday, are the quiet days, offering only rare occasions for entertainment. During the week clubs and discos organize theme evenings, and some of them operate a strict door policy. Places offering live music are also very popular; they often feature promising performers. The majority are located in the Navigli district.

DISCOS AND CLUBS

FOR THE ENERGETIC on the lookout for new trends in music and dance, Milan is a great place to be. The many discos and clubs in town offer different types of music and are so popular that they attract young people from all over Italy. The scene is quite volatile and with rare exceptions – some places have become positive institutions – Milan discos change their name, management and style periodically. It is quite common for a wildly popular club to fall out of favour, only to return to popularity once again some time later.

Some places charge an entrance fee; others are free but you are obliged to pay for drinks. Prices vary quite a lot; the so-called drinkcard system, whereby you pay for your drinks at the entrance, is fairly common.

One disco that has adopted this method is **Alcatraz**, a former factory converted into a multi-purpose venue for concerts, fashion shows and even conventions. Friday is given over to 1970s–80s revival dance music.

Next door is **Zenith**, which is more formal. There is a restaurant and also a private club called **De Sade**. Another chic disco that is popular with the prosperous younger generation is **Beau Geste**, where a range of music is performed. **Colony Dine & Dance** has live music and a students' night on Mondays. Sunday is cocktail evening with dancing.

Currently drawing in the fashion crowd is **Hollywood**. This is the place to go if you fancy celebrity spotting. The **Magazzini Generali**, which is also used for concerts and exhibitions, attracts a mixed crowd. The week opens on Wednesday and themed evenings include new musical trends and popular DJs. Friday is usually international night, with the latest music from around the world. Saturdays focus on the best of new dance, rock and contemporary pop music.

The **Shocking Club** is crowded every night from Monday to Saturday, and has become a Milanese institution. There is a strict door policy. A trendy multi-purpose disco is the **Café Atlantique**, which is a café, bar, restaurant and disco in one. **Rolling Stone** is a historic address where rock music reigns supreme. Thanks to its size, concerts are often held here.

The **Old Fashion**, inside the Triennale, is a disco with popular theme evenings. (The restaurant is also a big draw, especially for Sunday brunch.)

One of the largest discos in Milan is **Propaganda**. The place is also used for television programmes and music concerts.

For an alternative spot, try the **Rainbow**: it features rock and pop and on Friday and Saturday is mainly the haunt of teenagers. **Il Ragno d'Oro**, near the Spanish walls overlooking Porta Romana, is jam-packed in the summer.

NIGHTSPOTS WITH LIVE MUSIC

LISTENING TO LIVE MUSIC is a popular activity in the city and the choice of venues is wide. **Scimmie** is one of the city's historic nightspots. In the 1980s it was the place to go for live jazz, but recently has concentrated more on rock, blues and ethnic music. The place gets very crowded and it can be difficult to find a table unless you go early.

In the Navigli area, **Grillo-parlante** is worth checking out for up-and-coming bands. **Ca' Bianca** is the place to hear jazz and cabaret. You can sit outside in the summer, and there is also a restaurant.

Nidaba is small, dark and smoky, but people still love the atmosphere and it is always full. Promising young music bands are encouraged to perform here.

Lastly, concerts of current music are held at the **Tunnel**, a converted warehouse under the Stazione Centrale (main railway station). Tunnel also functions as a cultural centre, hosting shows and exhibitions as well as book launches for new publications.

DISCOPUBS

FOR THOSE WHO WANT TO dance without going to a disco there are so-called discopubs. In the early evening, these places are ideal for a relaxing drink and quiet conversation. Later in the evening the atmosphere livens up considerably. **Loola-paloosa**, for example, is an Irish pub with a happy hour extending from 5 to 9pm. Late at night it transforms into a totally different creature: the volume is turned up and every available spot is used for dancing, including the tables and the counter.

The **Indian Café**, in the Brera area, has a happy hour from 6 to 8pm, and turns into a discopub in the evening. There are three floor levels and concerts are put on for very reasonable prices. Music tends to be rock-oriented.

Another discopub is in the heart of the Brera quarter. **Soul to Soul** is always packed, and is a good place to hear black music. You need a membership card.

A great place for followers of fashion is the **Grand Café**, which is popular with celebrities and models. Happy hour runs from 6:30 to 9:30pm, after which you can dance downstairs. The house aperitifs are excellent.

Stonehenge is a bar and disco on two floor levels, inspired by Celtic culture. It is popular for theme evenings, live music and Latin-American dance courses. Happy hour extends from 6 to 9pm.

LATIN-AMERICAN

L ATIN-AMERICAN dance is increasingly popular in Milan. The place to go for uninhibited dancing is the **Tropicana**. It attracts mostly the over-thirty crowd and the best evenings to go are Thursday, Friday and Saturday.

If you find Cuban atmosphere intriguing and feel like trying out some Creole cuisine, the place to go is **Bodeguita del Medio**. Live music is on offer late at night and you can try salsa and merengue dancing.

A disco with Latin-American music only is **Planta Blanca**, where entry is free but drinks are obligatory.

Oficina do Sabor, on the other hand, alternates rock and blues evenings with nights entirely given over to Latin-American music. They also offer courses in salsa-merengue dancing, and anyone who wants to celebrate a special occasion can rent the club.

El Tropico Latino is a great place to try Mexican food while listening to music and sampling different types of tequila. Wednesday is the best evening to go.

MAJOR CONCERT VENUES

M ILAN'S LARGEST CONCERTS are sometimes performed in places normally associated with football. The stadium San Siro *(see p194)* is sometimes used, but the usual venue is the **Filaforum**, an ultra-modern sports arena with a seating capacity of 12,000. Other venues are the **Palavobis**, the former Pala-Trussardi, which can hold 9,000 people, and the **Palalido**, with 5,000 seats. Although space is limited at the **Leoncavallo** social centre, interesting concerts are put on. In the summer, concerts are also held at the Idroscalo or under the Arco della Pace. Sponsored by the Milan city council, entry is free.

Opera, Theatre and Cinema

THE THEATRE SEASON IN MILAN is undoubtedly one of the best and most varied in Italy. Visitors interested in a specific performance (especially if it is being put on in a well-known theatre such as the Scala or the Piccolo) should book well in advance, either directly through the theatre box office or by contacting one of the booking agencies in the city centre *(see p189)*.

For those who prefer films to the stage, Milan has a great number of cinemas. A bonus is that new releases are shown in Milan ahead of most other Italian cities. Many of the cinemas are multiplexes with plenty of screens, and the majority are concentrated in the city centre. Foreign-language films are also screened.

OPERA, BALLET & THEATRE

IT WOULD BE A SHAME to leave Milan without having seen an opera at **La Scala** *(see pp52–3)*. The season begins on 7 December, the feast day of Sant'Ambrogio, the city's patron saint. Lovers of ballet and classical music can also enjoy performances at the highest level from the theatre's ballet company and Filarmonica orchestra. It is important to book as far ahead of performances as possble, as, inevitably, there is much competition for seats at one of the world's most famous opera houses.

No less prestigious and world-famous is the **Teatro Grassi**. Founded just after World War II by Giorgio Strehler as "an arts theatre for everyone", its productions are known for their excellence. The **Teatro Strehler**, opened in 1998, was dedicated to the maestro, who had planned a state-of-the-art theatre worthy of his company's quality productions for over 40 years. The new theatre, with a seating capacity of 974, hosts the major Piccolo Teatro productions.

The **Teatro Studio**, in the former Fossati theatre, was originally meant to be a rehearsal hall for the Piccolo Teatro, but later became an independent company. Though interesting from an architectural standpoint, it is not all that comfortable.

The **Manzoni**, a favourite with the Milanese, presents a very eclectic programme, ranging from musicals to drama and comedy, always with top-level directors and actors.

Another historic theatre is the **Carcano**, first opened in 1803. It was restructured in the 1980s and has a capacity of 990 people. Its repertoire is classical, and dance is sometimes offered as well. For comedy, head for the **Ciak**, which usually stars leading comic actors.

For lovers of experimental and avant-garde theatre there are the **Teatridithalia-Elfo** and **-Porta Romana** theatres, which are dedicated to performing original works that are always fascinating and may sometimes shock.

The **Out Off** is also dedicated to avant-garde productions, but because of its limited seating capacity and location in the outskirts of town it is relatively unknown.

Milanese experimental theatre is performed at the **CRT Teatro dell'Arte**, which recently increased its seating capacity to 800.

The **San Babila** theatre offers a programme of more traditional theatre. Here the fame of the directors and actors attracts a large number of spectators, so that getting hold of a ticket may be hard.

The largest theatre in Milan is the **Smeraldo**, which can seat 2,100 people. Besides famous musicals, it plays host to dance performances, straight theatre and concerts.

Recently associated with the Smeraldo theatre is the **Nazionale**, which always features famous actors and has been concentrating more and more in recent years on dance and operettas.

The **Litta**, in Corso Magenta, is an elegant theatre which usually presents classic 20th-century plays. Another fascinating theatre is the **Teatro Franco Parenti**, which has a seating capacity of 500. The programme is quite varied, with particular attention being paid to new international works and music.

The small, intimate **Filodrammatici**, next to La Scala, presents a repertoire of classical works that also includes contemporary plays. The **Nuovo**, with its 1,020 seats, presents different kinds of theatrical productions, including musicals, comedies and dance, usually with famous actors. The recently renovated **Teatro Dal Verme** is also worth checking out.

CINEMAS

MOST OF THE leading cinemas in Milan are concentrated in the city centre, around Corso Vittorio Emanuele II. Most of these are multiplexes, which means there is plenty of choice. Ticket prices are reduced on Wednesday evening and in almost all cinemas on week-day afternoons as well. When popular new films are being shown there are always long queues, so go early.

Most non-Italian films are dubbed into Italian, without subtitles, so they will be difficult for anyone unfamiliar with the language. Visitors who want to see a film with the soundtrack in the original language *(in lingua originale)* can try the **Arcobaleno** on Tuesdays, or the **Anteo** or theatre 3 of the **Odeon Cinema 5**, where they have all-day showings of films in the original language on Mondays.

The **San Lorenzo**, with 170 seats, promotes various cultural events and programmes, such as the African Cinema Festival.

The **Auditorium San Fedele** is the home of three film clubs which offer different screening schedules and subject matter.

The **Odeon Cinema 5**, a multiplex, is the largest cinema in Milan, with ten theatres. On Corso Vittorio Emanuele II there are the **Pasquirolo**, with a seating capacity of 490, the **Mediolanum**, with 500 seats.

The **Excelsior** is situated in the Galleria del Corso. Another popular venue is the **San Carlo** in Via Morozzo della Rocca. The **Anteo** houses three theatres and also presents children's films.

The **Plinius**, in Viale Abruzzi, is a multiplex with five screens, while the **Colosseo**, in Viale Montenero, has three: the Visconti, Allen and Chaplin. The

President cinema in Largo Augusto can seat 250 people and is very comfortable. On Corso Garibaldi the **Brera Multisala** has two theatres. The **Ducale**, in Piazza Napoli, is an old cinema which has been converted into a multiplex with four theatres.

A popular newcomer on the scene is the **Arcadia**, just outside Milan at Melzo. The six cinemas here include Energia, the biggest in Italy.

The renovated **Gloria** now has two theatres (Garbo and Marilyn), huge screens and a good audio system. The Nuovo Arti *(see p189)* in Via Mascagni is entirely given over to programmes of children's cinema.

Fans of arthouse films can head for the recently renovated **Arioso**, the **Nuovo Corsica** or the **Sempione**. At the **De Amicis** cinema Milan city council organizes themed seasons of films, debates and film club showings.

Every year the Milan city council organizes cinema festivals, one of the best of which is the Panoramica di Venezia, held in September, when previews of the films competing in the Venice Film Festival are shown.

Many cinemas in Milan do provide wheelchair access, but it is always a good idea to telephone the box office beforehand for advice.

DIRECTORY

THEATRES

Carcano
Corso di Porta Romana 63.
Map 8 E3.
[02-55 18 13 77.
w www.teatrocarcano.com

Ciak
Via Sangallo 33.
[02-76 11 00 93.
w www.teatrociak.com

CRT Teatro dell'Arte
Viale Alemagna 6. **Map** 2
F3. [02-89 01 16 44.

Filodrammatici
Via Filodrammatici 1.
[02-869 36 59.

Litta
Corso Magenta 21. **Map**
A5. [02-86 45 45 45.

Manzoni
Via Manzoni 42.
Map 3 C5.
[02-76 02 05 43.
w www.teatromanzoni.it

Nazionale
Piazza Piemonte 12.
Map 1 C5.
[02-48 00 77 00.
w www.teatro
nazionale.com

Nuovo
Piazza San Babila 37. **Map**
4 D5. [02-76 00 00 86.
w www.teatronuovo.it

Out Off
Via Dupré 4.
[02-39 26 22 82.
w www.teatroutoff.it

San Babila
Corso Venezia 2/a. **Map** 4
E4. [02-76 00 29 85.

Smeraldo
Piazza XXV Aprile 10.
[02-29 00 67 67.

Teatridithalia-Elfo
Via Ciro Menotti 11.
[02-71 67 91.

Teatridithalia-Porta Romana
Corso di Porta Romana
124. **Map** 7 C2.
[02-58 31 58 96.

Teatro Franco Parenti
Via Pierlombardo 14. **Map**
8 F3. [02-55 18 40 75.

Teatro Grassi
Via Rovello 2. **Map** 3 B5.
[02-72 33 32 22.

Teatro alla Scala
Via Filodrammatici 2 (entrance from Piazza Scala).
[02-72 00 37 44.

Teatro Strehler
Largo Greppi 1.
[02-72 33 32 22.

Teatro Studio
Via Rivoli 6.
[02-72 33 32 22.

Teatro Dal Verme
Via Sangiovanni Sul Muro.
Map 3 B5.
[02-87 90 52 01.
w www.dalverme.org

CINEMAS

Anteo
Via Milazzo 9. **Map** 3 C2.
[02-659 97 75.

Arcadia
Via Martiri della Libertà 5,
Melzo. [02-95 41 64 44.

Arcobaleno
Viale Tunisia 11. **Map** 4
E2. [02-29 53 76 21.

Arioso
Via Arioso 16. **Map** 2 E4.
[02-48 00 39 01.

Auditorium San Fedele
Via Hoepli 3b. **Map** 4 D5.
[02-86 35 22 30.

Brera Multisala
Corso Garibaldi 99. **Map**
3 B2. [02-29 00 18 90.

Centrale
Via Torino 30. **Map** 7 B1.
[02-87 48 26.

Cinema Cavour
Piazza Cavour 3. **Map** 4
D4. [02-659 57 79.

Colosseo
Viale Montenero 84. **Map**
8 E2. [02-59 90 13 61.

Corallo
Largo Corsia dei Servi 9.
[02-76 02 07 21.

De Amicis
Via Caminadella 15. **Map**
7 A2. [02-86 45 27 16.

Ducale
Piazza Napoli 27. **Map** 5
C3. [02-47 71 92 79.

Excelsior
Galleria del Corso 4.
[02-76 00 23 54.

Gloria
Corso Vercelli 18. **Map** 2
D5. [02-48 00 89 08.

Mediolanum
Corso Vittorio Emanuele II
24. **Map** 8 D1.
[02-76 02 08 18.

Nuovo Corsica
Viale Corsica 68. **Map** 6
F3. [02-70 00 61 99.

Odeon Cinema 5
Via Santa Radegonda 8.
[02-87 45 47.

Pasquirolo
Corso Vittorio Emanuele II
28. **Map** 8 D1.
[02-76 02 07 57.

Plinius
Viale Abruzzi 28–30.
[02-29 53 11 03.

President
Largo Augusto 1. **Map** 8
D1. [02-76 02 21 90.

San Carlo
Via Morozzo della Rocca 4.
Map 6 F1.
[02-481 34 42.

San Lorenzo alle Colonne
Corso di Porta Ticinese 45.
Map 7 B2.
[02-58 11 31 61.

Sempione
Via Pacinotti 6.
[02-39 21 04 83.

Sports and Outdoor Activities

P EOPLE VISITING MILAN ON BUSINESS may want to
continue with a routine of practising a sport or
exercising. If so, there are many facilities in the city,
including health clubs and gymnasiums, that will suit
the purpose. These centres often offer a range of
activities under one roof so that you can make the
most of your free time. Visitors preferring to spectate
rather than participate can go and see the local football
(soccer), basketball and hockey teams. All are in
the first division and offer top-quality sport.

SPORTS FACILITIES

F OOTBALL (SOCCER) fans
should go to a match at
the **Meazza** (or **San Siro**)
Stadium *(see p195)* at least
once in their lifetime. Called
the "Scala of football", this
stadium has a seating capacity
of over 80,000. One particularly popular competition
from both the sporting and
the theatrical point of view is
the local derby between the
city's two teams, Inter and AC
Milan. However, it is best to
plan attendance in advance as
tickets sell out pretty quickly.

For horse-racing fans there
is the **Ippodromo**, where
races are held all year long,
except for December. Night
races are held from June to
September.

The Filaforum arena at
Assago *(see p191)* is the
home of the local basketball
(Pallacanestro Olimpia) and
volleyball (Gonzaga) teams.
The arena also plays host to
various tennis tournaments,
first and foremost the Inter-
nazionale di Milano, which
takes place in spring.

Ice hockey buffs can follow
the matches of the Devils
(the only remaining local
team after the disbanding
of Milano 24), who play at
the **PalAgorà** arena.

FIVE-A-SIDE FOOTBALL

O NE OF THE MOST popular
sports at the moment in
Milan is *calcetto* – five-a-side
football (soccer). Those wish-
ing to play should go to the
Centro Peppino Vismara,
where they play 11-, 7- and
5-a-side. Another good leisure
facility is the **Palauno**, where
there are five pitches.

GOLF

T HERE ARE SEVERAL golf
courses in the Milan area.
The closest one to the city
is **Le Rovedine Golf Club–
Sporting Mirasole**, which
is about 7 km (4 miles)
from the city centre. There is
also a restaurant for the use
of players at the club.

SWIMMING

F OR A RELAXING SWIM, one
good swimming pool is
the **Piscina Solari**, which has
five lanes. A good alternative
is the **Piscina Giovanni da
Procida**, which boasts a half-
size Olympic pool with six
lanes. There is also a gym
at this site which is ideal for
warming up.

The **Lido** is the city's most
popular outdoor swimming
pool. Visitors who are not
daunted by large crowds and
enjoy slides can come here
to swim during the heat of
the Milanese summer.

SKATING

T HOSE KEEN ON roller skating
will enjoy themselves at
the multi-purpose **24 Sport
Village**, which has rinks for
roller skating, roller hockey
and aerobic roller skating.
They also offer facilities for
many other sporting activities,
including tennis, basketball,
swimming and mountain
biking. Ice-skaters can go to
the **Palazzo del Ghiaccio**,
which has an indoor rink
where people can skate at
their leisure from Tuesday
to Saturday in the evening.
It is also open in the
afternoon at the weekends
from 3 to 6pm.

The PalAgorà welcomes ice
skaters from Wednesday to
Saturday in the evening and
also from 3 to 6pm at weekends. All the rinks have skates
for rent. During the Christmas
season an ice-skating rink is
usually set up in Piazza del
Duomo enabling people to
skate by starlight.

SQUASH

T HIS SPORT IS IDEAL for fit-
ness, and players are
welcome at the **Squash Vico**.
There are ten courts. Private
and group lessons are available, and equipment can be
hired. The centre is open
every day, including the
evening. However, to use
these facilities visitors must
buy a membership card,
valid for two months.

TENNIS

T ENNIS PLAYERS CAN play in
an ideal setting at the
**Associazione Sporting Club
Corvetto**. The Club does not
operate a membership card
scheme, and there are 13
indoor courts as well as a
gymnasium, bar and rest-
aurant and parking space
reserved for customers.

The **Centro Sportivo
Mario Saini** has 12 courts,
either covered or open to the
air, depending on the season.
It is best to book ahead by
telephone. Another place
where it is possible to play
in peace and quiet, in a sporting club reserved exclusively
for this sport, is the **Tennis
Club 5 Pioppi**, in the Fiera
district. There are four courts
that can be used both in
summer and winter.

JOGGING

T HE BEST AND healthiest
place for running is the
Monte Stella park (also
known as the "Montagnetta"),
near the San Siro Stadium.
This large area of greenery
is a good place to jog, following marked paths, or even
for cycling around on mountain bikes. In the summer the
park is often filled with numbers of apartment-dwelling
Milanese, catching some sun.

DIRECTORY

SPORTS FACILITIES

Ippodromo
Via Piccolomini 2.
02-48 21 61.
www. trenno.it

Meazza Stadium (San Siro)
Piazzale Axum.
02-622 81.

PalAgorà
Via dei Ciclamini 23.
02-48 30 09 46.

FOOTBALL

Centro Peppino Vismara
Via dei Missaglia 117.
02-826 58 23.

Palauno
Largo Balessa 55.
02-423 53 15.
www.palauno.com

GOLF

Le Rovedine Golf Club–Sporting Mirasole
Via C Marx 16,
Noverasco di Opera.
02-57 60 64 20.

SWIMMING

Lido
Piazzale Lotto 15.
02-39 266100.

Piscina Giovanni da Procida
Via Giovanni da Procida 20.
Map 2 D2.
02-33 10 49 70.

Piscina Solari
Via Montevideo 11. **Map** 6 E2. 02-469 52 78.

SKATING

Palazzo del Ghiaccio
Via Piranesi 14.
02-739 81.

24 Sport Village
Via Assietta 19.
02-662 16 11.

SQUASH

Squash Vico
Via GB Vico 38.
02-48 01 08 90.

TENNIS

Associazione Sporting Club Corvetto
Via Fabio Massimo 15/4.
02-53 14 36.

Centro Sportivo Mario Saini
Via Corelli 136.
02-756 12 80.

Tennis Club 5 Pioppi
Via Marostica 4. **Map** 5 A1. 02-404 85 93.
www.tennis-cinquepioppi.it

SAN SIRO STADIUM

KEY

○ ticket office

1 stadium entrances

▢ area for Milan guests

▢ area for Inter guests

— block of seats

— block of seats

— block of seats

— block of seats

GETTING THERE

Avoid going by car, as parking space is very hard to find. The best way to get there is to take line 1 of the metro to the Lotto stop; from there a shuttle bus goes to the stadium. At the end of the match the No. 24 trams (under the blue area) go to the city centre. Another option is taking a taxi (from the Lotto metro as well).

ENTERTAINMENT AT THE LAKES

The logo of the Caneva aquatic
amusement park

AT THE LAKES it is possible to devote a considerable amount of leisure time to entertainment and sport. At Lake Garda in particular, you will be able to practise any type of aquatic sport, have a go at trekking in the hinterland and dance the night away at the discos. Of the lakes, Garda also has the liveliest nightlife and is the most popular with young people. Lake Como, Lake Maggiore and the smaller lakes still offer a variety of opportunities for entertainment. In recent years the enterprising local APT tourist offices, sponsored by the town administrations, have been quite successful in promoting initiatives aimed at making holidays more interesting for visitors. Outdoor markets, feasts, festivals and other events have therefore become more and more frequent. The lakes offer breathtaking scenery, an entertainment in itself, and every year there are programmes of cultural events. In addition there are fine architectural and artistic works to be seen, lovely gardens to explore, and nature reserves to wander through.

SPORTS

IF KEEPING IN top physical shape is a priority, there are plenty of activities that serve the purpose at the lakes. Lake Garda is the domain of windsurfing; Torbole and Riva in particular being the most popular places for surfers both in summer and winter. Sailing fans will enjoy the Centomiglia, an annual regatta organized by the Circolo Vela Gargnano sailing club and held on the second weekend of September. For a more relaxing time, there are also opportunities to go fishing.

In the Garda hinterland, hiking has become very popular, and touring the area on a mountain bike is the most recent vogue. More adventurous souls can take lessons in paragliding.

Lake Maggiore offers not only many aquatic sports but is quite popular with golf enthusiasts. There are state-of-the-art golf courses in lovely natural settings which are enjoyed by Italian and foreign golfers alike.

The hills and valleys around the lake are ideal places for horse riding, hiking, mountaineering, free climbing, hang-gliding and paragliding and, in the winter, when snow covers the high ground, skiing and snow-boarding.

The most popular sports at Lake Como are sailing and water skiing. Lessons are available from qualified instructors, whatever your age and experience.

Another enjoyable activity is canoeing. All the lakes have clubs where you can rent canoes and equipment.

**A water skiing instructor
and his pupil at Lake Como**

For the more sedentary, there are many spas *(terme)* at the lakes or in the vicinity. These centres offer a variety of treatments.

OTHER ACTIVITIES

VISITORS TO Lake Garda, especially families with children, might want to visit the Gardaland amusement park *(see pp148–9)*. It is recommended for children and adults alike, the ideal place to enjoy yourselves and even experience the occasional thrill. However, in peak season, be prepared for a very long wait at the most interesting attractions.

About 2 km (1 mile) from Gardaland is **Caneva**, the

A group of windsurfers in action at Lake Garda

Camels in the Natura Viva zoological park, at Bussolengo-Pastrengo near Lake Garda

The **Parco Giardino Sigurtà** lies 8 km (5 miles) from Peschiera. This 50-ha (123-acre) garden is a temple to ecology.

At Lake Maggiore the Villa Pallavicino park *(see p133)* has a lovely 20-ha (49-acre) botanic garden with 40 different species of animals.

L'**Ultimo Caffè** and **Skagen**.

At Lake Maggiore, do not miss **La Rocchetta**, a disco situated in a splendid Art Nouveau villa with a view of the lake, and **Dancing Mirage**. At Verbania, go to **Tam Tam**, and **Byblos**, at Arizzano, is a lively spot.

largest water amusement park in Italy. Shows, water games and other displays, plus an area reserved for small children, make this a big aquatic attraction.

To take a closer look at some rare and endangered animal species, visit the **Parco Natura Viva**, a zoo located at Bussolengo-Pastrengo. A pleasant walk among ancient oak trees and plants takes visitors around the home of the 1,000 specimens in this lovely park. Cars are also allowed into the safari park, where a 6-km (4-mile) tour brings you into closer contact with some of the wild animals of the savannah.

Another popular place for lovers of interesting plants is the **Giardino Botanico della Fondazione André Heller** at Gardone Riviera: 1.5 ha (3.7 acres) of land with over 8,000 plants from every climatic zone in the world.

Logo of the Natura Viva zoological park

NIGHTLIFE

THE BEST AREA for night life is Lake Garda, which boasts internationally known nightspots. Desenzano, in particular, has a number of pubs and other spots for evening entertainment, while in the outskirts are some of the largest discotheques in Italy. The undisputed king is **Genux**, a gigantic and extremely popular place, especially in the summer. Another famous and very popular nightspot is **Fura**, a multimedia disco where theme evenings feature. On Friday there is funk, soul and "rare groove" music, while the other evening (and night) programmes are more unconventional.

At Lake Como the most popular disco is **Mascara,** where live music is played until midnight, after which there is dancing with a disc jockey. For live music, go to

One of the bars at the Genux discotheque at Lake Garda

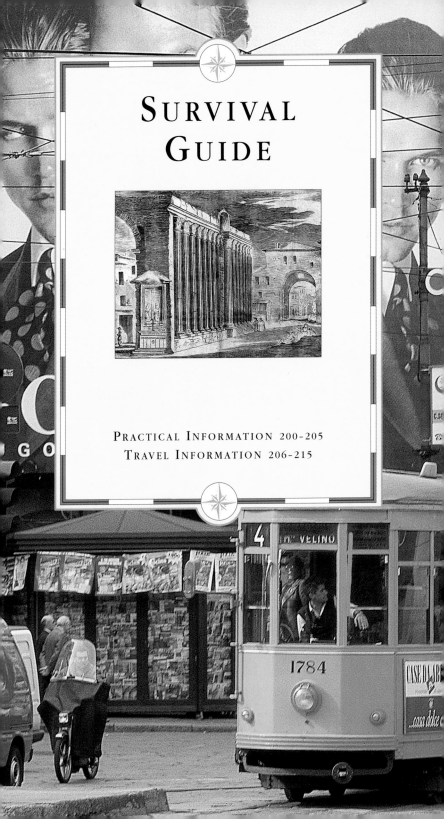

SURVIVAL GUIDE

PRACTICAL INFORMATION

ILAN IS ONE of Italy's most efficient and business-like cities, with an excellent public transport network and good public services. In the capital of fashion, appearances do matter, and you are likely to receive better service and attention if you are smartly dressed. Milan has its share of petty crime, and it is advisable to take some basic precautions in order to enjoy your stay to the full. Keep bags and cameras close to you at all times, and take extra care travelling on public transport, where pickpockets

Logo of the City of Milan

may be operating. The public transport system is, however, the best way to get around the city. Walkers should stay alert in the chaotic traffic, and take particular care crossing streets. Tourist offices are the best places to go for practical information including maps. At the lakes, brochures are available from APT offices, with information on local festivals and other entertainment. Information can be obtained ahead of your visit from the Italian tourist office (ENIT) in your home country.

TOURIST INFORMATION

THE Italian tourist board, the Ente Nazionale Italiano per il Turismo (ENIT) has offices in many major capital cities including London, New York and Montreal, where maps and information on hotels, etc. are available. In Milan itself, the Informazione e Accoglienza Turistica (IAT) and Azienda di Promozione Turistica (APT) tourist offices provide detailed information about the city, including free lists of hotels and restaurants as well as information on cultural events.

Logo of the APT in Milan

At the lakes, look for APT offices or IAT offices in larger towns, or Pro Loco offices in smaller towns and villages (usually in the town hall).

English is spoken and understood in most hotels and shops and frequently used on planes and tour buses. However, a few words of Italian will always be welcome.

PASSPORTS AND VISAS

EUROPEAN UNION nationals need a full passport to enter Italy, but can then stay as long as they like. Citizens of the US, Canada, Australia and New Zealand are in possession of a full passport can stay in Italy for up to three months. For longer stays, special visas are needed from an Italian embassy.

All visitors must declare their presence to the police within eight days of arrival. If you are staying in a hotel, this will be done for you.

The *Milano Dove, Come, Quando* listings guide

USEFUL PUBLICATIONS

EVERY WEEK the daily newspapers *Corriere della Sera* and *La Repubblica* publish a special supplement (*Vivi-Milano* and *Tutto Milano* respectively) packed with up-to-date information about cultural activities in the city and the surroundings.

The Milan daily newspapers such as *Il Corriere* have local news sections, which also include theatre and music entertainment and venues and a cinema guide.

The APT office distributes free copies of *Milano Mese*, a brochure with listings of the various cultural events.

Another publication, *Milano Dove, Come, Quando* is a practical guide that will help you to get around the city. It is also obtainable from the Milan APT office.

The main APT tourist office in Milan (on the left)

People with access to the Internet will find a mass of information available on the web. One especially useful website is www.itwg.com.

MUSEUMS, MONUMENTS AND TOURS

MILAN's artistic and architectural masterpieces are housed in a variety of institutions, from art galleries and churches to palazzi and castles. In general, most state-owned museums are open from Tuesday to Sunday, churches are open daily. Privately owned museums will operate their own individual timetables.

Discounts are available for residents of the EU under 18 and over 60 in the majority of state-run places.

A good way of gaining an overview of the city is to travel on the **Tram Turistico**, a tour tram that departs from Piazza Castello. The tour lasts for about 1 hour 45 minutes, and audio tapes provide recorded descriptions of sights in Italian, English, French, German and Japanese.

Another tour is the **Giro della Città**, which begins at Piazza del Duomo in the centre. This tour is available from Tuesday to Sunday and covers all the main monuments of Milan in approximately 3 hours.

In recent years the local administrations at the lakes have also been involved in a variety of cultural promotions. The Associazione Albergatori della Provincia di Varese (Varese hotel owners' association) has introduced a Welcome Card. Distributed free at hotels locally, it allows visitors to obtain a 10 per cent discount on the admission charge at many museums and sights in the area.

INFORMATION FOR STUDENTS

THE CENTRO TURISTICO Studentesco (CTS) offers discount tickets to young people under 26, which can be used for travel not only in Milan, but in the rest of Italy and Europe as well.

As far as student accommodation is concerned, there is one youth hostel in Milan, the **Ostello della Gioventù P Rotta**. You need to present an annual membership card (which can be bought at the hostel itself).

Membership cards of the CTS, or Centro Turistico Studentesco

For more detailed information on youth hostels around the lakes, contact the Associazione Italiana Alberghi per la Gioventù (Italian Youth Hostelling Association).

ITALIAN TIME

MILAN IS ONE HOUR ahead of Greenwich Mean Time. This means that London is one hour behind Italian time and New York and Los Angeles are 6 and 9 hours behind respectively, and Moscow is 2 hours ahead. Tokyo and Sydney are 8 and 9 hours ahead respectively.

Personal Security and Health

**Italian pharmacy
sign**

IN MILAN, there is widespread petty crime, a problem common to all large cities. Stay wary and keep a close eye on your personal property such as bags or cameras, especially in the evening and, in some quarters, during the day as well. The towns and villages around the lakes are very safe areas however, and there should be no cause for concern. Should you fall ill during your stay, Italian pharmacists can advise on minor ailments.

HINTS FOR TRAVELLERS

IT IS NOT advisable to walk around alone in the evening in poorly lit streets far from the city centre. Unaccompanied women should take particular care.

Petty theft is a perennial problem, so keep a tight grip on your bag or case in crowded places, particularly in trams and on the metro. Pickpockets work their way around the public transport system and can operate un-noticed in crowds of people. Always keep handbags closed and do not carry haversacks (backpacks) or shoulder bags on your back. It is always best to keep valuables such as a wallet or mobile phone well out of sight.

When walking along the street, keep handbags on the inside, away from the road, to foil purse snatchers on scooters (*scippatori*).

Visitors who are getting about by car should take all the usual precautions appropriate in a big city. Do not leave personal belongings or car radios visible inside the car, since they might attract potential thieves. It is best to try to leave your car in an attended parking space (*parcheggio custodito*). Make sure you have adequate travel insurance before you leave.

HEALTH AND MEDICAL ASSISTANCE

THE CITY HAS state-of-the-art health facilities, should you become ill during your stay in Milan. All EU citizens should be armed with the E111 form, available from post offices, which entitles the holder to free emergency treatment and reciprocal health care in Italy. It is wise, however, for visitors to have health insurance.

If the ailment is minor, go initially to a pharmacy (*farmacia*). Italian pharmacists are well

**A municipal policewoman
directing traffic in Milan**

trained to deal with routine problems. Each pharmacy can be identified by a neon green cross over the door. There is also a free emergency number: 800-80 11 85. A list of pharmacies open at night (*servizio notturno*) and on public holidays will be on display. A useful chemist (drugstore) is the **Farmacia della Stazione Centrale**, at the main railway station, open 24 hours a day. If you need urgent medical assistance, call the **Emergenza Sanitaria/ Ambulanze** (Health Emergencies/Ambulance), or go straight to the *Pronto Soccorso* (Casualty Department/ Emergency Room) at the nearest hospital.

If you need a doctor at your hotel, call the **Guardia Medica** (Night Duty Physician). In the unlikely event of poisoning, contact the **Centro Antiveleni** (Poison Control Centre).

MOSQUITOES

IN SUMMER mosquitoes (*zanzare*), which appear at the first sign of warm weather, can be a real pest. Despite the various anti-mosquito devices, such as citronella candles or electrical gadgets which burn insect-repellent tablets, it is difficult to fend them off altogether, especially when sitting at outdoor cafés (the Navigli quarter is fairly bad). People who are particularly allergic to mosquito bites should always apply insect repellent cream or spray.

Milanese police at a road block

Tap water is safe to drink in Italy, but many people prefer to drink bottled water *(acqua minerale)*, which may be either fizzy *(frizzante* or *con gas)* or still *(naturale)*.

Fire brigade jeep

EMERGENCIES

THE POLICE and fire brigade emergency services operate 24 hours a day. The various police stations *(Questura)* and hospitals *(Ospedale)* with a casualty unit/emergency room *(Pronto Soccorso)* are shown in the Street Finder *(see pp222–9)*. There are several different police forces in Italy. State police *(la Polizia)* wear blue, traffic police *(Vigili Urbani)* wear blue and white in winter, white in summer, and are responsible for traffic and parking. *Carabinieri* deal with general crime, public order and drug-related offences.

LOST PROPERTY

IF YOU LOSE documents or other personal property, it is advisable to report the loss immediately at the nearest police station. An official report will be needed for insurance claims. It may be worth contacting the city **Ufficio Oggetti Smarriti** (Lost Property Office). If you lose items on a train or in a station, contact the Left Luggage office *(Deposito)* in the Stazione Centrale.

Should an interpreter be needed, ask at your hotel or try the Yellow Pages *(Pagine Gialle)*, where agencies will be listed (there is also a website at www.paginegialle.it). The Associazione Italiana di Traduttori e Interpreti (AITI) has a list of qualified translators and interpreters. The various embassies should also be able to provide interpreters. It is wise to take photocopies of all important documents, including passport pages, before travelling.

Ambulance

Police van

SAFETY OUTDOORS

MILAN HAS a number of green open spaces, but the city air is still quite polluted. In certain weather conditions this produces a high concentration of smog, and people are advised to wear anti-pollution masks.

The air is much cleaner and fresher at the lakes, and visitors are unlikely to experience anything more alarming than the odd mosquito. The more adventurous keen to practise watersports should follow certain guidelines. At Lakes Maggiore and Como, cold water and strong currents challenge even experienced swimmers. On Lake Garda, windsurfers may be taken by surprise by sudden gusts of wind, particularly in the areas around Torbole and Riva (the northern part of the lake).

DIRECTORY

EMERGENCY NUMBERS

General Emergencies
(113.

Carabinieri
(112.

Fire
(115.

Emergenza Sanitaria/ Ambulanze (Health Emergencies/Ambulance)
(118.

Municipal Traffic Police
(02-772 71.

Guardia Medica
(02-345 67.

Centro Antiveleni (Poison Control Centre)
(02-66 10 10 29.

Farmacia della Stazione Centrale
(02-669 07 35.

Pronto Farmacia
(800-80 11 85 (free).

ACI – Accidents and Breakdowns (80 31 16.

LOST PROPERTY

Ufficio Oggetti Smarriti
Via Friuli 30. **Map** 8 F4
(02-5419 7249, 02-5419 7257.

Stazione Centrale (Left Luggage)
Piazza Duca d'Aosta. **Map** 4 E1
(02-6371 2212, 02-6371 2667.

Canoeing, one of the most popular outdoor activities in the lakes in Lombardy

Banking and Communications

MILAN HAS VERY GOOD public services. There is a bank on almost every corner of the city, and almost all of them have automatic cash dispensers. In general the post offices are well organized and run smoothly, despite the fact that the Italian postal system has a reputation for notoriously slow delivery. Public telephones can be operated by coins or phone cards and are well maintained. Business visitors may find it useful to know that it is possible to hire a mobile phone. At the lakes there are fewer banks and post offices because of the small size of the towns and villages, but the service is good.

Telecom Italia phone cards, now collectors' items

USING TELEPHONES

TELECOM ITALIA runs the network of public telephones throughout Italy, including Milan and around the lakes. Milan is well supplied with telephone booths, which usually operate with telephone cards (*schede telefoniche*) (sold at tobacconists or newsstands). Public phones take coins although cards are widely used. There are also public phones at Telecom offices. The largest branch is in Galleria Vittorio Emanuele II and it is open every day from 8am to 9:30pm. The Telecom bureau also offers a fax service.

The Telecom office in the Stazione Centrale (main station) is usually open from 8am to 8pm daily. From here you can telephone anywhere in the world. You can also receive faxes, and consult telephone directories for the whole of Italy, the rest of Europe and countries around the Mediterranean basin.

The cheapest phone rates are between 10pm and 8am Monday to Saturday, and all day on Sunday. It is convenient to make calls from your hotel room, but the charges will be much higher than at a public phone.

The area code (*prefisso*) for Milan is 02. The code should be included even when phoning within Milan. It is now necessary to dial numbers in full throughout Italy, even for local calls.

For information concerning international calls, dial 176; to make an international reverse charge (collect) call, the number to dial is 170.

New telecommunications companies such as Infostrada and Wind now compete with Telecom Italia, and telephone rates have become much more competitive.

GSM mobile phones work in Italy (but make sure they are turned off on aeroplanes). It is possible

Logo of Telecom Italia

DIAL THE RIGHT NUMBER

- Area code for calls to and within Milan: 02.
- Italian Directory Enquiries: 12.
- International Directory Enquiries: 176.
- Reverse charge international calls: 170.
- To call Great Britain from Italy, dial 0044, then the area code deleting the first zero, and the number of the person you are calling.
- To call the US: 001.
- To call Ireland: 00353.
- To call Australia: 0061.
- To call Canada: 001.
- To call France: 0033.
- To call South Africa: 0027.
- To call New Zealand: 0064.

to rent a mobile phone. These are available from three firms: TIM (Telecom Italia Mobile), Omnitel and Wind, all of which use the GSM network. Be careful, as charges can vary quite a bit. Another useful place should you need to hire a mobile phone, is the **Eurochange Business Centre** at Malpensa airport.

The Telecom office in Galleria Vittorio Emanuele II

Main branch of the Credito Italiano, in Piazza Cordusio

BANKS

MILANESE BANKS are open from Monday to Friday from 8:30am to 1:30pm, and in the afternoon from 3 to 4pm, though this may vary by about quarter of an hour from bank to bank. Almost all banks have cashpoint machines, or ATMs, which take all major credit cards, including American Express and Visa.

CURRENCY EXCHANGE

THE EURO came into circulation in Italy on 1 January 2002. Cash will be needed in smaller shops, in bars and for items like taxis, but it is better not to carry large amounts on you. The safest way to carry money is to buy euro travellers' cheques, which can be refunded if unused.

It is a good idea to bring

some euros with you, but it is possible to change money at the airports. At Linate, **Euro-change Linate**, at international arrivals, is open daily from 7am–midnight, and the office at international departures is open from 6am–10pm.

Both arrivals and departures at Malpensa have branches of **Eurochange Malpensa**, open daily from 7am–11pm. The **Banca Ponti** in Piazza del Duomo has an automatic exchange machine. **CIT** travel agents in the centre can also offer exchange facilities from Monday to Saturday.

CREDIT CARDS

BOTH IN MILAN and at the lakes, businesses accept major credit cards such as American Express, Visa, Diners Club International and MasterCard (Access).

Most banks have automatic cash dispensers *(bancomat)* where you can obtain money with credit cards or bank cards, using a PIN number. In the event of the loss or theft of your credit card, you should immediately contact the numbers listed in the directory below.

Logo of cashpoint machines *(bancomat)*

POSTAL SERVICES

POST OFFICES in Milan are open from Monday to Friday from 8:00am to 2:00pm and on Saturday from 9:30am to 1:00pm. There are also

thirteen post offices that have extended trading hours: weekdays from 8:00am to 7:00pm and on Saturday from 9:30am to 1:00pm. The **Ufficio Centrale** (central post office) is open all day and also has a poste restante *(Fermo Posta)* and express service *(Postacelere)*.

At **Linate Airport Post Office** you can send parcels, letters and registered letters, and a telegram office is open from 8am to 2pm every day.

This service is also offered at the **Ufficio Stazione Centrale** (main railway station) from Monday to Friday from 8:00am to 7pm and on Saturday from 9:30am to 1:00pm. Throughout Italy, stamps can be bought at post offices and also at tobacconists *(tabaccai)*.

E-MAIL

E-MAIL is a convenient way to keep in touch when travelling through Italy. Telecom Italia is setting up Internet services in major train stations and public phone centres. Time is purchased using a regular phone card.

Some Internet-access chains sell cards with credit that can be used in any of their Italian stores. Internet points can often be found around train stations and university areas. Users can often buy computer time in blocks as short as 15 minutes, and there are usually student discounts available.

DIRECTORY			
MOBILE HIRE	**Mondadori** Via Marghera 28. **Map** 1 C5 📞 02-48 04 73 03.	**Banca Ponti** Piazza Duomo 19. **Map** 7 C1 📞 02-72 27 71.	**Diners Club** 📞 800-86 40 64. **MasterCard** 📞 800-87 08 66.
Eurochange Business Centre Malpensa airport. 📞 02-58 58 10 74.	**CURRENCY EXCHANGE**	**CIT** Galleria Vittorio	**POSTAL SERVICES**
INTERNET CAFES	**Eurochange Linate** International arrivals 📞 02-756 13 72.	Emanuele II. **Map** 7 C1 📞 02-86 37 02 32.	**Ufficio Centrale** Via Cordusio 4. 📞 02-72 48 21 26.
Internet Enjoi Via Medici 3. **Map** 7 B2 📞 02-86 68 00.	**Eurochange Malpensa** International arrivals	**CREDIT CARDS** (MISSING/STOLEN)	🖥 www.poste.it **Other Post Offices** 📞 02-40 09 93 32
Metaverse Internet Point Via Plinio 48. 📞 02-29 53 62 70.	📞 02-58 58 03 05. International departures 📞 02-58 58 03 05.	**American Express** 📞 800-86 40 46. **Visa** 📞 800-87 72 32.	(Malpensa). 📞 02-717 847 (Linate). 📞 02-67 39 51 Via Sammartini 2. (Central Railway Station).

TRAVEL INFORMATION

TWO AIRPORTS link Milan with the rest of the world. Linate airport is only a few kilometres from the city centre and connects the capital of Lombardy with all the main Italian and European cities. It is conveniently located for European business travellers. Malpensa is an intercontinental airport about 50 km (30 miles) from Milan. There are car hire offices at both airports though it is usually cheaper to book a fly-drive deal ahead rather than arrange hire on arrival. For those travelling by train, there are excellent train links between

An Alitalia airplane

Milan and other cities in Italy. The city is also well connected to the rest of Europe, with fast, easy routes to France and Switzerland, and to Austria and Germany via Verona. Visitors arriving by car will use the excellent road and motorway networks. Exits from the ringroad around Milan are clearly marked. However, these roads are always congested with traffic, so journey times can be slow. In the early morning, when commuters begin to make their way into the centre, getting into town may take twice as long as you expect.

ARRIVING BY AIR

VISITORS ARRIVING IN Milan by air will fly into either Linate or Malpensa airports. Milan is a major point of entry into Italy, along with Rome. Frequent flights between London and Milan are operated by Alitalia, British Airways and low-cost airlines Buzz and Go. Alitalia offers the best choice of direct flights from the US, linking Milan with Boston, New York, Chicago, Miami and Los Angeles. Alitalia also has good connections from Toronto, Vancouver and Sydney.

LINATE AIRPORT

THIS AIRPORT has always been popular with the Milanese because of its proximity to the city centre. However business has been

scaled down as a result of the government's decision to concentrate on the total renovation and enlargement of Malpensa airport. At present Linate handles the Milan–Rome flights of all carriers except Meridiana; two daily Alitalia and AirOne flights to Naples; two Alitalia flights to Sicily and Sardinia; three to five daily flights to London, Paris, Amsterdam, Madrid and Frankfurt.

The airport has Left Luggage facilities, car rental offices including Avis and Hertz, and plenty of car parking space.

In the future the majority of international flights will be handled at Malpensa.

How to Get to Milan

Getting from Linate to the centre of Milan is very straightforward. Visitors

unfamiliar with the city and burdened with a great deal of luggage would do best to take a taxi. Official taxis are white and line up at the taxi stand right in front of the airport exit. In general, the service is prompt.

An alternative is going by bus, which is perfectly comfortable and much cheaper: tickets cost only €1 and are sold at the vending machine near the bus stop.

There are two bus lines serving Linate airport. ATM bus number 73 passes at regular intervals from 5:30am to 0:20am and connects the airport with the city centre, going as far as Piazza San Babila. The STAM bus runs from 5:40am to 7pm every 20 minutes and from 7 to 9pm every 30 minutes, connecting Linate and the main station.

A view of the new Malpensa airport

The Milan airport, Linate

The ring road *(tangenziale)* around Milan, often congested with traffic

MALPENSA AIRPORT

ONE OF EUROPE'S most modern airports, Malpensa was refurbished and enlarged in 1998.

How to Get to Milan
In June 1999 a new railway line connecting Malpensa and the city centre came into operation. Trains to the airport depart from Piazza Cadorna every 30 minutes, at 10 and 40 minutes past the hour; those to Milan leave at 20 and 50 minutes past the hour.

Two efficient coach lines also offer a good airport service. The Malpensa Shuttle is scheduled as follows: Malpensa–Stazione Centrale every 20 minutes from 6:40am to 10pm and every 30 minutes from 10:30pm to 12:30am; Stazione Centrale–Malpensa every 20 minutes from 5:20am to 10pm; Malpensa–Linate every hour from 6:20am to 1:20am and Linate–Malpensa every hour from 4am to 11:30 pm. The Malpensa Express train timetable is: Malpensa–Piazzale Cadorna every 30 minutes from 6:45am to

12:15am; Cadorna–Malpensa every 30 minutes from 5:30am to 10:30 pm (every hour from 1 to 3pm). Tickets for Malpensa– Stazione Centrale and Malpensa–Cadorna cost €6, and the Malpensa–Linate ticket is €9. Tickets for children aged 2 to 12 are half-price. You can check in at the Air Terminal in the Milan Stazione Centrale.

ARRIVING BY CAR

VISITORS ARRIVING IN Milan from the *autostrada* (motorway) will approach the city via the ring roads, *tangenziale est* (east) and *tangenziale ovest* (west), which are often congested with heavy traffic. Approaching the centre, it is best to look for an official car park *(see p211)* and then use public transport. The alternative is to use the ATM parking areas *(see chart below)*, which are on the outskirts but are well served by the metro. These are open from 7am to 8pm, cost one euro for half a day and two euros for a whole day up to 8pm. On Sundays and public holidays (and after 8pm), ATM parking is free *(see pp212–3).*

ARRIVING FROM	MOTORWAY EXITS	CAR PARK	NUMBER OF CARS	METRO AND BUS	DISTANCE FROM CITY CENTRE
Trieste Venice Verona Brescia	Cavenago/Cambiago	Gessate	500	M 2 (30/35 min.)	23 km
	Sesto San Giovanni/V.le Zara	Sesto Marelli	250	M 1 (20 min.)	8 km
	Tang. est/Cologno Monzese	Cologno Nord	500	M 2 (30 min.)	9 km
	Tang. est/Viale Palmanova	Cascina Gobba/ Crescenzago	800 600	M 2 (20 min.)	6 km
	Tang. est/Viale Forlanini	Forlanini	650	🚋 12 🚌 73	6 km
Turin Aosta Como Chiasso Varese Gravellona	Viale Certosa	Lampugnano	2,000	M 1 (20 min.)	5 km
	Pero	Molino Dorino	450	M 1 (25 min.)	8.5 km
	Tang. ovest/Milano Baggio	Bisceglie	900	M 1 (20/25 min.)	6 km
Ventimiglia Genoa	Viale Liguria/Centro Città/ Filaforum	Romolo/ Famagosta	250 560	M 2 (20 min.)	4–5 km
Naples Rome Florence Bologna	Milano/Piazzale Corvetto	Rogoredo/ San Donato	350 2,400	M 3 (20 min.)	5–7 km

An ETR departing from the Stazione Centrale in Milan

ARRIVING BY TRAIN

THE MAIN RAILWAY STATION in Milan is the **Stazione Centrale**, where all the major domestic and international trains arrive. Connections with your destination in town can be made by taxi, metro (underground) lines 2 and 3 and many trams and buses, all of which are just outside the entrance. **Porta Garibaldi**, in the Centro Direzionale area, and Milano Lambrate (near Città Studi), are much smaller railway stations. Both can be reached via metro line 2. Metro line 3 links the **Rogoredo** station, near San Donato Milanese, with central Milan.

A regional train service connects the city with Como, Varese and the Brianza region, run by the Ferrovie Nord Milano. Trains depart from Piazzale Cadorna, where metro lines 1 and 2 converge.

There is also the recently opened Passante Ferroviario, a suburban railway link network that connects various metro lines with the Porta Garibaldi station, run by the Ferrovie dello Stato (state railway), and the Milano-Bovisa station, run by Ferrovie Nord.

A number of different types of train operate on Italy's railways. The fastest train linking Milan and the main national and international cities is the **ETR Eurostar**, which is first-class only. The ticket price includes a supplement and obligatory seat reservation. Free drinks and newspapers are provided. **Eurocity** trains also offer fast links between Milan and major European cities such as Paris and Barcelona. **Intercity** trains link Milan and the main cities within Italy such as Florence and Rome. On both Eurocity and Intercity services tickets should be booked ahead. A supplement is charged.

The other types of train are slower, but the fares are reasonable, and calculated by the kilometre. Espresso trains stop at main stations, Diretto trains at most stations, and the Locale stops at every single station on the route.

There are also trains with sleeping cars for people travelling at night. A *cuccetta*

The new Ferrovie dello Stato logo

(bunk bed) in a compartment can be reserved. Compartments hold 6 or 4 beds. A more expensive but more private alternative are the Wagons-Lits carriages (*vagoni letto*). Compartments have washing facilities, and breakfast is provided. A first-class ticket is obligatory for a one-bed cabin.

Train tickets can be purchased at railway stations or in travel agencies. Tickets must be validated before departure, by date-stamping them at the station. This is done at small yellow stamping machines which are found normally at the entrance to each platform (*binario*).

Tickets are valid for two months from the time of purchase, but once date-stamped, they are only good for 24 hours. If you are adversely affected by a railway strike, tickets for travel should be stamped by a ticket inspector or cashier in order to claim a refund. Seats, *cuccette* and sleeping car bunks can be booked at railway stations or at any travel agency with terminals linked to the stations. Reservations can be made two months before departure time. Should your travel plans change and you need to alter a ticket, there is a charge. Cancellations cost 20 per cent of the price of the ticket if you cancel 24 hours before departure; after this you will be charged 50 per cent of the price.

The ticket counters at the Porta Garibaldi railway station

Coaches parked at Piazza Castello in Milan

ARRIVING BY COACH

COACH TRAVEL is a common means of getting about in Italy. Coaches (in Italian, *pullman*) arriving in Milan end their journey at the coach terminus at Piazza Castello.

The most important coach carrier connecting Milan with northern, central and southern Italy, including Sicily, is **Autostradale Viaggi**, with direct connections with the motorway. **SGEA**, **SIA** and **STIE** cover many key destinations in Lombardy, including most of the major holiday centres around the lakes. For destinations in Europe, the principal firm is **Eurolines**.

Long-distance coaches are comfortable, with reclining seats, air conditioning, toilets and television. There are regular stops at motorway service stations.

Tickets for coach travel can be purchased directly at the Piazza Castello termini.

Timetables and rates vary according to the length of the journey and the seasons. Reductions are sometimes available for small children and those over 60.

DIRECTORY

AIRPORTS

Information
Linate – Malpensa
📞 02-74 85 22 00.
W www.sea-aeroportimilano.it

Lost and Found
📞 02-70 12 44 51
(7:30am–9pm).

Left Luggage
📞 02-71 66 59.

First Aid
📞 02-74 85 22 22.

Lost and Found
📞 02-58 58 00 70 (T1).
📞 02-74 85 42 15 (T2).

Left Luggage
📞 02-58 58 02 98 (T1).
📞 02-40 09 93 63.

First Aid
📞 02-74 86 44 44 (T1).
📞 02-74 85 44 44 (T2).

CONNECTIONS WITH MALPENSA

Malpensa Express
From Milan (Piazzale Cadorna).
📠 02-27 76 31.

Malpensa Shuttle
From Milan (Stazione Centrale).
📠 02-6698 4509.

Autolinea
Linate – Malpensa
📠 02-58 58 31 85.

AIRLINES

Air France
📠 848-88 44 66.
📞 02-76 07 323.
W www.airfrance.co.uk

Air One
📞 848-84 88 80.
W www.flyairone.it

Alitalia
📞 848-86 56 41 (national).
📞 848-86 56 42
(international).
📞 02-24 99 27 00.
W www.alitalia.it

British Airways
📞 02-72 41 61.
📞 848-81 22 66.
W www.britishairways.com/italy

Buzz
📞 02-69 68 22 22.
W www.buzzaway.com

Go
📞 147-88 77 66.
W www.go-fly.com

Lufthansa
📞 02-80 66 30 25.
W www.lufthansa.co.uk

Meridiana
📞 02-58 41 71.
W www.meridiana.it

Qantas
📞 02-86 45 01 68.
W www.qantas.com

RAILWAY STATIONS

Stazione Centrale
📞 848-88 80 88
(State Railway info).

📞 02-67 07 09 58
(Reception Centre).

📞 02-63 71 22 12
(Left Luggage).

📞 02-669 45 25
(Railway Police).

Ferrovie Nord (Cadorna)
📞 02-202 22.

Porta Garibaldi
📞 02-655 20 78
(Information).

Rogoredo
📞 02-569 33 55.

COACHES

Autostradale Viaggi
Piazza Castello 1.
📞 02-80 11 61.

Eurolines
c/o Autostradale Viaggi
Piazza Castello 1.
📞 02-72 00 13 04.
📞 Florence: 055-35 71 10
(main office).
W www.eurolines.it

SGEA Lombardia
Via Ricasoli 12.
📞 02-72 02 32 98.

SIA
Piazza Castello 1.
📞 02-86 46 23 50.

STIE
Via Paleocapa 1.
📞 02-86 45 06 14.

GETTING AROUND MILAN

ALTHOUGH THERE ARE some traffic-free areas in Milan, such as the Brera and the historic centre, where you can stroll in relative peace and quiet, the city is not really very pedestrian-friendly. Milanese traffic is always heavy and often chaotic. This, combined with the great difficulty in finding parking space, would discourage anybody from using a car in Milan. Double parking, collisions and traffic jams are

Ticket for a car park in Milan

everyday matters, to say the least. Public transport (*see p212*) and, for the brave, scooters, offer the best solution to the problem of getting around. The tram, bus and metro network is efficient and ticketing is straightforward, with a flat fare operating in the city centre. One-day tickets offer good value. Tickets should be bought in advance and must be date-stamped before use. Fines are imposed on anyone caught having a "free ride".

WALKING IN MILAN

SOME AREAS of Milan are very pleasant to walk around. Strolling around the fashion district, for example, window shopping, is always an enjoyable aspect of Milan. Another good area for people on foot is the Navigli quarter, which is a pedestrian zone after 8pm. However, oases like these are few and far between in Milan, and the pedestrians' lot is by no means an easy one.

The main problem is the heavy traffic. Drivers tend to treat the streets as race tracks, and even where people crossing the streets are using the zebra crossings, the road markings may be ignored by motorists. An additional problem is that the chronic lack of parking space means that cars are usually parked on the pavements (side-

Corso Buenos Aires on a weekday

walks), leaving pedestrians very little room to manoeuvre. This is a particular problem for those trying to get around with prams or pushchairs.

DRIVING AROUND MILAN

VISITORS SHOULD try to avoid getting around Milan by car if possible. The heavy, chaotic traffic, motorists who sound their car horns for no apparent reason, one-way streets and no-entry areas are enough to turn a tour of the city into a nightmare. However, if you absolutely must use a car, it is possible to park (for a fee) without risking a fine.

The authorized ATM sales points, usually tobacconists, bars and newsstands, sell SostaMilano cards, which are pay-ahead car parking tickets. They are also sold by the ATM personnel near the official car parks. The price varies according to the length

of time: a 1-hour ticket costs €2, the 2-hour one €3. Both can be used from 8am to 8pm. In the evening from 8pm to midnight you can use the 2-hour ticket. Just scratch off the gilded part of the ticket so that the year, month, day, hour and minute of the beginning of your parking time is clearly visible and then place it either over the dashboard or on the rear-view mirror. SostaMilano cards are also used in those areas marked and bordered by blue lines.

Areas with yellow lines are reserved for residents only. From 8am to 8pm parking is allowed for a maximum of two hours in the blue areas, and the price is €2 per hour. From 8pm to midnight there a single fee of €3 for four hours. An alternative is the garages (*autorimesse*), (*see p211*).

Ask the staff at the car parks if you need help.

Looking down Corso Vittorio Emanuele to Piazza del Duomo

Motorbikes and scooters parked in Piazza Cordusio

SCOOTERS, MOPEDS AND BICYCLES

SCOOTERS AND MOPEDS *(moto)* are certainly a good means of getting around Milan. They are fast and agile, allowing you to avoid long queues and traffic jams.

Bicycles *(biciclette)* can also provide an alternative, provided you are confident and keep your wits about you. The tram tracks can be a nuisance for bicycle wheels. A number of companies offer moped or bicycle hire (rent).

TAXIS

ONE OF THE MOST common means of transport used in Milan, particularly for business purposes, is the taxi. Official taxis are generally white, but you may see yellow ones or taxis with the livery of their sponsors. Taxi stands are located throughout the city; all taxis have telephones and the numbers are listed in the telephone directory. At the beginning of the ride the meter should read €3, to which is added a supplement for holidays and night runs and for luggage. To call a taxi, ring the radio taxi service.

DIRECTORY

BICYCLES AND SCOOTERS FOR HIRE

AWS *(bicycles)*
Via Ponte Seveso 33.
02-67 07 21 45.
@ awssnc@tiscalinet.it

Bianco Blu *(scooters)*
Via del Ricordo 31.
02-26 30 81 58.
w www.biancoblu.com

Orizzonte
Via Bertini 3a.
02-33 10 30 41.
w www.comunic.it/orizzonte

RADIO TAXI

02-85 85 or 02-67 67 or 02-53 53.

CAR PARKS IN THE CITY CENTRE

KEY

P Tariff A	P Free car park	— Resident parking	→ To city centre
P Tariff B	— Pay car park	— Public transport park	City centre

Travelling by Public Transport

Logo of the Azienda Trasporti Municipali

To AVOID STRESSFUL driving and parking problems, the best and least expensive way to get around town is to use public transport. Milan has a very efficient city transport system, run by the Azienda Trasporti Municipali (ATM), which comprises trams, buses, trolleybuses, and the three lines of the underground railway *(metropolitana)*.

TRAMS AND BUSES

TRAMS AND BUSES in Milan are all orange – except for the tourist trams *(see p201)*, which are green – and virtually serve the entire city. They are always extremely crowded, especially during rush hour, and generally pass by every ten minutes.

Bus and tram stops are easy to recognize. Each has a yellow sign displaying the route taken. Stops are often located on islands with seats for waiting passengers.

The yellow signs also have a timetable, but be careful to distinguish the summer *(estate)* from the winter *(inverno)* schedules, as they are posted side by side. Italian timetables always use the 24-hour clock, so that 20:00 hours is 8pm, for example.

The doors of trams and buses have signs indicating which to use to get on and off *(uscita* means exit), but they are often ignored, so do not be surprised if you see someone getting off where you are getting on, and vice versa.

Tickets should be bought before you get on, and your ticket should be date-stamped on the bus or tram. There is a small machine to validate *(convalidare)* your ticket; it is usually at the front, behind the driver, but on longer vehicles there are at least two, one in the front and one at the back.

When you want to get off, press the red button to tell the driver you want to do so. A sign saying *"fermata prenotata"* will flash until the next stop is reached.

Keep a close eye on your personal belongings, including luggage, when travelling on public transport, particularly on a crowded bus or tram. Pickpockets may be on the lookout for handbags, mobile phones and wallets, and you must be wary.

THE METRO

THERE ARE THREE underground railway (subway) lines: number 1 (red) was inaugurated in 1964, while 2 (green) and 3 (yellow) are newer. Extensions are planned

An escalator at the exit of a Milan metro station

for all three lines, due to complete in 2005. Stations all have escalators (some have lifts/elevators for the disabled) and are usually located close to tram and bus stops. The trains run from about 6am to 12:30am and are often crowded. Once stamped, tickets can also be used for other means of public transport.

MILAN UNDERGROUND RAILWAY (METRO)

M1   MOLINO DORINO
P   S. Leonardo
Bonola
Uruguay
P   Lampugnano
QT8
Lotto
Amendola Fiera
Buonarroti
M1
P   BISCEGLIE   Inganni   Primaticcio   Bande Nere   Gambara   De Angeli   Wagner

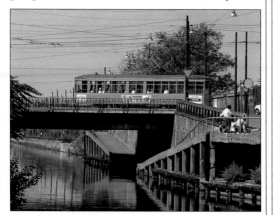

A tramcar going through the Navigli quarter

One of the Milan tourist trams (see p201), painted green

PASSANTE FERROVIARIO

THIS TRAIN SERVICE links the northwest of Milan with the metro. The line goes from Porta Venezia to Bovisa, with intermediate stops at Piazza della Repubblica, Stazione Garibaldi and Via Lancetti.

TICKETS AND TIMETABLES

ALL TICKETS CAN be used for above-ground transport, the metro and the new Passante. Tickets are valid for 75 minutes on all lines. However, they cannot be used twice on the metro.

Tickets should be bought in advance as you cannot buy them on board. They are sold at newsstands, tobacconists and automatic vending machines, which operate with both coins and banknotes. The tourist tickets are good value. They cost from €2 and are valid for 24 hours, or about €4 (48 hours). Weekly and monthly passes *(abbonamenti)* are also available.

Milanese public transport, including the metro, usually operates from 6am to midnight, but some buses and trams stay in service until 1:30am. For detailed information, make enquiries at the ATM information bureaux.

DIRECTORY

ATM (Public Transport)
Linea Verde ATM
☎ 800-01 68 57.

Season Ticket Sales
Via Ricasoli 2.
🕐 8:45am–12:45pm, 2–3:45pm Mon–Fri.
Viale Stelvio 2.
🕐 8:30am–12:30pm, 2–4:15pm Mon–Fri.
Viale P Custodi 11. 🕐 8:30am–12:30pm, 2–4:15pm Mon–Fri.
You can purchase various passes at the Cadorna, Centrale FS, Duomo, Garibaldi FS, Loreto, Romolo and San Donato stations.

KEY

— Line 1
— Line 2
— Line 3
— Automatic light railway
🅿 ATM car parks
🚉 Railway station
✈ Shuttle to the airports
🚌 Local bus terminus
♿ Wheelchair access
🚆 Passante Ferroviario train

Arriving at the Lakes

The funicular at Como in 1894

THE LAKES ARE EASILY ACCESSIBLE from Milan, both by car and by train. Visitors arriving by car will take the Autostrada dei Laghi motorway or the Valassina *superstrada*. There are good train links with all the lakes using either the Ferrovie dello Stato (FS) or the Ferrovie Nord (FNM) railways. Both offer frequent services. Bus services link the various towns and villages around the lakes, or you may well prefer to use the ferries in order to avoid traffic jams on the crowded roads, especially at weekends.

A Ferrovie dello Stato regional train

LAKE MAGGIORE

TO GET TO LAKE Maggiore from Milan by car, take the A8 autostrada and then the exit for Sesto Calende. From here take the road to Angera to go to the Lombardy side of the lake, or the road to Arona to go to the Piedmontese side.

To get to the upper part of the lake, proceed northwards, turn off at Gravellona Toce and then follow the signs for Fondotoce and Verbania.

Should you decide to go to Lake Orta, take the Borgomanero turnoff and follow the signs for Gozzano-Orta San Giulio. The A8 autostrada is also the easiest way to get to Lake Varese from Milan: take the Varese exit and continue to Gavirate.

The lake is also accessible by train from the Porta Garibaldi railway station in Milan, where the local trains go as far as Luino, via Gallarate. Another rail company, the **Ferrovie Nord** railway operates from the station in Piazzale Cadorna. There are frequent daily train services to Laveno.

The most enjoyable way of travelling from one town to another on Lake Maggiore is to use the hydrofoils and ferries. The main towns are connected by the **Navigazione Lago Maggiore** service, which has a fleet of 30 vessels, including steamboats, motor boats and ferries. The timetables are posted at local hotels, restaurants and all the ports, and are subject to seasonal changes.

If you are travelling to Lake Maggiore from outside Italy, the Malpensa 2000 airport (about 50 km, 30 miles from Milan) *(see p207)* is the closest to Lake Maggiore.

LAKE COMO

THE SHORTEST ROUTE from Milan to Lake Como by car is to take motorway *(autostrada)* A9, better known as Milano-Laghi, and exit at the Como Nord signs. To get to the western side of the lake, from Como take the statale 340 road, the ancient Via Regina, which goes as far as Sorico. If however you are headed for the other side, you have to go up the state road 583, which passes through Bellagio and goes as far as Lecco.

Traffic can be very heavy during the weekend, and as there is not much parking space around, the best solution may be to use a combination of car followed by one of the frequent hydrofoil or car ferry services. The hydrofoils are particularly frequent on the Como–Colico line, with intermediate stops, while the ferries stop only at Cadenabbia, Bellagio, Menaggio and Varenna. For detailed information, make enquiries at **Navigazione Lago di Como**.

The town of Como is also served by the Ferrovie dello Stato and Ferrovie Nord railways. The FS trains go to Como along the Milan–Chiasso line. The Nord trains leave from Piazzale Cadorna in Milan and arrive in the centre of town at Piazza Cavour. If you travel by air, the Malpensa 2000 airport is the closest one to Lake Como.

A ferry connecting the main towns around Lake Como

LAKE GARDA

VERONA IS THE NEAREST main town to the lake. It is on routes linking Milan with Venice, both road and rail. To reach Salò from the Milan–Venice A4 motorway, exit at the Brescia Centro signs and then go eastwards on the *tangenziale* (ring road) until you see signs for the Salò *superstrada* (highway). Alternatively you can exit at the Desenzano sign 118 km (73 miles) from Milan, cross the town and then go up the *statale* 572 road for 20 km (12 miles). A few kilometres past Salò is Gardone. Sirmione can be reached from Desenzano by following the southern side of Lake Garda for 9 km (6 miles), or by turning off the autostrada at the Sirmione-San Martino della Battaglia exit. To get to the Veneto side of the lake, take the A22 autostrada to Brennero and then exit at Affi.

To get to Lake Idro from Milan, take the A4 autostrada to Brescia Ovest and then proceed to Lumezzane.

Those coming from the east should take the state road that goes from Salò to Barghe, and then follow the signs for Madonna di Campiglio.

Lake Garda is also well served by trains. Desenzano del Garda and Peschiera del Garda are stops on the Milan–Venice line and coaches will take you onwards from these stations to Sirmione, Salò, Gardone and Limone. For more information, contact the **Azienda Provinciale Trasporti**.

A pleasant alternative is to travel on the lake: 21 boats offer continuous service on Lake Garda. The hydrofoils are the fastest means of crossing the lake and will save you time, while ferries go directly from Maderno to Torri del Benaco and back, for those who do not want to stop at every town on the route. Boat services are run by **Navigazione Lago di Garda (Navigarda)**.

The nearest airport is Catullo in Verona Villafranca. Other possibilities are Orio al Serio in Bergamo, Linate in Milan and Marco Polo in Venice.

Navigarda tickets

LAKE ISEO

THE EASIEST WAY to get to Lake Iseo by car is to take the A4 Milan–Venice motorway. Come off at the Ponte Oglio and Palazzolo exits to get to Sarnico, and at the Rovato, Ospitaletto and Brescia Ovest exits to get to Iseo. If you go to the lake by train, the state railway takes you to Brescia, and from there you can go on the Ferrovie Nord Brescia-Iseo-Edolo line; passengers can take bicycles with them if required.

The best way to get to Sarnico and Lovere is to take a boat from Iseo.

Direzione Naviseo will provide information on timetabling. In the summer (from June to September) there is a train service to Sarnico on the Palazzolo-Paratico-Sarnico line, run by the Ferrovia del Basso Sebino, which operates in the Oglio River Regional Park in cooperation with the WWF and other environmental associations.

DIRECTORY

RAILWAYS

Ferrovie Nord
Piazzale Cadorna 14, Milan.
Map 3 A5. **C** 02-202 22.
W www.ferrovienord.it

BUS SERVICE

Azienda Provinciale Trasporti
Via Lungadige Galtarossa 5, Verona.
C 045-805 78 11.

FERRY AND BOAT SERVICES

Navigazione Laghi Maggiore–Garda–Como
Via Ariosto 21, Milan.
C 800-55 18 01.

Navigazione Lago Maggiore
Isola Bella, Stresa.
C 0323-303 91.

Viale delle Magnolie, Verbania.
C 0323-50 32 20.
W www.navlaghi.it

Navigazione Lago di Como
Via Cernobbio 18, Como.
C 031-57 92 11.
W www.navigazionelaghi.it

Navigazione Lago di Garda (Navigarda)
Piazza Matteotti 2, Desenzano.
C 800-55 18 01.
C 030 91 49 511.
W www.gardanotizie.it/navigarda

Direzione Naviseo
Piazza Matteotti 2, Desenzano.
C 800-55 18 01.

The redeveloped Ferrovie Nord railway station, Milan

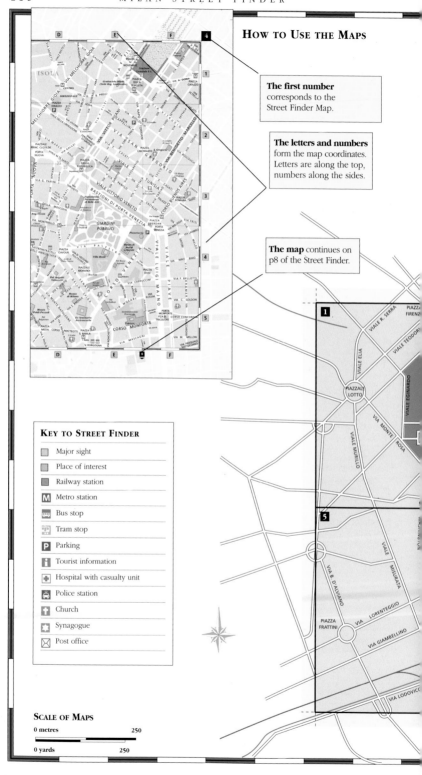

How to Use the Maps

The first number corresponds to the Street Finder Map.

The letters and numbers form the map coordinates. Letters are along the top, numbers along the sides.

The map continues on p8 of the Street Finder.

Key to Street Finder

▢	Major sight
▢	Place of interest
▢	Railway station
Ⓜ	Metro station
🚌	Bus stop
🚋	Tram stop
P	Parking
ℹ	Tourist information
✚	Hospital with casualty unit
🚓	Police station
✝	Church
✡	Synagogue
⊠	Post office

Scale of Maps

0 metres   250

0 yards   250

MILAN STREET FINDER

ALL THE MAP REFERENCES in this guide, both in the *Milan Area by Area* and in the *Travellers' Needs* sections, refer to the maps in this *Street Finder*. The page grid superimposed on the *Area by Area* map below shows which parts of Milan are covered by maps in this section. Besides street names, the maps provide practical information, such as tram and bus stops, post offices, hospitals and police stations. The key on the opposite page shows the scale of the map and explains the symbols used. The main sights are shown in pink. On page 211 there is a map of the Milan metro system, including the Passante Ferroviario. Inside the back cover is a map showing the main stops on the Milan public transport network.

Street Finder Index